THE CIVILIZATION OF THE AMERICAN INDIAN SERIES

INDIAN LIFE ON THE UPPER MISSOURI

INDIAN LIFE
ON THE
UPPER MISSOURI

BY JOHN C. EWERS

UNIVERSITY OF OKLAHOMA PRESS

NORMAN

By *John C. Ewers*

Plains Indian Painting (Stanford, 1939)
Gustavus Sohon's Portraits of Flathead and Pend d'Oreille Indians (Washington, 1948)
The Horse in Blackfoot Indian Culture (Washington, 1955)
The Blackfeet: Raiders on the Northwestern Plains (Norman, 1958)
(Editor) *Adventures of Zenas Leonard, Fur Trader* (Norman, 1959)
(Editor) *Five Indian Tribes of the Upper Missouri* (Norman, 1961)
Artists of the Old West (Garden City, 1965)
(Editor) *George Catlin's O-kee-pa* (New Haven, 1967)
Indian Life on the Upper Missouri (Norman, 1968)

LIBRARY OF CONGRESS CATALOG CARD NUMBER: 67–64641

Copyright 1968 by the University of Oklahoma Press, Publishing Division of the University. Composed and printed at Norman, Oklahoma, U.S.A., by the University of Oklahoma Press. First edition.

To my Daughter
JANE EWERS ROBINSON
in memory of her happy childhood
on the Upper Missouri

FOREWORD

✕═══✕═══✕

THE MISSOURI—North America's longest river—flows 2,546 miles through the heart of the continent from the Rocky Mountains to the Mississippi. Fur traders, who ascended this river during the early years of the nineteenth century, regarded the mouth of the Platte, below present-day Omaha, Nebraska, as the dividing line between the lower and the upper portions of the Missouri. From the mouth of the Platte, the Upper Missouri extended northward and westward more than 1,900 miles to its source. This distance is more than 500 miles longer than the overland automobile route from Boston to Omaha today.

The drainage basin of the Upper Missouri and its tributaries includes the southernmost portions of the Canadian provinces of Alberta and Saskatchewan and portions of the states of Montana, Wyoming, North and South Dakota, Nebraska, and Iowa. This basin comprises an area more than twice the size of the New England and Middle Atlantic states combined.

Only a small portion of the Upper Missouri region had been explored before Lewis and Clark traveled virtually the entire length of the Missouri on their overland expedition to the Pacific in 1804–1805. And they did not meet all of the tribes who were living in this vast Indian country. At that time half of the tribes of the Great Plains lived, hunted, traded, and/or fought in the Upper Missouri region. The resident tribes then included the Omaha and Ponca in present Nebraska; the Yankton, Yanktonai, and Teton Dakota (Sioux), and the Cheyenne, Arikara, Mandan, and Hidatsa in the Dakotas; and the Plains Cree, Plains Ojibway, Assiniboin,

Gros Ventre (Atsina), Crow, and Blackfoot (primarily Piegan, some Blood, and North Blackfoot) tribes north of the Missouri or west of the mouth of the Yellowstone. These tribes had suffered severe losses in a smallpox epidemic in 1781. Their combined population in Lewis and Clark's time may not have exceeded fifty thousand.

These tribes spoke dialects of three different languages—Algonquian, Siouan, and Caddoan. The Caddoan-speaking Arikaras and the Siouan-speaking Omahas, Poncas, Mandans, and Hidatsas lived in semipermanent villages and raised crops of corn, beans, and squash. The other Siouan-speaking tribes—Teton, Yankton, Yanktonai, Assiniboin, and Crow—and all of the Algonquian-speaking tribes of this region—Cheyenne, Cree, Gros Ventre, Ojibway, and Blackfoot were nomads who lived in portable tipis and subsisted primarily upon the great herds of buffalo which roamed over the grasslands.

Ever since the French fur trader La Vérendrye first heard of the Mandans in the early 1730's, the Indians of the Upper Missouri have held a strange fascination for non-Indians. Numerous field observers—French, English, and American fur traders, soldiers, missionaries, government officials, artists, scientists, and early settlers—have recorded their impressions of one or more of these tribes. Three of the most able ethnologists of the first half of the twentieth century—Alfred L. Kroeber, Robert H. Lowie, and Clark Wissler—did field work among them. Nevertheless, many problems involving the history and the culture of these Indians remain unsolved.

My interest in the Indian tribes of the Upper Missouri was aroused by Clark Wissler in his seminars in the Yale University Graduate School some thirty-five years ago. Since then I have devoted a major portion of my career to learning more about their history and culture. I have been fortunate to have known and to have obtained information from a goodly number of elderly Blackfeet, Assiniboins, and Sioux—men and women who were members of the last generation of Indians of the Upper Missouri to have participated actively in tribal life before the buffalo were exterminated in their homeland.

I believe my approach to the study of these tribes has been essentially ethnohistorical—combining field work with library and museum research. I have tried to use the methods and the resources of both history and ethnology. And I find both the historian's concern for accuracy in dating observations and events and the ethnologist's interests in cultural content and continuity have been helpful in my studies. The historian may point out that Blackfoot Indian culture changed markedly between 1730 and 1830, but the ethnologist will insist that we are still dealing with *Blackfoot Indian* culture at the end of the century. Regardless of the number and variety of new materials and ideas these Indians may have acquired from either white men or other Indian tribes during that interval, they valued and made use of these acquisitions in ways which were peculiarly meaningful and useful to them. At the same time they guarded against rapid changes in the most cherished aspects of their traditional life.

The resources of the ethnohistorian are many and varied. The written observations—whether published or in manuscript—of the persons who had firsthand knowledge of the Indians of the upper Missouri are indispensable. And a large part of the ethnohistorian's time must be devoted to locating and examining obscure publications and unpublished papers in libraries and archives. No less valuable is the verbal testimony of aged Indians who possess lively memories of Indian life in buffalo days. Field work with living informants does more than reveal unrecorded data to the ethnohistorian. It gives him a feeling for a culture and its values that enables him to appraise written sources more accurately and to identify basic misunderstandings on the part of some writers.

Visual materials add another dimension to ethnohistorical research. Adequately documented artifacts in museum collections give form and substance to the words of informants and writers and provide another primary resource for defining and interpreting Indian life during the period these objects were in actual use. The drawings and paintings executed by artist-observers of Indian life and the photographs taken by pioneer cameramen in field and studio are especially helpful to studies of Indian material culture. Yet these sources must be as critically evaluated as the written words of field observers, because a picture is of little value to the ethnohistorian if it is not an accurate representation of its subject matter. In this book the illustrations are employed as visual evidence—not as decoration of the text. They have been carefully selected to serve this purpose.

I look upon the chapters of this book as demonstrations of the results that can be obtained from the critical study of the various ethnohistorical sources I have mentioned, as well as a contribution toward a better understanding of some aspects of the history and culture of the Indian tribes of the Upper Missouri. The fifteen chapters were written over a period of a quarter of a century (since 1943) and were separately published in scientific or historical journals in the United States and in Canada.

For permission to reprint these papers, with some modifications based upon my additional studies, I am grateful to the following institutions, journals, and editors: Historical Society of Alberta, *Alberta Historical Review*, Hugh A. Dempsey, editor; American Anthropological Association, *American Anthropologist*, Ward Goodenough, editor, and Charles Frantz, executive secretary; The Saskatchewan Natural History Society, *The Blue Jay*, George F. Ledingham, editor; Hudson's Bay Company, *The Beaver*, Malvina Bolus, editor; Washington Academy of Sciences, *Journal of the Washington Academy of Sciences*, S. B. Detwiler, Jr., editor; Missouri Historical Society, St. Louis, *Missouri Historical Society Bulletin*, George R. Brooks, director; Montana Historical Society, *Montana, The Magazine of Western History*, Vivian Paladin, editor; The New-York Historical Society, *The New-York Historical Society Quarterly*, Jane N. Garrett, editor; Museum of New Mexico, Museum of New Mexico Press, *Probing the American West*, Delmar M. Kolb, director; Southwest Museum, Los Angeles, *The Masterkey*, Bruce Bryan, editor; University of New Mexico, *Southwestern Journal of Anthropology*, Harry Basehart and Stanley Newman, editors; and the Smithsonian Institution, The Smithsonian Press, *Smithsonian Annual Report, 1965*, and *Miscellaneous Collections*, Anders Richter, director.

CONTENTS

xv

PART IV
THE PERSISTENT IMAGE

ILLUSTRATIONS

xvii

PART III

PART IV

MAP

PART ONE

❖═❖═❖

WARRIORS, TRADERS, AND WOMEN

SEVENTY YEARS before Meriwether Lewis and William Clark became the first American explorers to meet the Indians of the Upper Missouri, a French fur trader, Pierre La Vérendrye, learned from the Assiniboin Indians near Lake Winnipeg of a strange people who lived in large villages on a great river to the southwest from whom the Assiniboins obtained corn. That was in 1734. Four years later La Vérendrye accompanied an Assiniboin trading party overland to see for himself what these strangers were like.

On the Missouri, near the mouth of Heart River in present North Dakota, he found the Mandan Indians living in six large, fortified villages of earth-covered lodges. They cultivated the alluvial bottom lands and operated a flourishing trading center at which they exchanged the produce of their fields for products of the chase brought to their villages by nomadic, buffalo-hunting Indians of other tribes.

There can be little doubt that this pattern of trade between farming and hunting tribes existed among the Indians of the Upper Missouri before they met white men. And it was through this preexisting network of intertribal trade that the first items from the white man's world reached the Indians of this region before the time of La Vérendrye.

The most valued of these new acquisitions to the nomadic tribes were the horse and the gun, which reached them from opposite directions. The horse was diffused northward from tribe to tribe from the Spanish Southwest. The gun was traded southward and westward from the French and the English through Indian inter-

3

mediaries. When La Vérendrye visited the Mandans in 1738 he observed that those Indians had already received a few guns from the Assiniboins. The following summer two Frenchmen, whom he left among the Mandans to make observations of their life and customs, witnessed a visit of horse-using tribes to the Mandan villages for purposes of trade. Thus before 1740 the expanding frontier of the horse met the expanding frontier of the gun at that great native trading center. Indians equated the horse with the gun in trade values, and intertribal trade was further stimulated.

But it was among the nomadic tribes, whose movements on foot had been slow and whose warfare had been relatively ineffectual in pedestrian days, that horses and guns exerted the strongest influence during the second half of the eighteenth century. Mounted on swift horses and armed with firearms, nomadic Algonquian and Siouan tribes pushed westward and southwestward into the valley of the Missouri, displacing other and less-well-armed tribes from the richest buffalo-hunting region of the northern plains—the drainage basin of the Missouri west of the mouth of the Yellowstone. Before Lewis and Clark's time the Blackfeet and the Gros Ventres had driven the Shoshonis, Flatheads, and Kutenais from lands north of the Missouri, and the Assiniboins followed them into this region. The Crows pushed the Shoshonis out of the middle Yellowstone, and the powerful Tetons crossed the Missouri into western South Dakota and on into the Black Hills and beyond.

It was during this period also that the first white men, Frenchmen in the employ of the British trading companies, gained a precarious foothold in the Mandan villages, and a trickle of direct trade developed between the parties of visiting white men and the Mandans.

White influences touched the lives of Indian women as well as men. The acquisition of horses relieved women of the backbreaking task of carrying heavy burdens when camps were moved. Moreover, a few Indian women who married white traders acquired roles of considerable importance as intermediaries between the whites and their own people. As mothers of the mixed bloods such women were destined to play increasingly important roles in Indian-white relations on the Upper Missouri in future years.

Lewis and Clark found an Indian trade flourishing at the Mandan trading center in 1804. But the Mandans and the neighboring Hidatsas could furnish few beaver pelts themselves, and demands of the Indians for metal weapons and tools—guns, tomahawks, knives, and awls—continued to exceed the supply of these useful items which reached them. The richest of the Upper Missouri's resources in beaver were to be found in the headwaters area toward the mountains, and those regions had not been tapped by white traders at the Mandan villages. As yet traders were the only whites the Upper Missouri tribes had met. It is understandable, therefore, that they should have looked upon the Lewis and Clark expedition as an advance party of trader-explorers from downriver.

✷≡✷≡✷

CHAPTER ONE

A Blood Indian's Conception of Tribal Life in Dog Days*

ON JANUARY 14, 1950, one of the strongest living links between the modern Blackfoot Indians and their traditional past was severed by the death of a little old man bearing the name of Weasel Tail on the Blackfeet Reservation in Montana. Weasel Tail's exact age, like that of other illiterate, full-blood Indians of his generation, was uncertain. The official census for the Blackfeet Reservation for the year 1901 listed Weasel Tail, then the father of a twenty-year-old daughter, as forty-two years of age. On the basis of this record he must have been some ninety-one years old at the time of his death, and in his middle eighties during the period 1941–47 when he served as one of my principal informants.

When I last saw Weasel Tail in the summer of 1947, he was still physically active. His eyes were bright. His mind was clear and sharp. And he still possessed a delightful sense of humor which had made association with him a particular pleasure.

Weasel Tail was born and raised among the Blood Indians in Canada, but he had spent most of his adult life among the Piegans south of the border. In his youth and young manhood he had hunted buffalo and had been on a number of horse-stealing raids against neighboring tribes. His memory of the details of Blackfoot life in those days was remarkable. He was also well versed in the rich mythology of his tribe. But unlike most other aged full bloods, Weasel Tail tried to distinguish between mythological explanations of Blackfoot life in the dim and dateless past and testimony of older Indians whose descriptions were of a more personal nature.

* Reprinted in revised form from *The Blue Jay*, Vol. XVIII, No. 1 (March, 1960).

As a young man Weasel Tail had repeatedly questioned some of the oldest men and women of his tribe about the life of the Blackfeet in earlier times. Among his informants was a very elderly woman (whom Weasel Tail firmly believed was over one hundred years old), Two Strikes Woman, whom he had befriended and who had told him stories of her great-grandfather's time handed down to her by her father.

Another elderly Blood Indian, Victory All Over Woman, recounted to him stories which she had heard during her girlhood from the lips of her aged grandparents who had claimed to remember tribal life in the days before the Bloods obtained horses. From his memories of such conversations as these, Weasel Tail described to me some aspects of Blood Indian life in dog days.

Certainly I do not contend that these third- or fourth-hand reminiscences of an elderly Indian probably born in 1859 present an unadulterated word-picture of Blackfoot life in dog days. But in the total absence of any contemporary observations of Blackfoot customs by literate people in those early times, I believe Weasel Tail's testimony is worth preserving and worth recording for the consideration of students of history and archaeology who are seeking to trace the course of human occupation of the northwestern Great Plains. Weasel Tail's account, which follows, may be of particular interest to students of Saskatchewan history and prehistory because it is most probable that the Blackfoot tribes dwelt within the present boundaries of this province before they acquired firearms and horses and moved westward toward the Rocky Mountains and southward into present Montana.

For the convenience of the reader I have organized Weasel Tail's testimony as follows:

Camp Movements in Dog Days

When the Indians moved camp, all the able-bodied men, women, and children old enough to keep up with the others walked. Sometimes old people too feeble to walk were transported on a litter consisting of two cross poles tied between the frames of two travois poles, each of which was pulled by a strong dog.

8

Lodges were small. Their covers were of but five or six buffalo skins. These covers were made in two parts, one for the right and one for the left side of the tipi. In setting up the lodge, the two sections were laced together along the vertical line of the center of the back of the tipi, then pinned together above the doorway in front. When a lodge was taken down one half of the cover was folded and placed upon the back of a dog. The other half was packed on the back of a second dog. Thus two dogs were needed to transport the skin covering of a tipi. The relatively short poles needed to support a lodge of this size were grouped in small bundles and tied to the cross-frames of dog travois so that the ends of the poles dragged on the ground behind.

Cooking pots and soft skin bags containing other household furnishings and utensils were placed upon the oval cross-frames of dog travois for transportation.

Surrounding the Buffalo

After swift-running men located a herd of buffalo, the chief would tell all the women to get their dog travois. Men and women would go out together, and approach the herd from down wind so that the animals would not get their scent and run off. The women were told to place their travois upright in the earth, small (front) ends up. The travois were spaced so that they could be tied together, forming a semicircular fence. Women and dogs hid behind them while two fast-running men circled the herd, approached them from up wind and drove them toward the travois fence. Other men took up their positions along the sides of the route and closed in as the buffalo neared the travois enclosure. Barking dogs and shouting women kept the buffalo contained within the enclosure. The men rushed in and killed the buffalo with arrows and lances.

After the buffalo were killed, the chief went into the center of the enclosure, counted the dead animals, and divided the meat equally among the participating families. He also distributed the hides to the families for making lodge covers. This was called "surround of the buffalo." The women hauled the meat to camp on their dog travois.

Women also fleshed the hides with a buffalo shank bone, one end of which was hewn to a sharp edge. They scraped the hides with a sharp flint bound to an antler handle. They softened them by pounding them with rocks.

A Trap for Deer

Men dug a deep hole in the ground about fifteen to twenty feet in diameter. They placed supporting posts in the hole and covered it with slim willows, over which they placed grass so that the hole was completely hidden. The men then drove the deer toward the pit. When the deer stepped on the willow covering it gave way and the animals fell into the pit. Then the men killed them with clubs. This was called a "deer fall."

(Weasel Tail said that old Two Strikes Woman showed him a pit of this type, located about five miles south of Macleod, Alberta. At the time it was overgrown with vegetation.)

A Trap for Wolves and Coyotes

A smaller hole to trap wolves and foxes was dug. The men covered it with sticks and grass, and placed manure, entrails, and bones of buffalo on top of this covering. At intervals around the exterior of the pit they placed bent willows in the ground to which were attached snares. Then they built a fire nearby in which they melted some fat. Animals could smell the burning fat a long way off, and were attracted to the location. When they went for the bait atop the pit, they either became caught in the snares or fell into the lightly covered hole.

Pottery Making

Women made pottery from crushed rock mixed with sand and water. They dug a little pit in the ground and made a fire in it to harden the earth walls. Then they lined the bottom and sides of the pit with the pottery mixture. While this was still fresh and soft they pushed small stones into the clay at two points opposite each other and near the top of the pit sides. Then they built a fire inside to harden the pot. When it was sufficiently hardened the fire was extinguished and the pot was lifted out of the hole by the two stone handles.

[Note: On September 2, 1947, Double Victory Calf Robe, an aged woman on the Blood Reserve in Alberta, told me a variant tradition of Blackfoot pottery-making. She said that quantities of sandstone and selenite were ground to powder and mixed with water into a dough. A hole was dug in the ground and the dough was spread over the inner surface of the hole. Boiling water was poured into the hole and allowed to stand for a period. Then the pot was removed, smoothed on the outside, and later used for boiling meat.]

Marriage

If a young man fell in love with a girl and wanted to make her his wife he hitched a good travois dog to a travois and took it to the girl's father, saying to him, "I will give you these for your daughter." A father of a girl might offer the same kind of gift to a young man whom he wanted for a son-in-law.

Warfare with the Snakes

Long ago the Snakes (Shoshonis) and Blackfeet were friendly. But one time a group of Snake and Blackfoot boys were playing a kind of football game, and a Snake boy was hurt. His father became angry and clubbed to death the Blackfoot boy he accused of injuring his son. This started the fighting between these tribes.

Scabby Robe was the first Blackfoot Indian to take a Snake scalp. The opposing forces of Snakes and Blackfeet confronted each other on opposite sides of the Bow River near present Gleichen, Alberta. A Snake Indian challenged a member of the Blackfoot party to meet him in single combat. Scabby Robe answered his challenge and the two met in the middle of the river. The Snake threw his "big arrow" [lance] at Scabby Robe. It missed, and Scabby Robe picked it up and killed the Snake with his own weapon. Scabby Robe brought the body of the Snake ashore and took the scalp as a war trophy. From that time on there was continuous warfare between the Snakes and the Blackfeet.

In those days, however, any man who didn't wish to fight would

11

sit down in the midst of a battle, throw up his hands, and the enemy would not bother him. But once a Blackfoot Indian did this and the Snakes killed him. Thereafter, the Blackfeet had no mercy for their enemies.

The Blackfoot tribes didn't use shields in their warfare before they obtained guns. Rather, they clothed themselves in long shirts of three thicknesses of buckskin. These shirts reached to below the wearer's knees. They were good protection against enemy arrows.

Acquisition of the First Firearms

The Blackfeet began to acquire guns before they got horses. Before they had any guns the bow and arrow was their principal weapon. They were then friendly with the Crees. One time a party of Blackfeet were in the woods north of the Saskatchewan. They heard a frightening noise and began to run away. Some Crees, who had made the noise by shooting a gun, motioned to the Blackfeet and told them to come to them. The Crees then showed the Blackfeet how to load a gun from the muzzle and to fire it by pulling the trigger.

Later one of the Cree young men married a Blackfoot girl and gave one of the new weapons to his father-in-law. Soon thereafter another Cree married a Blackfoot and gave the girl's father a gun. That is how the Blackfeet obtained their first guns.

Still later, the Blackfeet obtained two guns from a trader. When a war party set out against the Crows and Shoshonis to the south, they took guns along. And when the enemy heard the noise of these guns they were so frightened that they fled southward from their location near present Calgary, leaving their tipis, their horses, and all of their camp equipment behind. The Blackfeet drove the Crows, Snakes, Flatheads, and Nez Percés from the Bow River southward to the Sweetgrass Hills and beyond. The Crees helped the Blackfeet to do this.

Acquisition of the First Horses

Shaved Head led a war party southward to about the location of the present Blackfeet Reservation in Montana. There they discovered a camp of Indians from west of the Rockies who owned a lot of horses. The Blackfeet stole some of these animals. When some of the warriors tried to mount the horses, the latter began to walk and the frightened would-be riders quickly jumped off. They led the horses homeward. When the people heard that Shaved Head had brought back a pack of "big dogs," they gathered around the strange animals and looked at them in wonder. They put robes on the horses, but when the animals began to jump they ran. After a time a woman said, "Let's put a travois on one of them just like we do on our small dogs." They made a larger travois and attached it to one of the gentler horses. It didn't kick or jump. They led the horse around with the travois attached. Finally a woman mounted the horse and rode it.

The Blackfeet called the first horses "big dogs." Later, because the animals were about the size of an elk, they called them "elk dogs." And that, of course, is still the name for horses in the Blackfoot language.

CHAPTER TWO

The Indian Trade of the Upper Missouri
before Lewis and Clark*

EVERY FRONTIER has two sides. The historian has approached the frontier of the Indian trade on the Upper Missouri from the viewpoint of the white trader operating in Indian country far in advance of the frontier of white settlement. He has found his studies a rewarding means of interpreting progress in western exploration and international and inter-company competition for territory and/or commercial advantages, as well as a means of describing details of the fur trade, the major economic enterprise of whites on the Upper Missouri throughout the historic period prior to white settlement in that region.

The anthropologist, however, looks at the problem of the Indian trade of the Upper Missouri from the other side of this frontier—the Indian side. His interests lie primarily in determining the effects of trade upon the lives of the Indian tribes engaged in it. Some of these tribes were the aboriginal occupants of the region. Others migrated to the Upper Missouri country subsequent to the late years of the seventeenth century.

Both approaches to this study are legitimate. Ideally they should serve to complement each other in producing a truer and better-rounded picture of the significance of early trade in this region. Eventually the researches of archaeologists should provide valuable new data regarding both the prehistoric and the historic Indian trade of the area. Their activities have been greatly intensified in the postwar years through the Missouri River Basin Archaeological

* Reprinted in revised form from The Missouri Historical Society *Bulletin*, Vol. X, No. 4 (1954).

Survey, sponsored jointly by the National Park Service, the Smithsonian Institution, and collaborating institutions. These field explorations, however, are too recent and are not sufficiently advanced to provide us with a comprehensive study of archaeological findings bearing upon the problem of Indian trade along the Upper Missouri. For the time being, the anthropologist must rely primarily upon the same sources utilized by the historian—the writings of early fur traders and explorers—for his basic data on this subject. His contribution must lie in the presentation of new interpretations of available data rather than in the presentation of additional facts. I hope, however, that this interpretation of the Indian trade of the Upper Missouri before the Lewis and Clark expedition may serve to provide greater historical depth to the historian's perspective of this problem, which may help him in his own interpretations.

Because the available source materials on the Indian trade of the Upper Missouri prior to the period of the Lewis and Clark explorations (1804–1806) are extremely limited, it appears advisable to begin with a consideration of the intertribal trade of this region as it existed at the time of their expedition. On the accompanying map I have plotted the known intertribal trading relations at that time as recorded by the explorers themselves and their contemporaries.[1]

Two primary trading centers then existed on the Upper Missouri. One was located at the Mandan and Hidatsa villages in the vicinity of Knife River, in present North Dakota. For all practical purposes this may be considered a single Mandan-Hidatsa center. The other trading center on the Upper Missouri was at the Arikara villages north of the mouth of Grand River, in present South Dakota. These

[1] The principal contemporary sources on the Indian trade of the Upper Missouri during the years 1803–1806 are: Meriwether Lewis and William Clark, *Original Journals of the Lewis and Clark Expedition, 1804–1806*; Pierre-Antoine Tabeau, *Tabeau's Narrative of Loisel's Expedition to the Upper Missouri*; François Larocque, *Journal of Larocque from the Assiniboine to the Yellowstone, 1805*; Charles Mackenzie, "The Missouri Indians, 1804–1805," in *Les bourgeois de la Compagnie du Nord-Ouest*, I; Alexander Henry and David Thompson, *New Light on the Early History of the Great Northwest*. Abraham P. Nasatir's *Before Lewis and Clark, Documents Illustrating the History of the Missouri, 1784–1804* offers important source materials on the trade of the previous decade. *David Thompson's Narrative of His Explorations in Western America, 1784–1812* includes Thompson's firsthand observations of the Mandan trade in 1797.

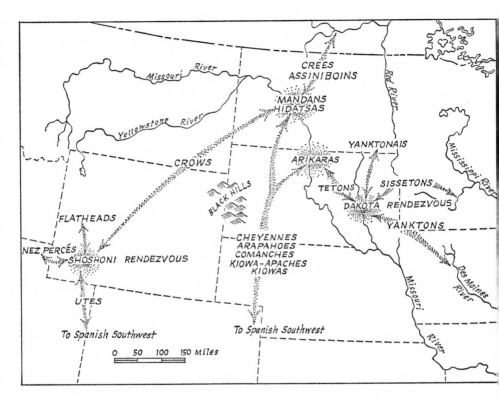

Routes and Centers of Intertribal Trade in 1805

three tribes—Mandan, Hidatsa, and Arikara—lived in semi-permanent villages of earth-covered lodges and grew crops of Indian corn, beans, and squash in the fertile river bottoms.

To the Mandan trading center (as indicated on the accompanying map) came a number of nomadic hunting tribes of the plains at the time of Lewis and Clark. These included the Assiniboin and Plains Cree from the northeast, the Crow from the middle Yellowstone, and the Cheyenne, Arapaho, Kiowa, Kiowa-Apache, and Comanche who lived on the plains southwest of the Mandan-Hidatsa. The five tribes last named also traded at the Arikara center, as did the powerful nomadic Teton Dakota (primarily Oglala, Brûlé, and Miniconjou).

Turning again to the map, we see that the tribes who exchanged goods at the primary centers on the Missouri were engaged in a trade that had far wider ramifications. Not only did the Assiniboins and Crees trade with the Mandan-Hidatsas, but they also traded with the English of the Hudson's Bay and North West companies at their posts on the Assiniboine and Souris rivers. The Crows traveled to a trading rendezvous in the west with the Shoshonis, Flatheads, and Nez Percés, and the Shoshonis in turn traded, through the Utes west of the Rockies, with the Spaniards of New Mexico.[2] The Cheyenne, Arapaho, Kiowa, Kiowa-Apache, and Comanche tribes not only traded with both the Mandans and the Arikaras but also traveled to the Spanish settlements of the Southwest by way of the western high plains. The Tetons were accustomed to meet other Dakota groups each spring at a great rendezvous on the James River where they received some of the goods supplied to the Sissetons and Yanktons by North West Company traders on the St. Peter (Minnesota) and Des Moines rivers.[3]

[2] No contemporary source definitely located this Shoshoni rendezvous. On my map I have placed it in its most probable location, in the river valleys of southwestern Wyoming west of the South Pass. This was the same region in which the Mountain Men later held their annual rendezvous.

[3] In 1795, Jean-Baptiste Truteau first mentioned this Dakota rendezvous, at which the Tetons traded with related Dakota tribes who obtained goods from white traders on the Minnesota and Des Moines rivers (Truteau in Nasatir, *Before Lewis and Clark*, I, 301–11). Both Lewis and Clark (*Original Journals*, VI, 45, 98) and Tabeau (*Tabeau's Narrative*, 121–23) knew of this rendezvous. The former considered it

Thus we see that at the time of Lewis and Clark the Indian tribes of the Upper Missouri were engaged in a complex system of trade extending for thousands of miles from the Spanish Southwest through nomadic intermediaries to the English trading posts on the western tributaries of the Red and Upper Mississippi rivers.

In this widespread system of trade we can now distinguish not only the two primary trading centers on the Missouri but also two important secondary centers, the Shoshoni and Dakota rendezvous (one east and one west of the Missouri), as well as the peripheral centers manned by white traders in the Spanish Southwest and on the Assiniboine, Souris, Minnesota, and Des Moines rivers. The nomadic tribes played important roles as intermediaries between these trading centers. This network of intertribal trade involved no fewer than nineteen Indian tribes.

Upon analysis of the articles employed in this trade at the time of Lewis and Clark this trade appears to have comprised a combination of two patterns of intertribal trade, one chronologically older than the other. Let us term these (1) the aboriginal intertribal trade pattern, and (2) the protohistoric or transitional trade pattern. The latter may be considered as transitional from the aboriginal pattern to a third or historic pattern of direct trade between Indians and whites on the Upper Missouri, which also will be considered in the following characterization of these three trading systems.

During the winter of 1738–39, La Vérendrye left two Frenchmen with the Mandans to learn their language and observe their customs as a means of facilitating future trade with these peoples. On their return from the Mandans, in September of 1739, the two reported to La Vérendrye the visit of allied nomadic tribes from the west to the Mandans for purposes of trade. They spoke of this trade as if it had been a yearly occurrence for some time prior to their witnessing it, noting that these savage tribes came "every year, at the beginning of June," and that in 1739 they remained "over a

---

particularly important to the fur trade of the Upper Missouri, because it rendered the aggressive Tetons independent of the traders on that river and hostile to those traders' commerce with other Missouri River tribes. The Dakota trading fair dates back to at least 1700, although before the Teton movement westward to the Missouri it was held farther east, on Minnesota River. George E. Hyde, *Red Cloud's Folk*, 8.

18

month with the Mandan." They observed that the visitors brought "dressed skins trimmed and ornamented with plumage and porcupine quills, painted in various colors, also white buffalo-skins," and that the Mandans gave them in exchange "grain and beans of which they have an ample supply."[4]

It is noteworthy that although these unnamed nomadic tribes possessed horses, there is no mention of their trading any of those animals of European origin or descent to the Mandans. The trade consisted solely in the exchange of products and by-products of the chase for the agricultural products of the Mandans. This appears to have been an aboriginal trade pattern which was widespread in the Great Plains. Although we have no comparable description of an exchange of solely native products by the Arikaras, it is noteworthy that Spanish explorers of the Southern Plains recorded a similar exchange between the nomadic tribes of that region and the horticultural Plains and eastern Pueblo tribes in the sixteenth century.

In 1541 Coronado's chronicler observed that the nomadic Querechos and Teyas "follow the cows, hunting them and tanning the skins to take to the settlements in the winter to sell, since they go there to pass the winter, each company going to those which are nearest, some to the settlement of Cicuye, others toward Quivira, and others to the settlements situated in the direction of Florida. . . . They exchange some cloaks with the natives of the river for corn."[5] Again, four decades later, the Rodríguez Expedition learned of Apache nomads who came to the eastern Pueblos with "articles of barter such as deer skins and cattle hides for making footwear, and with a large amount of meat in exchange for corn and blankets."[6]

In aboriginal times there was little incentive for trade between two horticultural tribes or two hunting peoples, as neither possessed an abundance of desirable articles which the other did not have.

---

[4] Pierre G. V. la Vérendrye, *Journals and Letters of Pierre Gaultier de Varennes de la Vérendrye and His Sons*, 336–38.

[5] George Parker Winship (ed.), *The Coronado Expedition, 1540–1542*, 527–28.

[6] G. P. Hammond and Agapito Rey (eds.), "The Gallegos Relation of the Rodríguez Expedition to New Mexico," *Historical Society of New Mexico Publications in History*, IV, 91.

But barter between hunting and gardening peoples enabled each group to supplement its own economy with the products of the other's labor. It was a mutually profitable exchange.

Of major importance in this aboriginal type of exchange was the barter of foodstuffs. The nomadic tribes who traded at the two primary centers on the Missouri appear to have been particularly eager to obtain quantities of corn to supplement their primary meat diet. In January, 1734, Assiniboin chiefs of the lower part of Lake Winnipeg told La Vérendrye that they "were leaving as soon as spring opened to go to the [Mandan] to buy corn." He also learned that the Assiniboins had been to the Mandans the previous fall, probably for the same purpose.[7] Lewis and Clark and their contemporaries observed that the Mandans and Hidatsas traded corn to the Assiniboins, Plains Crees, and Crows, and that the Arikara furnished it to the Teton Dakotas, Cheyennes, Arapahoes, Kiowas, Kiowa-Apaches, and Comanches.[8] The Crows and Cheyennes, both of which tribes had formerly been horticulturalists, seem to have been particularly fond of corn. The Crows offered leggings, robes, and dried meat for cooked or raw corn,[9] while the Cheyennes found it difficult to go without this vegetable.[10]

Other products of the fields of the gardening tribes also were offered to the nomads. These included beans, "pumpkins," and a variety of native tobacco (*Nicotiana quadrivalvis, Pursh.*) cultivated by the village tribes.[11]

The foodstuffs offered in exchange by the nomadic tribes con-

[7] La Vérendrye, *Journals*, 153, 160. In 1736, Father Alneau also learned that the Assiniboins started "every year just as soon as the streams are frozen over" to the Mandan villages "to procure their supply of corn." *The Jesuit Relations and Allied Documents* (ed. by R. G. Thwaites), LXVIII, 293.

[8] Trade in corn at the Mandan-Hidatsa center was mentioned by Truteau (in Nasatir, *Before Lewis and Clark*, II, 381), as well as by Lewis and Clark (*Original Journals*, VI, 89); and Tabeau (*Narrative*, 131, 151, 154) describes the corn trade at the Arikara center.

[9] Larocque, *Journal*, 22.

[10] Tabeau, *Narrative*, 151.

[11] Truteau in Nasatir, *Before Lewis and Clark*, II, 381; Lewis and Clark, *Original Journals*, VI, 90; Larocque, *Journal*, 66; and Henry and Thompson, *New Light*, I, 398, mention this trade at the Mandan-Hidatsa center. Lewis and Clark, *Original Journals*, VI, 89, and Tabeau, *Narrative*, 131, 151, 154, refer to it at the Arikara center.

sisted primarily of dried buffalo meat.[12] However, Tabeau observed that the western nomadic tribes also traded flour made from the wild turnip (*Psoralea esculenta*) to the Arikaras in 1804.[13] This product may have been a minor item in the trading inventory at the Mandan center, even though it was not specifically mentioned by Lewis and Clark and their contemporaries.

In addition, the nomads traded the horticulturists other products and by-products of the chase, including dressed skins of the buffalo and deer, buffalo-skin lodge covers which would be useful to the villagers on their hunting excursions, and articles of dress clothing, particularly skin shirts, leggings, and moccasins.[14]

It is noteworthy that this trade between nomadic and horticultural peoples, as reported by early white observers, was primarily a direct exchange between producer and consumer. The articles of trade were grown, collected, obtained in the hunt, or manufactured by the offering tribe. The articles received were eaten or used by the receiving tribe. This aboriginal trade was not a fur trade. As we know it from the records of early white observers, it was primarily an exchange of perishables—foods and leather goods. These are not the types of articles which would normally be found by archaeologists except under the most favorable conditions of preservation,

[12] Larocque, *Journal*, 22, is the principal source on the dried meat trade at the Mandan-Hidatsa center; Tabeau, *Narrative*, 131, 158, on this trade at the Arikara center.

[13] Tabeau, *Narrative*, 158. All of the nomadic tribes of the Upper Missouri collected quantities of this root in early summer. It was known to the French as *pomme blanche* or *pomme de prairie*.

[14] Larocque (*Journal*, 22, 66, 71), Mackenzie ("The Missouri Indians," 346), and Henry and Thompson (*New Light*, 398) noted the buffalo-robe trade at the Mandan-Hidatsa center. Tabeau (*Narrative*, 131, 158) tells of Arikara receipt of dressed leather from the Tetons and deerskins from the western nomads. Lewis and Clark (*Original Journals*, VI, 90, 103) mentioned the trade in "leather lodges" at the Mandan-Hidatsa center. Skin shirts and leggings were traded at that center also (Larocque, *Journal*, 66, and Mackenzie, "The Missouri Indians," 346). Lewis and Clark (*Original Journals*, VI, 103) simply noted that the Crows traded "many articles of Indian apparel" to the Mandans and Hidatsas. Although Truteau (in Nasatir, *Before Lewis and Clark*, I, 310) told of "clothes" being traded to the Arikaras by the Tetons in 1795, he did not mention specific garments. Tabeau (*Narrative*, 158) named antelope skin shirts and shoes (moccasins) among the articles the Arikaras received from the nomadic tribes west of the Missouri. Probably ornaments and other items of clothing, which the white observers deemed of too little consequence to specify, also were traded at both centers.

such as might be afforded by dry caves. Undoubtedly other raw materials or native manufactured articles of less perishable nature must have been exchanged. But the absence of mention of such articles by the early writers should be a warning of the impossibility of trying to reconstruct a true picture of the aboriginal trade pattern of the Upper Missouri on the basis of archaeological finds alone.

This aboriginal pattern of trade must have had the effect of intensifying the labors of the nomads and the horticulturalists in their own specialties. In order for the nomadic tribes to enjoy the advantages of a vegetable diet without the necessity for raising crops themselves, they had to kill more wild game, to dry more meat, and to dress and work more skins than would have been the case had they attempted to supply their needs solely by their own labors. Conversely, in order to decrease their reliance upon the buffalo hunt and to free themselves of the necessity of dressing large numbers of skins and of making dress clothing, the gardening peoples had to plant, cultivate, and harvest much larger crops than were required for themselves alone.

Not only did this aboriginal trade pattern survive on the Upper Missouri until the time of Lewis and Clark, but it persisted for many decades thereafter. Thus, in 1833, Maximilian found that the leather shirts worn by the Mandan men were obtained as presents from or in barter with neighboring nomadic tribes.[15] Kurz referred to Hidatsa trading of corn to the Crows in 1851.[16] At the same time the Teton Dakotas were making yearly visits to the Arikaras to exchange buffalo robes, skins, meat, and other commodities for corn.[17] In the summer of 1953, elderly Assiniboin Indians living on the Fort Peck Reservation told me that in the decade prior to the extermination of the buffalo their tribe visited the Mandan-Hidatsas at Fort Berthold to exchange products of the chase for corn, and that they carried the corn with them on their hunts in sacks made from buffalo calf hides. That was nearly a century and a half after La Vérendrye first recorded trading visits

[15] Alexander Phillip Maximilian, *Travels in the Interior of North America*, XXIII, 262.

[16] Rudolph Friederich Kurz, *Journal*, 198.

[17] Edwin Thompson Denig, *Five Indian Tribes of the Upper Missouri*, 47.

of the Assiniboins to the Mandans for purposes of obtaining a supply of corn.

The distinguishing characteristic of the protohistoric or transitional trade pattern was the use of articles of European origin in intertribal trade. Through the medium of this trade, horses and objects made in Europe were diffused from the peripheral white men's trading centers by Indian intermediaries to remote tribes of the Great Plains long before some of those tribes first were met by white explorers. Nearly five years before La Vérendrye's party made the earliest recorded visit by white men to the Mandans, he noted that the Assiniboins were trading a few axes and knives to that tribe. Before his visit he also learned that the Assiniboins were trading guns, powder, bullets, firesteels, kettles, and awls to the Mandans. When he reached the Mandans in December, 1738, he had an opportunity to observe this trade at the villages. He noted that the Mandans "are sharp traders and clean the Assiniboin out of everything they have in the way of guns, powder, ball, knives, axes, and awls."[18]

At the time of Lewis and Clark, articles of European origin employed in the trade of the Upper Missouri included horses, mules, riding gear, weapons, tools, household utensils, and articles of clothing and adornment. Of major importance in the development of this trade in the years between La Vérendrye's visit to the Mandans in 1738 and Lewis and Clark's contact with the same Indians in 1804 was the exchange of guns for horses. Horses were diffused from the Spanish settlements of the Southwest (New Mexico and Texas). The pedestrian Plains Indians readily adopted the new animals to their use in hunting buffalo, in moving camp, and in warfare. The Southwestern Spaniards continued, however, to abide by the law prohibiting sale or distribution of offensive or defensive arms to Indians, which was first promulgated by Ferdinand and Isabella, September 17, 1501.[19] English and French traders ap-

[18] La Vérendrye, *Journal*, 160, 254, 323, 332.

[19] *Recopilación de Leyas de los Reynos de las Indias*, Tomo II, Libro VI, Titulo I, 196. In 1805 the Shoshonis complained to Lewis and Clark that "the Spaniards will not let them have fire arms and ammunition, that they put them off telling them that if they suffer them to have guns they will kill each other." Lewis and Clark, *Original Journals*, II, 383.

proaching the Great Plains from the north and east had no horses to trade, but they were not restrained from bartering firearms to the natives. Consequently, horses were diffused northward from the southwest, while guns and ammunition were diffused southward and westward from the French and English of Canada. At the horticultural villages on the Upper Missouri the expanding frontier of the horse met the expanding frontier of the gun. This placed the Mandans, Hidatsas, and Arikaras in an admirable trading position in the protohistoric as well as in the aboriginal trade. It strengthened the importance of their villages as trading centers.

As we have seen, the Assiniboins were already trading firearms to the Mandans when the latter tribe was first met by white men in 1738, while the nomadic tribes visiting the Mandans from the Southwest at that time already owned horses. Thus the expanding frontier of the gun and that of the horse had already met at the Mandan villages at the time of the first white contact. There is no mention, however, of any trade in either firearms or horses between the Mandans and the nomadic tribes southwest of the Missouri at that time. La Vérendrye also learned that the Arikaras south of the Mandans on the Missouri possessed horses at that time, but it is unlikely that the Arikaras then had any guns.[20]

The Plains Indian needed both the mobility offered by the horse and the firepower of the gun to make him most efficient as a warrior. Any tribe possessing one without the other was at a disadvantage in competition with a tribe possessing both. Consequently there was a lively demand for guns on the part of the mounted tribes living south and west of the Missouri, and no less of a demand for horses by those tribes of the Great Plains north and east of that great river. It is unlikely, in the face of this golden opportunity, that the strategically located Mandans, Hidatsas, and Arikaras long delayed taking advantage of their strategic location for trading both guns and horses. Probably the Mandans and Hidatsas began to take an active part in this trade soon after La Vérendrye's visit, perhaps as early as the 1740's. The Arikaras, however, may have been delayed in entering the trade because of lack of firearms until

20 La Vérendrye, *Journal*, 335-37.

after the Teton Dakotas moved west to provide them with this article of commerce after 1750.[21]

The value of the horse was equated with that of the gun in the intertribal trade of the Upper Missouri during the latter years of the century, although canny traders sometimes insisted that in addition to the gun a supply of ammunition and possibly some other small items be thrown in to seal the bargain.[22]

At the time of Lewis and Clark, horses reached the horticultural tribes on the Upper Missouri by two main trade routes. The more direct and probably the older route was through Arapaho, Cheyenne, Kiowa, Kiowa-Apache, and Comanche nomadic intermediaries via the western high plains. The other route was through the Shoshonean tribes west of the Rockies and the Flatheads and Nez Percés (previously supplied with horses by the Shoshonis), and thence through the Crows who obtained horses at the Shoshoni rendezvous. By these routes not only horses, but also mules (particularly desired as pack animals because of their strength and endurance), and some Spanish saddles, bridles, and other horse trappings reached the tribes of the Upper Missouri.[23] A few other

[21] Hyde, *Red Cloud's Folk*, 17–18, has dated the Tetons' arrival on the Missouri and their initial trading contacts with the Arikaras about 1760. The Tetons themselves had possessed some firearms since 1700. On November 27 of that year Le Sueur presented six guns and a quantity of ammunition to the Mdewakantons and Oglala Sioux who visited his post near Mankato, Minnesota (Jacques Le Sueur, *Le Sueur's Voyage Up the Mississippi*, 192).

[22] Tabeau (*Narrative*, 158) observed that in their trade with the western nomads the Arikaras ordinarily exchanged a gun, a hundred rounds of ammunition, and a knife for a horse.

[23] Jacques d'Eglise, the first white visitor to the Mandans after La Vérendrye to leave a description of those Indians, found in 1791 that the Mandans possessed "saddles and bridles in Mexican style." Three years later Juan Fotman observed that "almost all" the Mandan and Hidatsa horses, as well as many of their mules, were marked "with well-known letters" (Spanish brands). Nasatir, *Before Lewis and Clark*, I, 161, 333.

The trade in horses and mules at both primary centers on the Missouri was mentioned repeatedly in the writings of Lewis and Clark and their contemporaries (Lewis and Clark, *Original Journals*, VI, 89, 90, 100–101, 103; Tabeau, *Narrative*, 151). Truteau (1794) first mentioned Arikara trade of horses to the Tetons. He also encouraged the Cheyennes to trade horses to the Arikaras for European goods (Nasatir, *Before Lewis and Clark*, I, 306, 310). Henry accompanied the Hidatsas on a horse-trading journey to the Cheyennes in the summer of 1806 (Henry and Thompson, *New Light*, I, 377–89). Trade in horses at the Shoshoni rendezvous was noted by both Larocque (*Journal*, 71–72) and Lewis and Clark (*Original Journals*, VI, 103).

items of southwestern origin also appear to have been carried in this trade, including "thick, striped blankets," possibly of Navaho or Pueblo weave, and possibly trade beads.[24]

In addition to firearms and ammunition, the articles of European manufacture that crossed the Missouri in the opposite direction through trade at the Mandan-Hidatsa and Arikara centers were arrowheads of iron and brass, tomahawks, axes, knives, metal kettles, awls, brass and iron bracelets, buttons, and probably some trade cloth, as well as manufactured articles of cloth material.[25] The new articles replaced those of stone, bone, pottery, and skins previously manufactured by the natives themselves. However, the Indians displayed remarkable ingenuity in their use of some of the strange articles of white man's make they received in trade. Thus the Arikaras remelted trade beads and made pendants of some of

---

The latter also saw Spanish bridles and stirrups among the Shoshonis and noted that those Indians traded bridles to the Crows (Lewis and Clark, *Original Journals*, III, 19; VI, 103). The trade in horses at the Dakota rendezvous was noted by Tabeau (*Narrative*, 121–25) and Lewis and Clark (*Original Journals*, VI, 95).

24 Larocque (*Journal*, 72) mentioned Shoshoni acquisition of "Spanish blankets" through trade with the whites of New Mexico. Lewis and Clark (*Original Journals*, VI, 103) learned that blankets passed from the Shoshonis to the Crows and thence to the Mandans and the Hidatsas. Larocque (*Journal*, 68) observed the Crows' fondness for small, blue glass beads "that they get from the Spaniards but by the second or third man." Although beads from Spanish traders may have reached the primary centers on the Missouri through Indian intermediaries, Tabeau (*Narrative*, 149) stated that it was a Spanish prisoner who taught the Arikaras how to melt and rework glass beads.

25 Trade in guns and ammunition at the Mandan-Hidatsa center is described by Truteau (in Nasatir, *Before Lewis and Clark*, II, 381), Lewis and Clark (*Original Journals*, VI, 90, 103), Tabeau (*Narrative*, 160–61), Larocque (*Journal*, 66, 71), Mackenzie ("The Missouri Indians," 346), and Alexander Henry (*New Light*, I, 377, 387, 398). The gun trade at the Arikara center is noted by Truteau (in Nasatir, *Before Lewis and Clark*, I, 306, 310), Tabeau (*Narrative*, 158), and Lewis and Clark (*Original Journals*, VI, 89). Tabeau (*Narrative*, 121–23) and Lewis and Clark (*Original Journals*, VI, 95) mentioned the gun trade at the Dakota rendezvous. Larocque (*Journal*, 64, 73) claimed the Crows traded no firearms to the Flatheads and Shoshonis prior to the summer of 1805. However, Lewis and Clark (*Original Journals*, II, 341), in August of that year, observed that the Lemhi Shoshonis possessed "a few small fusils of Northwest Co. trade type" obtained from Indians on the Yellowstone.

Trade in other materials listed above is mentioned by Lewis and Clark (*Original Journals*, III, 19; VI, 89, 90, 95, 96, 103), Mackenzie ("The Missouri Indians," 346), Larocque (*Journal*, 64, 71), Henry (*New Light*, I, 398), Truteau (in Nasatir, I, 310), and Tabeau (*Narrative*, 158).

them.[26] They also cut a section off the end of the barrel of the gun to make it easier to handle, and fashioned metal arrowheads from the cut-off portion.[27] The distant Flatheads did not employ for cooking the few brass kettles they received, but cut them into small pieces with which they decorated their garments and their hair.[28] The Shoshonis used the buttons they obtained in trade as hair ornaments.[29] The Crows were clever in fabricating knives out of broken pieces of iron.[30]

Contemporary accounts give us some idea of the magnitude and conduct of this transitional intertribal trade on the Upper Missouri shortly before or at the time of Lewis and Clark. In June, 1805, the Crows traded 250 horses to the Hidatsas while the latter offered the Crows 200 guns.[31] The very next year the Hidatsas offered the Cheyennes 200 guns, hoping to receive at least an equal number of horses in exchange.[32] A mark-up of 100 per cent was commonly demanded by tribes trading at the Mandan-Hidatsa center. The Crows sold horses to the Mandans and Hidatsas at double the cost to them at the Shoshoni rendezvous, while the horticultural tribes doubled this price again in their dealings with peoples northeast of the Missouri.[33] It was not necessary for an entire tribe itself to be well supplied with either horses or guns in order for some of its members to participate actively in trading them to other tribes. Thus, David Thompson, in 1797, noted the relative poverty of the Mandans in horses: "Even for the purpose of hunting their horses are too few," although the Mandans were trading horses to northeastern tribes at that time.[34] There is no indication that the Mandans, Hidatsas, or Arikaras were rich in horses at any time in buffalo days. They must have retained few of the animals they received

[26] Mathew W. Stirling has summarized the information available on Arikara glass bead-making in "Arikara Glassworking," *Journal of the Washington Academy of Sciences*, XXXVII, No. 8 (1947).
[27] Tabeau, *Narrative*, 199.
[28] Larocque, *Journal*, 58.
[29] Lewis and Clark, *Original Journals*, III, 19.
[30] Larocque, *Journal*, 58.
[31] Mackenzie, "The Missouri Indians," 346.
[32] Henry and Thompson, *New Light*, I, 387.
[33] Larocque (*Journal*, 16, 64) and Henry and Thompson (*New Light*, I, 399).
[34] Thompson, *Narrative*, 230.

in trade for their own use. The Teton Dakotas certainly were trading guns to the Arikaras prior to 1794.[35] Yet, in 1806, Zebulon M. Pike estimated that only about 5 per cent of the Tetons possessed firearms.[36] The large profits to be realized in intertribal trade must have encouraged individual Indians who came into possession of desirable horses or guns to furnish them to foreign tribesmen rather than to men of their own tribes who lacked these valuable assets.

The protohistoric or transitional trade pattern differed from the pre-existing aboriginal trade pattern not only in its employment of articles of European origin, but also in that the commerce was largely in imperishables, including many weapons, tools, utensils, and articles of adornment which have been recovered by archaeologists. Items received in this trade were not limited in use to the receiving tribe, but commonly were retraded to another tribe at a handsome profit. It appears also that as trade routes were extended in this transitional trade some articles of native manufacture among distant tribes were added to the inventory of the nomadic intermediaries and through them reached tribes on the Upper Missouri. We know, for example, that catlinite pipes were traded to the Tetons by eastern Dakota tribes at the James River rendezvous.[37] The appearance of these pipes in protohistoric but not in aboriginal village sites of the Arikaras would suggest that the Tetons introduced them to the Arikaras through trade. Another native-made article probably distributed through the medium of this transitional trade is the bow. Bradbury, while among the Arikaras in 1811, noted that they used bows of mountain-sheep horn and ones of yellow wood (Osage orange). The former must have reached them from the west, the latter from the south in conjunction with the trade in horses.[38]

---

[35] Truteau, in Nasatir, *Before Lewis and Clark*, I, 310.

[36] Pike estimated the number of Teton warriors at two thousand, the number of their firearms at one hundred. (Zebulon M. Pike, *An Account of Expeditions to the Sources of the Mississippi*, Table following Appendix to Part I.) Lewis and Clark (*Original Journals*, I, 166) observed that the Oglalas, whom they met in September, 1804, were "badly armed with fusees."

[37] Tabeau, *Narrative*, 121–23.

[38] John Bradbury, *Travels in the Interior of North America in the Years 1809–11*, Vol. V of Thwaites' *Early Western Travels*, 170.

Historians have been concerned primarily with direct trade between Indians and whites. They are familiar with the known history of its extension to the Missouri from Canada and from St. Louis. There is no need for much detail, but this trade should be related to the pre-existing patterns of Indian trade in the region. Chronologically, it was a late comer, directed largely toward the old, established, primary centers on the Upper Missouri, the Arikara and the Mandan-Hidatsa centers. White traders were primarily interested in obtaining the Indians' furs, providing them with such articles as were necessary to achieve this end.

In the years prior to the Lewis and Clark expedition white fur traders approached the Missouri from two directions. The competing traders of the Hudson's Bay and North West companies sent out small groups periodically to the Mandan and Hidatsa villages from their established posts on the Assiniboine and Souris rivers. It is not known definitely when these brief visits to the Mandan-Hidatsa center were inaugurated with any degree of regularity, but it seems most probable that the Hudson's Bay Company, which was usually content to trade with distant tribes through Indian intermediaries, did not enter this direct trade until forced to do so by more active competitors from Montreal after the cession of Canada in 1763. Possibly the Frenchman, Pierre Menard, who was living among the Mandans in the 1790's, was among the first Canadians to engage in this trade. According to the best available estimate he came to reside with them in 1777 or 1778.[39] He and René Jesseaume (who began residence at that center about 1789) served as guides to Canadian trading parties and as their intermediaries in dealing with the Mandans and Hidatsas. At the time of Lewis and Clark the Canadians remained in control of such trade as the whites had at the Mandan-Hidatsa center. The sporadic, weak attempts of the St. Louisians to discourage them were unsuccessful. The Arikara center was regularly visited by traders from St. Louis after 1790, and in 1793 Joseph Garreau took up residence with that tribe.[40]

White traders at both centers found their stiffest competition

[39] In 1791, Jacques d'Eglise learned that Menard had been living among the Mandans for fourteen years. (Nasatir, *Before Lewis and Clark*, I, 82.)

[40] *Ibid.*, I, 82–83.

from the Indian intermediaries operating under the older, proto-historic trade pattern. Jean-Baptiste Truteau, in 1795, found that the prices he was allowed to pay would not permit him to compete successfully with the Teton Dakotas for the beaver trade of the Arikaras.[41] Both the nomadic and the horticultural tribes recognized the whites as competitors and sought to discourage their efforts to extend their trade by frightening them. In 1797 the Assiniboins tried to dissuade David Thompson's party from going to the Mandans by telling him of their great danger from hostile Sioux, who resented white men's furnishing their Mandan enemies with ammunition.[42] In 1805 the Hidatsas sought to prevent François Larocque from opening trade directly with the Crows by pointing out the dangers he would face from hostile Assiniboins, Cheyennes, and Arikaras, and by representing the Crows as thieves and liars.[43] Undoubtedly the Indian traders, jealous of their own rights as traders under the pre-existing trade patterns, resented white trading contacts with the more distant tribes. They sought to retain their old patterns of trade with those tribes while they themselves enjoyed direct trade with the whites. In the face of this Indian opposition white commerce on the Upper Missouri prior to Lewis and Clark's arrival was limited largely to trade with the three horticultural tribes. Furthermore, the quantity of furs collected was small. At the Mandan-Hidatsa center white employees of the trading companies gave a sizable part of their goods to Indian women in return for their favors. Traders secured horses, corn and meal, wolf and fox skins, but few valuable beaver pelts. As late as 1806, Charles Mackenzie was proud to be "the first north trader who crossed the Missouri with four packs of beaver."[44] The writings of Truteau and of Tabeau suggest that the returns from the Arikara trade were little if any more favorable.[45]

[41] *Ibid.*, 301.

[42] Thompson, *Narrative*, 212.

[43] Larocque, *Journal*, 16–21.

[44] Mackenzie, "The Missouri Indians," 393.

[45] Tabeau (*Narrative*, 83–86, 145) not only referred to the Arikara trade as "slight," but commented at length on the scarcity of beaver on the Missouri and its tributaries in the neighborhood of that tribe.

PLATE 1 Weasel Tail (1859?–1950), Blood Indian veteran of the intertribal wars.

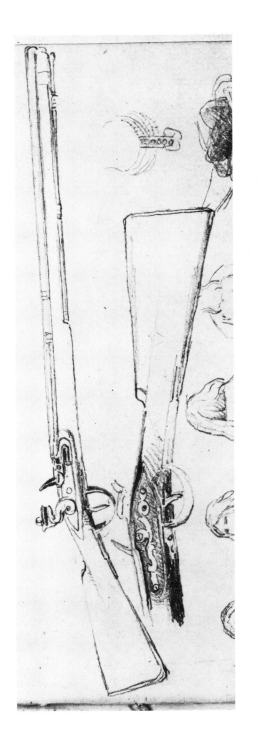

PLATE 2   North West Trade Gun, from Charles Wimar's sketchbook, 1858.

PLATE 3 Assiniboin-Cree attack upon a party of Piegan outside Fort
McKenzie, August 28, 1833. Engraving from a drawing by
Karl Bodmer.

COURTESY SMITHSONIAN INSTITUTION

PLATE 4   Black Moccasin, Hidatsa chief, painted by George Catlin in 1832. Lewis and Clark had known this Indian as a vigorous leader of his tribe in 1804–1805.

PLATE 5   Arikara Indian Village painted by George Catlin in 1832.
Lewis and Clark had visited this same village in 1804 and
1806 on their way to and return from the Pacific Coast.

COURTESY SMITHSONIAN INSTITUTION

PLATE 6   Interior of the earth lodge of a Mandan Indian chief. Engraving from an original water color by Karl Bodmer, 1833.

PLATE 7   Medicine Snake Woman, Blood Indian wife of the American
trader Alexander Culbertson.

PLATE 8   Deer Little Woman, Assiniboin Indian wife of the American trader, Edwin T. Denig.

In sum it appears that prior to the time of Lewis and Clark direct trade between Indians and whites on the Upper Missouri was not only limited geographically but restricted quantitatively. Prior to 1805, intertribal trade was the dominant commerce on the Upper Missouri. White activity was no longer peripheral, but it had not progressed to the point of replacing the pre-existing intertribal pattern of trade.

One of the major responsibilities of Lewis and Clark, on their epic-making voyage of exploration to the Pacific in 1804–1806, was obtaining reliable information on the Indian trade of the Upper Missouri and trans-Rockies region through which they passed.[46] Although they carried with them a carefully selected assortment of articles to be presented to chiefs and headmen of the tribes encountered, as gifts of their government, they were to be observers of the Indian trade rather than participants in it.[47]

The explorers' day-to-day accounts of happenings during their travels reveal the lively demand for metal and useful manufactured objects among the Indians. They had to be vigilant lest the Indians steal their weapons. At the Mandan villages they found "the Indians extravagantly fond of sheet iron of which they form arrowpoints and manufacture into instruments for scraping and dressing their buffalo robes." Part of a burned-out sheet-iron stove was traded to the Mandans by the expedition's blacksmith. For each piece about four inches square the natives were happy to give him seven or eight gallons of corn.[48] The explorers noted that the Mandans seemed quite pleased to receive a metal corn mill as a present. Yet, nine months later Alexander Henry found that the Indians were less impressed with the new machine as a device for grinding corn than with the possibility of re-using the precious metal for other purposes. They had demolished the mill to make arrowheads

---

[46] President Jefferson's instructions to Meriwether Lewis briefly but clearly defined the nature of that leader's responsibilities with respect to the Indian trade. Lewis and Clark, *Original Journals*, VII, 250.

[47] Both the choice of presents and their distribution to individual Indian leaders were painstakingly planned in advance. Lewis and Clark, *Original Journals*, VI, 270–77.

[48] Lewis and Clark, *Original Journals*, I, 255.

and employed a large piece of it, which they could not break, as a hammer fixed to a wooden handle for pounding marrow bones.[49] During the early months of 1805, Indians in the vicinity of the expedition's winter camp near the Mandan and Hidatsa villages kept the party's smiths busy making iron battle-axes for them in exchange for corn.[50] More than a year later Sergeant Ordway of the Lewis and Clark party observed Indians at the Pahmap Village at the mouth of Potlatch River in present Nez Percé County, Idaho, more than seven hundred airline miles distant from the Mandan-Hidatsa trading center, using war axes as stakes in gambling. He added, "The war axes these Indians have they got from the Grousevanntres [Hidatsas] on the Missouri & they got them from us at the Mandans."[51] Thus, unknown to them at the time, Lewis and Clark's smiths were supplying material for the far-flung proto-historic intertribal trade.

The careful description of the trading relations between the tribes of the Upper Missouri which Lewis and Clark prepared as a result of their own observations and their conversations with active traders in the field provide the best available contemporary information on the conduct of both the intertribal and Indian-white trade in this region at that time. These data include concise summaries of the trade of each tribe.[52] Hence they are more comprehensive than the more detailed observations of contemporary traders whose interests were primarily focused upon the limited number of tribes with whom they did business.

Lewis and Clark's firsthand observations of the extent of trade and trading interests of the Indians west of the Rockies are uniquely valuable. At the time of their visit to the Lemhi Shoshonis the protohistoric trade in European-manufactured articles was still expanding westward. By 1805 the Shoshonis possessed a small number of firearms obtained from the primary Mandan-Hidatsa center through Crow intermediaries at the Shoshoni rendezvous.[53]

[49] *Ibid.*, 211; Henry and Thompson, *New Light*, I, 329.

[50] Lewis and Clark, *Original Journals*, I, 251, 254–55, 263, 266, 268, 272.

[51] John Ordway, "Sergeant Ordway's Journal," *Wisconsin Historical Society Collections*, XXII, 353.

[52] Lewis and Clark, *Original Journals*, VI, 80–120.

The frontier of the gun had reached the Shoshonis and the tribes beyond were clamoring for firearms. Farther westward they found the Nez Percés wanting those very articles that had for three-quarters of a century or longer comprised an important part of the protohistoric trade inventory on the Missouri—guns, ammunition, knives, tomahawks, kettles, and awls for making moccasins.[54]

Not only did Lewis and Clark's report point out the need for action in wresting control of the Mandan-Hidatsa trade from the Canadians, but they for the first time revealed the potential sources of valuable furs in the country up the river beyond the Mandans and the trans-Rockies region. Prophetically Lewis and Clark pointed out sites for trading posts which became the locations of two of the most important centers of commerce on the Upper Missouri after the expansion of Indian-white trade in later years.[55] One of these, the mouth of the Yellowstone, became the site of the key post of Fort Union in 1828. The other site at the mouth of the Marias, which the explorers indicated as the best location for trade with the Blackfeet, became the site of Fort Piegan in 1831. For more than half a century, until the end of buffalo days, trading posts in this general vicinity continued to control the trade of the powerful and aggressive Blackfeet. Not only were Lewis and Clark keen and accurate observers and recorders of the Indian trade of the Upper Missouri in their own time, but they were also wise prophets of the expansion of the fur trade on the Upper Missouri, which took place in the quarter-century which followed.[56]

[53] They found no axes or tomahawks among the Shoshonis. Those Indians' supply of other European manufactured goods was limited. (Lewis and Clark, *Original Journals*, III, 190.)

[54] So eager were the Nez Percés to obtain firearms that in the summer of 1805 they sent a small deputation to the distant Mandan-Hidatsa center to obtain some of them. These travelers returned with six precious guns before Lewis and Clark reached the Nez Percés, May 12, 1806, on their return from the Pacific coast. Thus the gun frontier moved westward from the Shoshonis to the Nez Percés during the very period of Lewis and Clark's explorations. (Lewis and Clark, *Original Journals*, V, 23, 30.)

[55] *Ibid.*, 321; and VI, 52, 74.

[56] Meriwether Lewis' "Observations and Reflections on Upper Louisiana, 1809" not only reveals a thorough knowledge of current problems in the fur trade of that region but also offers a number of practical solutions for those problems. (*Ibid.*, VII, 369–88.)

꞉꞊꞉꞊꞉

CHAPTER THREE

The North West Trade Gun*

NO OTHER ARTICLE in the Indian trader's stock was so keenly desired by his redskinned customers as was the gun. Indeed the old muzzle-loading smoothbore, the pioneer trade gun, enjoyed a popularity among the Indians that was out of all proportion to its effectiveness as a hunting or fighting weapon. Respect for the white man's gun was kindled in the minds of the Indians when they first saw and heard this strange weapon in action. This curious hollow rod which made such a frightening noise when the little trigger was pulled, hurling such a tiny round missile so swiftly that the human eye could not follow its flight and with such force that it could kill or cripple wild game or an enemy at a distance, filled the primitive Indian with wonder and admiration. To the Indian this new thing which behaved so mysteriously was strong medicine.

During the third quarter of the seventeenth century, French explorers who introduced guns among the Indians of the western Great Lakes region noted that the natives explained the firing of the Frenchmen's weapons by saying there were spirits within them which caused the loud noises. Nicholas Perrot learned that members of a delegation of warlike Sioux on a visit to the Ottawas heard the report of a gun for the first time and were so terrified that "they imagined it was the thunder or the lightning of which the Outaouas had made themselves masters in order to exterminate whomsoever they would."[1]

* Reprinted in revised form from *Alberta Historical Review*, Vol. IV, No. 2 (Spring, 1956).

[1] Emma Helen Blair (ed.), *The Indian Tribes of the Upper Mississippi Valley and Region of the Great Lakes*, I, 163.

During the century following the establishment of English trading posts on Hudson Bay in 1670, the frontier of the gun moved southward and westward to the tribes on the Canadian plains and in the valley of the Upper Missouri River. Cree and Assiniboin Indians played important roles as middlemen in arming the more distant tribes of the northern Great Plains. The Crees themselves must have begun to obtain English guns from Hudson's Bay Company posts shortly after 1670. They made good use of these new weapons in their wars against Siouan tribes farther south. Within a few years the Crees so weakened the Assiniboins that the latter sued for peace. Then the Assiniboins forsook their Siouan kinsmen the Dakotas and formed an alliance with the better-armed Crees. To strengthen their new allies, the Crees supplied guns to the Assiniboins. This shift in allegiance and arming of the Assiniboins probably occurred prior to 1690, although it was not reported until 1700 by the French trader, Le Sueur.[2]

In 1729, La Vérendrye found that the Assiniboins still traded with his English competitors through Cree middlemen. Yet in the next decade the Assiniboins themselves were serving as middlemen in extending the trade in firearms southward to the Mandan Indian villages on the Missouri.[3]

At the same time Crees and Assiniboins were extending the gun frontier westward up the valley of the Saskatchewan to the Blackfoot tribes. When David Thompson was among the Piegans in the winter of 1786–87 he was told of the first employment of firearms in Piegan-Shoshoni warfare during the young manhood of his aged Cree Indian informant, Saukamaupee (Boy). The Shoshonis had gained an advantage in the prolonged intertribal warfare through the acquisition of some horses on which they rode swiftly into the ranks of the pedestrian Piegans and belabored them with their stone battle-axes. The Piegans then sought aid from their (then) allies the Assiniboins and Crees, who not only supplied warriors, but included among them ten men armed with guns. In the next large-scale battle with the Shoshonis the owners of these new secret

[2] Le Sueur, *Voyage*, 190.
[3] La Vérendrye, *Journals*, 61, 332.

35

weapons were stationed at intervals along the Piegan battle line. Confused and terrified by the deadly, incomprehensible action of this new weapon, the Shoshoni line broke. Most of their fighting men fled. The few who bravely stood their ground were overpowered and dispatched by the Piegan force. That action probably occurred about the year 1730.[4]

In 1754–55, Anthony Henday of the Hudson's Bay Company accompanied Assiniboin and Cree traders westward as far as present Alberta to see and make the acquaintance of those Indians whom the Crees called the "Archithinue" (a general term covering the three Blackfoot tribes as well as the Sarsi and the Gros Ventre). Henday found that the "Archithinue" were then horsemen who had no interest in taking the long canoe voyage to the bay to trade at the company's posts. This did not mean that they were not avidly interested in acquiring guns and other useful tools and utensils of European manufacture. On leaving these people to return eastward in May, 1755, Henday recorded in his journal: "We are above 60 Canoes and there are scarce a Gun, Kettle, Hatchet or Knife amongst us, having traded them with the Archithinue Natives."[5]

Throughout the remaining years of the eighteenth century the powerful Blackfoot tribes and their allies attempted to strengthen themselves by acquiring firearms from Indian middlemen and later through direct trade with whites. At the same time they tried to prevent firearms from falling into the hands of their enemies to the south and west. The mobile (mounted) and better-armed Blackfeet swept the Shoshonis, Flatheads, and Kutenais from the Alberta and Montana plains, forcing them to seek safety in the valleys west of the Rockies.

Duncan McGillivray, in 1795, learned that the Kutenais west of the Rockies attempted to bribe the Plains Indians by payments of horses to permit them to visit Fort George on the Saskatchewan to trade. But the Indians of the plains, realizing that this would en-

[4] David Thompson, *Narrative*, 330–32.

[5] Anthony Hendry, *York Factory to the Blackfeet Country: The Journal of Anthony Hendry, 1754–55*, 352.

able the Kutenais to obtain firearms which would be used against them, did not fall for that scheme.[6] A decade and a half later Alexander Henry found the Blackfoot tribes still unwilling to permit white traders to pass through their country with guns and other goods destined for enemy tribes beyond the mountains.

So the powerful and aggressive Blackfoot tribes tried to halt the advance of the gun frontier beyond the Alberta plains in the second half of the eighteenth and the first decade of the nineteenth century. Meanwhile, large numbers of guns were carried by Cree and Assiniboin middlemen to the great trading center at the Mandan and neighboring Hidatsa villages on the Missouri, where many of these guns were retraded to nomadic tribes living farther west and south. The fact that the Spanish government forbade colonists to trade firearms to Indians made it necessary for the Indian tribes of the Southern Plains to look elsewhere for these coveted weapons. They turned to the English and French traders who operated under no such restriction. Indians quickly learned to recognize the superiority of English guns over those of French manufacture. So, many far-off tribes from the south traveled to the Mandan trading center on the Missouri offering horses they had traded or stolen from the Spaniards or their Pueblo allies in exchange for firearms. Before the time of Lewis and Clark (1804) the Mandans and the Hidatsas were exchanging guns for the horses of the Kiowas, Kiowa-Apaches, Comanches, Arapahoes, and Cheyennes. They also traded guns to the Crow Indians on the Yellowstone, who in turn were beginning to offer a few of them to those old enemies of the Blackfeet, the Shoshonis and the Flatheads. Thus, by a round-about route, the Blackfoot barrier to the gun trade with the over-mountain tribes was beginning to be circumvented at the time of Lewis and Clark. Some idea of the complexity of this venture is indicated by the fact that the few guns reaching the Shoshoni, by 1805 had to pass through many Indian hands en route. In Canada the Assiniboins or Crees obtained them from Hudson's Bay Company or rival North West Company traders. They transported them in late fall or early

[6] Duncan McGillivray, *The Journal of Duncan McGillivray of the Northwest Company at Fort George on the Saskatchewan, 1794–1795*, 56.

37

winter to present North Dakota where they traded them to Mandans or Hidatsas, who, in turn traded them to Crow Indians who visited their villages the following summer. The Crows the following spring took the weapons to a trading rendezvous with the Shoshonis and the Flatheads west of the continental divide in present Wyoming. Thus fully a year and a half was consumed in the long journey of a gun from the Canadian plains to the Shoshonis via this circuitous route. Some conception of the scale of the gun trade by way of the Mandan-Hidatsa center is found in a record of some two hundred guns traded to the Crows by the Hidatsas in June, 1805, and of the same number of guns offered by the Hidatsas to the Cheyennes the following summer.[7]

Considering the thousands of guns that were traded to the Indians of the Northern Plains prior to the time of Lewis and Clark and the many thousands more supplied them before the buffalo disappeared and the Indians were placed upon reservations, it is surprising how few Indian trade guns have been preserved in public and private collections. One reason for their rarity may have been the reluctance on the part of ethnologists in collecting weapons which were not of Indian manufacture. Another reason may just as well have been their very commonness prior to 1890. Collectors could not foresee that Indian trade guns ever could be in short supply. There are many fine collections of western firearms that do not include an example of the North West gun—the most typical Indian trade firearm of the northern Great Plains of the historic period prior to the widespread introduction of breech-loading rifles in the 1870's.

So far as I have been able to determine, the name "North West gun" first came into use among traders in western Canada and the United States about the year 1800. Although the name was derived from that of the North West Company, organized in Montreal in 1784 as a competitor of the Hudson's Bay Company for the western Indian trade, the gun type must be much older than this name. Indeed, I have seen evidence that the North West Company itself,

[7] See chap. 2, Part I.

as late as 1798, was specifying that its trade firearms purchased in London should be "exactly the same as Hudson's Bay." So the North West gun and the earlier Hudson's Bay "fuke" or fusil were essentially the same weapon. Nevertheless, it was by the "North West" name that this gun became most widely known to traders in Canada and the United States and to many manufacturers in Europe and America during the nineteenth century.

Lewis and Clark recorded that the Lemhi Shoshonis possessed a "few small fusils of North West Co. trade type" in 1805.[8] The following winter Zebulon Pike observed that "N.W. Guns" were traded to Indians at the North West Company's fort on Leech Lake in present Minnesota.[9] In the National Archives in Washington, D.C., is a copy of an order from the superintendent of Indian trade, Georgetown, D.C., for "100 of the real N.W. guns by Barnett and Ketland" for sale at trading posts then operated by the United States government in the Indian country. This order was dated March 21, 1809. In September of the following year "74 Fusils, N. West at $8.00" each were listed in an inventory of goods on hand at the government trading post at Fort Osage on the Lower Missouri.

The North West gun was originally an English product. It was made to the same specifications by several firms in London and Birmingham. However, the great majority of specimens of this gun type known to me bear the imprint "Barnett" on the lock plate. The London gunsmith Barnett must have been a prolific maker of North West guns in the early years of the nineteenth century. A gun bearing the mark of that maker and dated 1805 has been preserved. Apparently the illiterate Indians became so accustomed to seeing that name ornamenting the firearms they most desired that they became distrustful of any guns offered them which failed to exhibit that familiar marking. Why else would the American Fur Company, largest trading organization on the Upper Missouri, have insisted that the five hundred North West guns which they ordered made in

[8] Lewis and Clark, *Original Journals*, III, 30.
[9] Zebulon M. Pike, *An Account of Expeditions*, Appendix, 39.

Belgium in 1829 bear the marking "Barnett"? For six years thereafter they continued to specify the inclusion of that name in their
orders for North West guns from Belgium.

Another indication of Indian influence upon the standardization
of the North West gun appears in the complaint of the American
Fur Company's St. Louis agent to the New York purchasing office
in 1832, which points out the Indians' unwillingness to accept inferior substitutes:

> The North West Guns are one of the articles most important in
> our business, and our traders in general complain of those of this
> year, especially in the posts of the Upper Missouri, where they make
> the most use of them. The Stocks are a little too heavy, and not
> crooked enough—but the worst of it is that every stock is made of
> two pieces joined at the breech and this the Indians cannot endure.
> When the Stock is new and varnished, you hardly discover this im-
> perfection, but when they have been used, or exposed to the wet, it
> has an ugly effect, and very often the Indians bring them back to
> be exchanged for better, or those who have them on credit will not
> pay for them.[10]

Enterprising Pennsylvania gunsmiths learned to duplicate the
English-made North West gun at least as early as 1828, when the
American Fur Company ordered 580 such guns from the Boulton
Gun Works, near Nazareth, Pennsylvania. Nevertheless, the private trading firms in the United States continued to order the bulk
of their North West guns from English and European makers because of the lower prices of the foreign-made articles. In 1843, the
American Fur Company acknowledged that North West guns
manufactured by Henry E. Leman of Lancaster, Pennsylvania,
were equal in quality to guns of the same type made abroad, yet
Leman could not compete successfully with foreign manufacturers
in the matter of price.[11]

The United States government did make sizable purchases of
Leman's North West guns for distribution to western Indians in
partial payment of annuities due them in the 1850's. In 1858 no

[10] John E. Parsons, "Gunmakers for the American Fur Company," *The New-York
Historical Society Quarterly*, Vol. XXXVI, No. 2 (1952), 183.

[11] *Ibid.*, 183–84.

fewer than 365 North West guns, 297 of which were flintlocks and the remainder of the improved percussion-cap firing mechanism were bought from Leman by the government for distribution to members of the Teton Dakota (western Sioux) tribes the following year.

A page in one of the original sketchbooks of Charles Wimar, contains excellent drawings of a North West gun seen by that artist when he visited the Upper Missouri tribes on his trip upriver in the summer of 1858. That page is here reproduced (Plate 2) through the courtesy of the City Art Museum of St. Louis. These pencil sketches clearly portray some of the salient characteristics of the North West gun. It was a fullstocked flintlock. Peculiarities were the large trigger guard designed to facilitate pull of the trigger by a mittened finger in the cold winter season and the brass counter-lock plate ornament in the form of a conventionalized dragon or sea monster.

The North West gun had a ⅝" smooth bore. It was supplied in barrel lengths ranging from 2'6" to 3'6". However, it was not uncommon for the equestrian Plains Indians to file off a section of the barrel, thus converting the gun into a makeshift carbine. In the summer of 1853, Governor Isaac I. Stevens observed that the "short northwestern gun" was the principal firearm of the Red River half-bloods as well as the Blackfoot Indians. He noted the Blackfoot custom of filing off "a piece of the barrel, leaving it but little longer than that of a horse-pistol." He characterized the North West gun as "an inferior kind of shotgun."[12] It is true that the North West smoothbore had neither the range nor the accuracy of the historically better-known Pennsylvania or Kentucky rifle. Yet this gun did answer the Indians' demand for a firearm that was deadly at close range, light in weight, sturdy, and inexpensive.

In the middle 1850's the Hudson's Bay Company exchanged North West guns to the Plains Crees for five buffalo robes or three silver fox pelts.[13] In late years of buffalo hunting Blackfoot men

[12] United States Commissioner of Indian Affairs, *Annual Report for 1854*, pp. 193–205.

[13] Edwin T. Denig, *Five Indian Tribes of the Upper Missouri*, 122.

gave as many as eight to ten robes for one of these guns. It was the policy of the trading companies to restrict their profits on such necessities as guns and ammunition in order to encourage Indian hunters to bring in larger numbers of valuable furs. The Plains Indians made relatively little use of North West guns in their favorite hunt of buffalo on horseback. Few Indians could reload this weapon on a fast-running buffalo horse. It was easier for them to shoot arrows from a bow at point-blank range when chasing buffalo on horseback.

Among the Plains Indians the gun was primarily a fighting weapon which was much used in intertribal wars and wars with the whites during the nineteenth century. However, several contemporary white observers of the northwestern Plains Indians expressed the opinion that these Indians were less skilled with the gun than with bows and arrows and that their gun marksmanship was not as good as that of men of the mountain tribes to the westward who were accustomed to use firearms in hunting small game at a distance.

In warfare as in hunting, the problem of reloading proved to be a handicap to the efficient use of the muzzle-loading gun. The experienced trader and Indian fighter, William T. Hamilton, claimed that he and a single Indian companion killed five Blackfoot braves during the time those Indians were trying to reload their Hudson's Bay flintlocks in a skirmish near Fort Benton in 1865.[14] Many Indians shortened their reloading time by carrying bullets in their mouths, dropping them into the powder without any wadding, and firing. This shortcut enabled them to fire, reload, and fire again—four or five times a minute. But omission of wadding further decreased both range and accuracy of fire.

Many Indian battles were fought at close range—distances of one hundred, even fifty yards or less. When they exposed themselves to gunfire in the open, Indians commonly kept moving, jumping from side to side to prevent their opponents from taking ac-

14 William T. Hamilton, "Council at Fort Benton," *Forest and Stream*, Vol. LXVIII, No. 17 (April 13, 1907), 607.

curate aim. The finest illustration of Plains Indian warfare I know of is the realistic lithograph after an original drawing by Karl Bodmer interpreting the historic attack of a large force of mixed Assiniboin-Crees upon a camp of Piegans outside Fort McKenzie on the Missouri in present Montana, August 28, 1833. The artist Bodmer witnessed this action from the elevated walk behind the stockade of the fort. His picture thus has the authenticity of a pictorial reminiscence by an observant eyewitness. It portrays the use of muzzle-loading flintlocks by some of the Piegan defenders. It also illustrates the heterogeneity of weapons employed in the intertribal warfare of that region at that time. In addition to using guns, the Indians are fighting with bows and arrows, lances, at least three types of war clubs, and two types of knives. (See Plate 3.)

This picture serves to remind us that there was no standard equipment in Indian warfare. Each man furnished his own weapons, and those weapons varied in accordance with the wealth and the preferences of individuals. Some Indians could not afford guns; so they continued to use the traditional bow and arrows as fire weapons. Other Indians preferred to carry into battle both the Indian-made bow and arrows and the European-made gun.

The use of the North West gun in Indian warfare continued for a number of years after breech-loading, repeating rifles (known to the Blackfeet as "many shots") were introduced among the tribes of the Upper Missouri, which is further proof of the individual variation in the use of weapons among these Indian tribes. Certainly Indians readily recognized the advantages of faster rate of fire, greater power, range, and accuracy of the breech-loaders over the old North West gun. But many Indians could not afford the more costly new-style weapons. Denny observed that the half-blood hunters he saw near Cypress Hills in 1874 were armed chiefly with "flintlock muskets purchased from the Hudson's Bay Company." The following year he noted the sale of "flint-lock muskets" at that company's store on Ghost River, not far from Morley.[15] A thorough study of firearms employed in the Custer battle suggests that

[15] Sir Cecil Denny, *The Law Marches West*, 29, 86.

the number of improved breech-loading rifles may not have exceeded the number of muzzle-loading flintlocks or percussion guns in the hands of the victorious Indians.[16]

When Sitting Bull finally returned to the States from Canada in the early summer of 1881, he and his few loyal followers surrendered their arms to the United States Army at Fort Buford. Although Sitting Bull himself turned over a model '66 Winchester to the post commander, Major Brotherton, we know that at least one of the other weapons surrendered at that time was a typical North West gun, a flintlock, bearing the familiar name of Barnett and the late date of 1876.

Perhaps it was only poetic justice that the outmoded North West gun, the gun that had played a prominent role in Plains Indian warfare throughout most of the historic period, should have been represented at the surrender of Sitting Bull, last of the great war leaders of the fighting Sioux.[17]

[16] John E. Parsons and John S. Dumont, *Firearms in the Custer Battle*, 33, 39.
[17] See chap. 14.

✖ ▭▭▭ ✖ ▭▭▭ ✖

CHAPTER FOUR

Reactions of the Plains Indians
to the Lewis and Clark Expedition*

ON THEIR historic overland journey during the years 1804–1806 the men of the Corps of Volunteers for North-Western Discovery, led by Captains Meriwether Lewis and William Clark, explored the valley of the Missouri to its headwaters, crossed the Rocky Mountains, descended the Columbia River to the shores of the Pacific Ocean, and returned safely to St. Louis on the Mississippi. They traveled more than nine thousand miles in, roughly, twenty-eight months. They logged some seven thousand of those miles and spent eighteen of those months east of the Rockies in the valley of the Missouri and its most important upper tributary, the Yellowstone. They met Indians from eleven of the fourteen tribes who then inhabited the Upper Missouri region from the mouth of the Platte to the Rockies, and they initiated the first official relations between the United States and these Indian tribes. They conferred with the chiefs of the three largest farming tribes on the Missouri—the Arikaras, Mandans, and Hidatsas. And they encountered men of the two strongest military powers on the Northern Plains—the nomadic Teton Dakotas (western Sioux) and the Piegan Blackfeet. The reactions of these Indians to their meeting with Lewis and Clark were important to the future relations of United States citizens with the native peoples of an area larger than that of the original thirteen united states.

Although the men of the Lewis and Clark expedition were the first from the United States to meet the Indians of the Upper Mis-

* Reprinted in revised form from *Montana the Magazine of Western History*, Vol. XVI, No. 1 (Winter, 1966).

souri, it would be a mistake to think of those Indians at that time as unsophisticated aborigines whose lives had been untouched by influences from the white man's world. Nor were they ignorant of the interests white men had in them and in the resources of their country.

Radical changes had taken place in the lives of the Indians of the Northern Plains since Henry Kelsey, a Hudson's Bay Company employee, first met some of them in their own country in 1691.[1] Then the Indians hunted buffalo and made war on foot, using weapons of their own manufacture. The farming tribes, living in sedentary villages and combining hunting with the growth of crops, enjoyed greater economic security than the nomads who depended largely upon buffalo-hunting for their subsistence. But the acquisition of the European horse by tribes of this region during the eighteenth century greatly increased the mobility of the nomads and decreased the feast-or-famine character of the hunters' life. Some tribes of farmers left their villages to become wandering nomads. Those who persisted in their horticultural practices found themselves surrounded by and largely at the mercy of the mounted nomads. Penned up in their compact villages, they suffered heavy losses from smallpox plagues, so that by the time of Lewis and Clark the numbers of villages as well as the populations of the farming tribes were greatly reduced.[2]

Horses were symbolic of wealth among all the Upper Missouri tribes in Lewis and Clark's time. Poor but ambitious young men found that the simplest way to acquire horses was to steal them from alien peoples—whether Indians or whites. There was no stigma attached to this action. Rather, the theft of a horse was recognized as a minor war honor. Consequently, horse raiding was, by 1804, a common action in the warfare of the region.[3]

Intertribal trade was almost as typical of Northern Plains Indian life as was intertribal warfare. When Pierre La Vérendrye first visited the Mandan villages on the Missouri in present North

[1] Henry Kelsey, *The Kelsey Papers*.
[2] John C. Ewers, "The Horse in Blackfoot Indian Culture," Bureau of American Ethnology *Bulletin 159*, pp. 332–36.
[3] *Ibid*., 176–91.

Dakota in 1738, he found a flourishing native trade center to which nomadic tribesmen brought products of the chase to exchange for the agricultural produce of the villagers. He observed that some articles of European manufacture, introduced by Indian intermediaries who traded directly with whites farther northeast, had already appeared in the trade at the Mandan villages. The Mandans, as well as the warlike nomads farther south and west with whom the Mandans traded, were eager to obtain firearms, ammunition, metal arrowheads, knives, and axes.[4] Although the trade in these items increased in volume by the time of Lewis and Clark, the supply still fell far short of the Indians' demands.

Before the end of the eighteenth century, direct trade between whites, involving the exchange of European-made goods for furs and peltries, developed on a rather modest scale. British traders built fixed posts on the Assiniboine River and the upper waters of the Saskatchewan and traded with the nomadic tribes of the plains south of the Saskatchewan. Several French Canadians established residences in the villages of the Mandans and of their neighbors, the Hidatsas; they learned the Indian languages, married Indian women, and exerted considerable influence in behalf of either the Hudson's Bay Company or rival North West Company traders who made periodic trading expeditions some 150 miles southwestward from their posts in the valley of the Assiniboine River.[5]

Employing similar methods, operating through white residents in Indian villages, businessmen from St. Louis extended their trade up the Missouri to the Arikara villages, less than 200 miles south of the Mandans. In 1796, John Evans, a Welshman acting in the interest of the St. Louis traders, pushed upriver as far as the Mandan villages, where he distributed flags, medals, and other presents to the chiefs, and urged them to recognize "Their Great White Father the Spaniard." He ordered the British traders to return to Canada, but since the Spaniards failed to establish a more permanent contact with the Mandans, British traders continued to do business at the Mandan trading center.[6]

[4] La Vérendrye, *Journals*, 153–60, 332–38.   [5] See chap. 2, Part I.
[6] A. P. Nasatir (ed.), *Before Lewis and Clark*, II, 495–98.

It is significant that before the time of Lewis and Clark not only the Mandans and Arikaras but all other tribes of the Upper Missouri had gained some knowledge of white men. Furthermore, most, if not all, of these tribes knew from experience that white men were in competition for their trade. And they had no reason to believe that there were any whites who were not closely associated with the fur trade.

For many years traders visiting the Upper Missouri tribes had been accustomed to making liberal gifts to prominent Indian chiefs in order to win their loyalty and obtain a share of their tribe's trade. Three articles—flags, medals, and ornate, semimilitary coats (known to the trade as "chiefs' coats")—had become standard traders' gifts to Indian chiefs. Presented in formal councils, these gifts appealed to a chief's vanity. Furthermore, possession of these articles became visual evidence to a chief's followers that he was recognized as a tribal leader by important whites, and this, in turn, strengthened his position in the eyes of his fellow tribesmen.

In a series of formal councils with the leaders of the Otos and Missouris, Yankton Dakotas, Arikaras, Mandans and Hidatsas on their way up the Missouri, Lewis and Clark presented flags, medals, and chiefs' coats to the principal chiefs. They also gave smaller medals to lesser Indian leaders.[7] These gifts must have confirmed the Indians' beliefs that all whites were traders.

Sixteen hundred and nine miles up the Missouri, and seven miles below the mouth of Knife River, the explorers spent the winter of 1804–1805 near the Mandan and Hidatsa villages. This was the only neighborhood actually on the Missouri River where British traders did business with the Indians. Because this was a critical location for the establishment of American prestige and because these Indians, over a period of five and one half months, had better opportunities to get to know the explorers than did any other tribes of the Great Plains, let us examine in some detail the reactions of the Mandans and Hidatsas to the expedition.

The two villages of the Hidatsas on the Knife River and the two Mandan villages on the Missouri were less than five miles apart.

[7] William Clark, *The Field Notes of Captain William Clark, 1803–1805*, 169–72.

Yet moving up the Missouri, the Lewis and Clark party was met and welcomed by Mandan Indians on October 24, 1804, three days before they met any Hidatsa Indians. The Mandans proceeded to take advantage of their timely friendship with the explorers to the disadvantage of their Hidatsa neighbors. At the grand council with the two tribes five days later, Lewis and Clark recognized a greater number of Mandan than Hidatsa chiefs.[8] After the explorers built their winter quarters—Fort Mandan, three miles downstream from the lower Mandan village—the ranking Mandan chiefs, Black Cat and Big White, made frequent visits to the fort, even in the dead of winter when the thermometer registered twenty degrees or more below zero. The chiefs enjoyed spending the night in the white men's quarters. They entertained the whites in their own villages, and invited some of them to take the parts of old men in their buffalo-calling ceremony, during which the wives of younger men gave themselves to the elders.[9] That Mandan women were more than friendly toward these whites is attested by the leaders' repeated comments in their journals upon the prevalence of "venereal complaints" among the enlisted men that winter.[10]

As the winter wore on and meat became scarce at the fort, the Mandans brought corn to exchange for the services of the expedition's smiths in mending tools and utensils and in making iron battle-axes. More significant as an indication of the friendship that developed between the Americans and the Mandan Indians was the captains' offer to assist these Indians in case of a Sioux attack upon their villages, and the later Mandan aid to Captain Lewis in the pursuit of his horses stolen by the Sioux.[11]

In marked contrast to the warm friendship of the Mandans was the aloofness and suspicion of Hidatsa relations with the explorers. Nearly a month passed following the first council with the chiefs before a Hidatsa visited Lewis and Clark. One Eye, the principal

[8] *Ibid.*, 164–72.

[9] Lewis and Clark, *Original Journals*, I, 218–47.

[10] *Ibid.*, 248, 250, 279.

[11] *Ibid.*, 243–72. On March 13, 1805, the explorers noted that so great was the Indian demand for battle-axes that "the Smiths have not an hour of idle time to Spare."

Hidatsa chief, made a single visit to Fort Mandan during the entire winter, and Captain Lewis visited the Hidatsas but once.[12]

Undoubtedly the Hidatsas' coolness toward the Americans was influenced by the agents of the Hudson's Bay Company and the North West Company, who spent considerable time in the Hidatsa villages that winter. These British traders not only wanted to maintain their foothold among the farming tribes of the Mandan region, but they were eager to expand their trade southwestward into the Crow Indian territory of the Yellowstone Valley where "beaver were as rich in their rivers as buffalo and other large animals were in their plains."[13] They feared that the expansion of trade into that region by men from the United States would deny golden opportunities. When Antoine Larocque of the North West Company visited Fort Mandan in late November, the American captains forbade him to give medals or flags to the Indians of the newly acquired United States territory in which he was trading. Word reached Lewis and Clark in January through their Hidatsa interpreter, Toussaint Charbonneau, that the North West Company's clerk had been speaking unfavorably of the Americans to the Hidatsas.[14]

Perhaps this explains why Alexander Henry, of the North West Company, on his visit to the Hidatsas in the summer of 1806, reported that those Indians believed the medals and flags Lewis and Clark had given their chiefs "conveyed bad medicine to them and their children" and "supposed they could not better dispose of those articles than by giving them to the natives with whom they frequently warred, in hope the ill-luck would be conveyed to them."[15]

Henry also claimed that the Hidatsas "are disgusted at the high-sounding language the American captains bestowed upon them-

---

[12] *Ibid.*, 226–80. Apparently the Mandans, jealous of their inside track with the Americans, tried to keep the Hidatsas from visiting Fort Mandan by starting a rumor that the white men would kill them if they came to the fort (249).

[13] Mackenzie, "The Missouri Indians," 341.

[14] Lewis and Clark, *Original Journals*, I, 228, 248–49.

[15] Henry and Thompson, *New Light*, I, 350.

selves and their own nation, wishing to impress the Indians with an idea that they were great warriors, and a powerful people, who if exasperated, could crush all the nations of the earth. This manner of proceeding did not agree with these haughty savages, who had too high an opinion of themselves to entertain the least idea of acknowledging any race to be their superiors."[16]

Nevertheless, Alexander Henry acknowledged that "the Mandan are more tractable, and appear well inclined toward the United States."[17]

Perhaps one prominent Hidatsa chief, Black Moccasin, whom Lewis and Clark recognized as the first chief of their smaller village, did not share the opinion of the American leaders that Henry claimed prevailed in that tribe. At least we know that a quarter of a century later this aged chief told George Catlin of his fond memories and high regard for "Red Hair" (Clark) and "Long Knife" (Lewis), and insisted that Catlin convey his best wishes to General Clark in St. Louis.[18]

Of the other members of the exploring party, York, Captain Clark's Negro servant, attracted the most attention from both the Hidatsa and the Mandan Indians. They had never before seen a Negro and did not know quite what to make of him. York himself, a dark, corpulent man, tried to make the Indians believe he had been wild like a bear and was now tamed. One Eye, the principal Hidatsa chief, examined York closely, spit on his own hand, and rubbed the Negro's skin, trying to rub off what he believed to be paint. Possibly this Indian reaction to York survives in the term for Negro in the languages of some of the Upper Missouri tribes, which may be translated as "black white man."[19]

The smiths of the Lewis and Clark party were highly regarded by the Indians of both tribes. The Mandans believed their bellows

---

[16] *Ibid.*, 350.

[17] *Ibid.*

[18] George Catlin, *Letters and Notes on the Manners, Customs, and Condition of the North American Indians*, I, 186–87.

[19] William Clark, *Field Notes*, 119; Donald Jackson (ed.), *Letters of the Lewis and Clark Expedition with Related Documents, 1783–1854*, 539.

were strong medicine. A Hidatsa chief, appraising the Lewis and Clark expedition to Charles Mackenzie, a North West Company trader, in 1805, said: "Had I these white warriors in the upper plains, my young men would do for them as they would for so many wolves, for there are only two sensible men amongst them, the worker in iron and the mender of guns."[20]

The explorers' brief contacts with the most powerful nomadic tribes of the Upper Missouri were hostile. The Teton Dakotas at that time were the scourge of the Missouri Valley in the present region of North and South Dakota. They were the aggressive enemies of the Mandans and Hidatsas. At that time the Tetons secured guns and ammunition in trade with more easterly Dakota tribes at a rendezvous on the James River. And they tried to prevent Missouri River traders from taking arms upriver to strengthen their enemies. Only by a show of force and determination to fight if necessary were the explorers able to prevent the Tetons from stopping them at the mouth of the Teton River on their way upstream, and they narrowly averted open conflict with these Sioux while descending the river in 1806. Lewis and Clark's initial encouragement of the Arikaras, Mandans, and Hidatsas to make peace with their enemies was of little avail without the co-operation of the most powerful enemies of those tribes—the Teton Dakotas. So the bitter intertribal warfare of the Upper Missouri continued unabated, little affected by the peace talks of the well-meaning American captains.[21]

On their journey westward in the spring of 1805, the explorers traveled from the mouth of the Little Missouri to the Rocky Mountains (a distance of nearly one thousand miles) without sighting an Indian. The country through which they passed was a marginal area between the warring Assiniboins, Gros Ventres, and Blackfeet on the north, and the Crows on the south. The travelers saw many timbered lodges that had been built as overnight shelters by Indian war parties among the trees on the banks of the Missouri. Some of these "war lodges" appeared to have been occupied recently. But

20 Mackenzie, "The Missouri Indians," 330.
21 Lewis and Clark, *Original Journals*, I, 162–70; V, 361–68.

the explorers deemed themselves lucky not to encounter any Indian warriors.[22]

They were much less fortunate on their return journey across the plains of present Montana. The expedition was then divided into two parties. One, under Lewis' command, descended the Missouri. In July, 1806, Lewis and three picked enlisted men explored the upper waters of the Marias River in order to ascertain the northwestern boundary of Louisiana. Lewis knew he was in the country of the aggressive Blackfeet and Gros Ventres. He had no desire to meet any of these Indians, but he was confronted by a party of red men who outnumbered his little force two to one. Mutually suspicious of each other, the groups exchanged untruths through the sign language. Lewis claimed he was happy to meet the Indians and had come in search of them. The Indians signed that they were Gros Ventres and that there were three chiefs among them. Although dubious of their chiefly claims, Lewis gave a medal, a flag, and a handkerchief to those three. Forced to spend the night with the Indians, the whites were roused at dawn by the red men's attempt to steal their guns and horses. In the ensuing melee one Indian was stabbed to death and another shot in the belly.[23]

This small-scale skirmish with the Piegans (not Gros Ventres) on July 27, 1806, in the valley of the Two Medicine River on the present Blackfeet Reservation, Montana, was the only mortal combat between the explorers and any Indians.[24] It was probably the most unfortunate incident in the entire expedition. The whites could not have been blamed for protecting their lives and property. Nevertheless, this action was the first cause of the prolonged Blackfoot Indian hostility towards Americans. In the next year David Thompson, a British trader on the Saskatchewan, noted that "the murder of two Peeagan Indians by Captain Lewis of the U.S. drew

[22] *Ibid.*, II, 80–249. Olin D. Wheeler, *The Trail of Lewis and Clark*, I, 279.

[23] Lewis and Clark, *Original Journals*, V, 218–28. More than half a century later Piegan Indians identified their tribesman killed in this action as He-that-looks-at-the-Calf. See James H. Bradley, "The Bradley Manuscript," Montana Historical Society *Contributions*, VIII, 135.

[24] A recent, detailed, illustrated study identifies the site of this historical skirmish. See Helen B. West, *Meriwether Lewis in Blackfeet Country*.

the Peeagans to the Missouri."[25] It was a quarter of a century before peaceful trade was established between Americans and Piegans. In the interval the aggressive Blackfeet killed many American trappers and twice forced the Americans to abandon their efforts to take beaver from the streams of the Montana region.[26]

William Clark, with ten men and some forty-eight horses, descended the Yellowstone Valley to that river's junction with the Missouri. On the Upper Yellowstone his party began to see smoke signals on the high points in the distance. They met no Indians, but awoke one morning to find half their horses missing. A diligent search of the vicinity revealed no tracks—only a moccasin and a robe left by Indians. This was the first, but by no means the last, theft of American horses by the Crow Indians, who became notorious as the cleverest horse thieves of the American West.[27]

In his instructions to Meriwether Lewis, penned nearly a year before that explorer started up the Missouri, President Jefferson specifically stated: "If a few of the[ir] influential chiefs, within a practicable distance, wish to visit us, arrange such a visit with them."[28] Surely Lewis and Clark placed a very liberal interpretation upon Jefferson's phrase "practicable distance." More than 2,500 miles above St. Louis on his return journey, Clark carefully prepared a speech for delivery to the Crow Indians (whom he never met) inviting them to send chiefs to Washington.[29] Farther downstream, at the Mandan and Hidatsa villages, 1,600 miles from the mouth of the Missouri, he offered similar invitations to the chiefs of both tribes. They declined, fearing that their enemies, the Sioux, would kill them en route. A young Mandan of poor reputation volunteered to make the hazardous journey, but Clark refused his offer. Only after the captain agreed to take the interpreter, René Jesseaume, and his wife along did that canny Frenchman persuade Big White, principal chief of the Lower Mandan village, to risk the long journey to a strange land to meet his new Great White

25 David Thompson, *Narrative*, 375.
26 John C. Ewers, *The Blackfeet: Raiders on the Northwestern Plains*, 48–71.
27 Lewis and Clark, *Original Journals*, V, 276, 279–81.
28 Jackson, *Letters of the Lewis and Clark Expedition*, 64.
29 Lewis and Clark, *Original Journals*, V, 299–300.

Father. And before he returned, Big White had good reason to regret his decision, for intertribal warfare on the Missouri prevented his reaching home until 1809.[30]

At the Arikara villages Clark was even less successful in soliciting chiefly delegates to Washington. The chiefs flatly refused to consider making the trip until their chief "who went down" the previous year returned home. Lewis and Clark during their trip up the Missouri had arranged for that chief's journey. They were very fortunate that, at the time of their meeting with the Arikaras on their return journey, those Indians had not yet learned of the death of their beloved leader in the nation's capital. When word of this chief's death reached them shortly thereafter, the Arikaras abused the interpreter who brought them this news along with President Jefferson's personal message of condolence and liberal presents for the family of the deceased. There was a strong suspicion among the Arikaras that the Americans had killed their leader.[31]

Prior to that time the Arikaras had been friendly to traders from St. Louis. But thereafter these Indians repeatedly demonstrated their hostility toward Americans, preventing the passage of trading parties upriver and killing many whites. In 1823 a battle between William Ashley's traders and the Arikaras led to the first campaign of the United States Army against any Plains Indian tribe. A quarter of a century after the Lewis and Clark expedition American traders still referred to the Arikaras as "the horrid tribe."[32]

Looking back upon the Lewis and Clark expedition after the passage of 160 years, it seems that this pioneer American venture into the wilds of the Upper Missouri was much less successful in the field of Indian diplomacy than in the fields of geographical exploration and scientific discovery. Lewis and Clark were handicapped from the start because the Indians of the region had never known any white men who were not fur traders. They did score a noteworthy success in winning and holding the friendship of the Mandans. Yet it seems most probable that even those Indians whom

[30] *Ibid.*, 338–45. Jackson, *Letters of the Lewis and Clark Expedition*, 382–83, 411–12, 414, 432–38, 445–50, 456–58, 460–61, 479–84.
[31] Lewis and Clark, *Original Journals*, V, 350–55. Jackson, *Letters*, 306, 437.
[32] Denig, *Five Indian Tribes*, 54–59.

they came to know best regarded the explorers as the advance party of a great trading company, "the United States," in whose name and interest Lewis and Clark spoke to them, and which was not much different from the Hudson's Bay Company or the North West Company, whose agents were well known to the northern tribes.

The explorers could not have been expected to make any great progress in wooing the Indian tribes from their allegiance to the entrenched British traders. It required a quarter of a century of courageous and ingenious activity on the part of American traders before they could compete favorably with the experienced Hudson's Bay Company for the fur trade of the nomadic tribes north of the Missouri.

Two persistent impediments to the progress of the American fur trade on the Upper Missouri were, in part, an unwanted legacy from the Lewis and Clark relationship with the Indians, *i.e.*, the prolonged Arikara and Blackfoot hostility toward Americans. In both cases the hostile feelings on the part of the Indians were the results of accident rather than of design. But in the minds of the proud members of those primitive tribes, the causes were very real.

CHAPTER FIVE

Mothers of the Mixed Bloods*

THE INDIAN COUNTRY of the Upper Missouri was a man's world before the white man's civilization penetrated that remote portion of the interior of our continent. Indian men were the big-game hunters and warriors. As partisans they led war parties. As chiefs they deliberated in tribal councils and negotiated intertribal peaces. They were the seekers of visions, the makers and the manipulators of powerful medicine bundles, and the conductors of prolonged and involved religious rituals.

Women were the diggers of roots and collectors of berries, the carriers of firewood and drawers of water, the dressers of hides and makers of tipis and clothing. As homemakers and housekeepers they performed scores of tasks necessary to the welfare of their families. But their role was a humble one.

The Indian woman's inferior status was revealed clearly in her marital relations. When a man returned from a buffalo hunt, he expected his wife to care for his horse, remove his moccasins, fill and light his pipe, and bring him food. A lazy wife might receive several sharp cuts from the rawhide lashes of her husband's riding quirt. Men acquired as many wives as they desired or could afford. Young men bragged of their conquests of married women. But the wife who was so indiscreet as to have a lover and to be found out might be assaulted by all of her husband's fraternity brothers—the fellow members of his men's society. Or, in his jealous wrath, her

---

* Reprinted in revised form from *El Palacio* (A Quarterly Journal of the Museum of New Mexico), Vol. LXIX, No. 1 (Spring, 1962).

husband might lop off the end of her nose with a sharp knife and so mark her as an unfaithful hussy for the rest of her life.

The first white men met by Indian women of the Upper Missouri were French fur traders, members of Pierre La Vérendrye's overland expedition from the Assiniboine River to the Mandan villages on the main stem in 1738. At that time, the villages of the horticultural tribes were thriving native trading centers to which the nomadic tribes brought products of the chase to exchange for the produce of the Indian farmers' fields. For more than seventy years thereafter these earth-lodge villages remained the major destinations of white trading parties moving southward from Canada or up the Missouri from St. Louis.

One of the principal attractions of these villages for the illiterate French Canadians, who comprised the greater number of these parties, were the Mandan and Arikara women, who became noted both for their charms and for their ease of conquest. David Thompson, while among the Mandans in 1797, observed that relations with the Indian women was for many members of his party "almost the sole motive for their journey hereto. The goods they brought they sold at 50 to 60 per cent above what they cost; and reserving enough to pay their debts, and buy some corn: spent the rest on Women."[1]

Fourteen years later the naturalist Brackenridge was shocked by the speed with which Manuel Lisa's stalwart boatmen, upon reaching the Arikara villages, "disposed of almost every article they possessed, even their blankets and shirts," in eager exchange for the favors of red-skinned damsels. The extraordinary prowess of Lisa's men caused the Arikara chief to ask, "Do you white people have any women amongst you? . . . your people are so fond of our women, one might suppose that they had never seen any before."[2]

Most of these transients had no more interest in matrimony than would merchant seamen on shore leave in an exotic port after a long, hard ocean voyage. Nevertheless, they left some permanent

[1] Thompson, *Narrative*, 234.

[2] Henry M. Brackenridge, *Journal of a Voyage up the River Missouri Performed in Eighteen Hundred and Eleven*, 129–30.

impression upon Indian society in the form of mixed-blood children.

More prolonged contacts between the two races at the Mandan, Hidatsa, and Arikara villages led to the earliest known marriages between Indian women and white men on the Upper Missouri during the last quarter of the eighteenth century. As early as 1779, Menard took up residence among the Mandans. He was joined by René Jesseaume in the early nineties. Joseph Garreau settled among the Arikaras in 1793. And in 1795 a fourth Frenchman, Toussaint Charbonneau, began to live among the Hidatsas on Knife River. The three Frenchmen at the Mandan and Hidatsa villages sometimes guided trading parties traveling between the English posts on the Assiniboine River and the Indian villages on the Missouri. They also collected furs and interpreted for white traders who visited the Indian villages in which they lived. They became part of the Indian community, readily adopted Indian customs, and learned to think and to act much like Indians. When David Thompson (in 1797) wrote of a French Canadian, "He was in every respect as a Native," he might have been referring to any of these pioneer white residents on the Upper Missouri.[3]

Little is known of the history of Jesseaume's and Garreau's marital experiences, and even less of Menard's, but Charbonneau is remembered as the French husband of one of the most famous women in American history—Sacajawea. This Shoshoni Indian girl, captured by a Hidatsa war party near the Three Forks of the Missouri, became Charbonneau's wife after he purchased her (or won her as a stake in gambling). Sacajawea, known as Bird Woman, was still in her teens and carrying her two-month-old baby on her back when she and her husband left the Mandan villages in April, 1805, with the Lewis and Clark expedition bound for the shores of the far-off Pacific Ocean. In spite of the romanticists' claim, she was not the guide for this famous exploring party. The two Virginia gentlemen who were its co-leaders took her along in the hope that she would be useful as an interpreter when they encountered the Shoshoni Indians. She more than fulfilled that hope in establishing cordial relations between their party and her Shoshoni people. But

[3] Thompson, *Narrative*, 230.

59

that was not her only important contribution to the success of the venture. This frail Indian girl's courage, stamina, and uncomplaining disposition buoyed the morale of the thirty-one strong white men with whom she traveled. Her very presence among them helped to convince the many strange tribes of Indians they met on the long journey of their good and peaceful intentions. Indian women with infants on their backs did not accompany war parties. Their only bloody encounter with Indians took place when the party was split on the return journey. And Sacajawea was not with Lewis' small reconnoitering group who battled the Piegans on the Upper Marias.[4]

William Clark thoroughly appreciated Sacajawea's services to the exploring expedition, and he had a particular fondness for her little boy. Just four days after he bade good-bye to the Charbonneaus at the Mandan villages, Clark wrote to Toussaint offering to educate the boy and to help the father establish himself in business if the family would come downriver to the settlements. Some time later they accepted his kind offer. Charbonneau bought a tract of land on the Missouri in Saint Ferdinand township and sought to settle down to a more civilized life. But it was not to be. When Brackenridge accompanied Manuel Lisa up the Missouri in the spring of 1811, he noted:

> We have on board a Frenchman named Charbonet, with his wife, an Indian woman of the Snake nation, both of whom accompanied Lewis and Clark to the Pacific, and were of great service. The woman, a good creature, of a mild and gentle disposition, greatly attached to the whites, whose manners and dress she tries to imitate, but she has been sickly, and longed to revisit her native country; her husband, also, who has spent many years among the Indians, had become weary of civilized life.[5]

Whether Sacajawea died of "putrid fever" at Fort Manuel on the

---

[4] Lewis and Clark's own journals provide the best basis for determining Sacajawea's contributions to the success of their explorations. An able recent evaluation of her services appears in John E. Rhees, "The Shoshoni Contribution to Lewis and Clark," *Idaho Yesterdays*, Vol. II, No. 2 (1958).

[5] Brackenridge, *Journal*, 32–33.

Upper Missouri on December 20, 1812, or whether she lived to old age on the Wind River Reservation in Wyoming is of little significance to this discussion. What does matter is that Sacajawea was the first unschooled, full-blood Indian woman of the Upper Missouri who is known to have served as an intermediary between her own people and the whites, and who, having had a taste of the white man's civilization, had to make the difficult decision whether to accept it or to return to the Indian way of life.

In their concept of "The Marginal Man" sociologists have a ready-made characterization of a person such as Sacajawea. Regardless of sex, this marginal individual is "one whom fate has condemned to live in two societies and in two not merely different but antagonistic ones."[6] Although they have not applied this term specifically to Indian women who married white traders, the sociologists have recognized that these marginal individuals appear wherever peoples of different cultures and different races come together.[7] Sacajawea, then, may be regarded as the first and the most famous marginal woman of the Upper Missouri. There were hundreds more of them during the heyday of the fur trade in that region. Before generalizing on the roles these women played, it seems advisable to review briefly two more case histories.

About the year 1840, Alexander Culbertson, bourgeois of Fort Union at the mouth of the Yellowstone—the American Fur Company's largest and most important post on the Missouri—sent nine horses to be tied in front of the tipi of Seen-From-Afar, a Blood Indian. Shortly thereafter Seen-From-Afar sent a return gift of nine horses, and with them went his younger sister, Medicine-Snake-Woman, to live with "Major" Culbertson in the finely furnished big house near the center of the palisaded fort. In this typical Blackfoot marriage ceremony a fifteen-year-old Indian girl became the wife of the most important businessman on the Upper Missouri, a man of another race and of twice her age.

[6] Everett V. Stonequist, *The Marginal Man, a Study in Personality and Culture Conflict*, xv.

[7] *Ibid.*, xviii. Stonequist credits the concept of "The Marginal Man" to Professor Robert E. Park of the University of Chicago, who published "Human Migration and the Marginal Man" in the *American Journal of Sociology* in 1928.

White men who met Mrs. Culbertson during the next quarter of a century wrote enthusiastically of her beauty, intelligence, and strength of character. She loved to wear the finest white women's gowns when she attended balls held in her honor at the various trading posts. She was fond of jewelry—if it had plenty of color in it. She was a gracious hostess, an expert horsewoman, and a good swimmer. Yet, like other Indian women of her time, she ate the raw brains of freshly killed buffalo, enjoyed a feast of fat, broiled puppy, was proud of her skill as a porcupine quillworker, insisted upon calling in an Indian medicine woman to doctor her sick child, and cut her long, shining, black hair short when a brother was killed in battle.

Medicine-Snake-Woman did not learn to speak English. But her husband could speak her native tongue. Her brother, Seen-From-Afar, aided by liberal gifts of ammunition and tobacco (obtained through Mr. Culbertson) to his fellow tribesmen, rose to the position of head chief of the Blood tribe prior to 1855. He is remembered as the most able and wealthiest Blood chief of his generation. Her cousin, Little Dog, became head chief of the Piegan tribe, the first Blackfoot Indian to try his hand at farming, and a strong advocate of peace with the Flatheads and the Crows as well as with the whites. He was murdered in 1866 by some of his own people who thought he was too friendly with the whites.[8]

Like Sacajawea before her, Medicine-Snake-Woman played an important role in establishing peaceful relations between white explorers and her people. When Governor Isaac I. Stevens' Pacific Railway Survey party approached the Blackfoot country in the summer of 1853, he was fearful of the reception his soldiers might receive from those "most bloodthirsty Indians of the Upper Missouri." Wisely, he employed Alexander Culbertson to aid him, and cited as an important point in making his decision that this trader's wife was a Blood Indian. Medicine-Snake-Woman mixed with the Indians, kept them in good spirits with jokes and funny stories of her experiences among the whites, listened to their conversations, and reported their reactions to Governor Stevens through her hus-

[8] Ewers, *The Blackfeet*, 225–35, 242.

band. Her cousin, Little Dog, journeyed northward into Canada and brought back prominent chiefs to confer with the Governor at Fort Benton. Little Dog also played a prominent part in preparing for and in negotiating the first Blackfoot treaty with the United States near the mouth of the Judith River in the fall of 1855.

When Lewis Henry Morgan, often called "the Father of American Anthropology," traveled up the Missouri in 1862, Mrs. Culbertson furnished him detailed information on both Blackfoot and Gros Ventre Indian kinship systems which were valuable in his pioneer comparative studies of the social organization of American Indian tribes.

Medicine-Snake-Woman and Culbertson had five mixed-blood children. After the second child was drowned in the Missouri, they sent the other children downriver to be educated in a convent and a military school. By 1858, Culbertson had amassed a fortune in the Indian trade. He and his Indian wife retired to Peoria, Illinois, where they were formally married in a Christian ceremony. Their large and beautiful home, Locust Grove, became one of Peoria's showplaces. It was magnificently furnished. Original paintings by John Mix Stanley adorned its walls, and Medicine-Snake-Woman enjoyed its comforts; but in the summertime she pitched a Blackfoot tipi on the spacious lawn, donned her Indian dress, and played Indian. Finally, ten years of lavish living, coupled with some poor investments, caused Culbertson's fortune to dwindle away. In 1868, he and his wife returned to the Upper Missouri where he sought to make a living, but his wife, at last disillusioned with life in the white man's world, left her white husband and returned to her own people. Having no home of her own, she lived in the log house of her nephew, Chief Old Moon. After the buffalo were exterminated, Medicine-Snake-Woman drew the regular Indian ration from the Canadian government. About age seventy this longtime wife of the leading Indian trader on the Upper Missouri died on the Blood Reserve in 1893. She was buried in the Indian cemetery near Standoff, Alberta.[9]

[9] The best biographical sketch of the life of this woman was published by Anne McDonnell in the Montana Historical Society *Contributions*, X, 243–46. See also

Edwin Thompson Denig, who succeeded Culbertson as factor at Fort Union, had two Indian wives. The more remarkable of them was Deer-Little-Woman. She was one of the many children of Iron Arrow Point, chief of the Stone Band of the Assiniboins, who was reputed to have selected the site of Fort Union for an American fur-trading post. Her brother, The Light, was the first Assiniboin Indian to visit the Great White Father in Washington. Another brother, First-to-Fly, represented his tribe at the Fort Laramie Treaty Council in 1851, and thereafter was considered to be the second ranking chief among the Assiniboins.

Deer-Little-Woman's marriage to Denig must have helped her brother First-to-Fly win political recognition. It also must have aided her husband's career as a trader and as a writer, for he was unusually successful in both endeavors. By 1855 he had become known as the leading authority on the Indian tribes of the Upper Missouri in general and the Assiniboins in particular, although his voluminous writings had not yet been published. Denig and his wife lived like civilized folk in the great house at Fort Union, importing fine clothes and rare foods from St. Louis. Yet in 1855 they decided to leave the Indian country in order to educate their children. That summer on a trip to Columbus, Ohio, to visit Denig's relatives, they stopped in St. Louis to be formally married. Had it not been for the Columbus summer heat, the Denigs might have settled there. On their return to Fort Union they found the Red River Settlement in Canada more to their liking. The following year Denig established himself as a private trader on the White Horse Plains, west of present Winnipeg, and placed his eldest daughter in school. He died in the fall of 1858, leaving a considerable estate to his Indian wife and their children. His widow and children continued to live on the White Horse Plains until 1879, when Deer-Little-Woman and her son, Alexander, homesteaded in the Pilot Mound district of Manitoba. A few years before her death Deer-Little-Woman remarried and took the name of Christiana Olson. She died May 31, 1889, in

---

Lewis Henry Morgan, The Indian Journals, 1859–62. I am indebted to Hugh Dempsey, Glenbow Foundation, Calgary, Alberta, for information on Mrs. Culbertson's life on the Blood Reserve in her later years.

her sixty-sixth year, and was buried in the Christian cemetery at Pilot Mound. Unlike Medicine-Snake-Woman, this full-blooded Assiniboin marginal woman seems to have made a satisfactory and permanent adjustment to civilized life.[10]

Many more case histories of marginal women among the Upper Missouri tribes could be cited. But I think these three—Sacajawea, Medicine-Snake-Woman, and Deer-Little-Woman—are sufficient to show that the lives of these women followed no standard pattern. Their individual personalities and those of their husbands were factors of importance in charting the courses of their marital careers.

It may help us to assess the roles played by these marginal women in the history of the Upper Missouri if we examine the motives for the mixed marriages themselves. At Fort Union, in 1851, Edwin T. Denig frankly told Rudolph Kurz:

> Men in charge of trading posts like to marry into prominent [Indian] families. . . . by such a connection they increase their adherents, their patronage is extended, and they make correspondingly larger profits. Their Indian relatives remain loyal and trade with no other company. They have the further advantage of being constantly informed through their association with the former as to the demands of the trade and the village or even the tent where they can immediately find buffalo robes stored away.[11]

Denig was no less objective in stating the equally practical reasons why Indian women married white traders: "An Indian woman loves her white husband only for what he possesses—because she works less hard, eats better food, is allowed to dress and adorn herself in a better way—of real love there is no question."[12]

Charles Martin, an experienced trader, made much the same points in 1860. He thought that these women really preferred Indian men to white men, but that they married whites "from such motives as the certainty of more and finer clothes than an Indian can pro-

[10] Denig, *Five Indian Tribes of the Upper Missouri*, xv–xxv. Information on Mrs. Denig's later years appears in Chris Vickers' "Denig of Fort Union," *North Dakota History*, Vol. XV, No. 2 (1948).
[11] Rudolph Friederich Kurz, *Journal*, 156.
[12] *Ibid.*, 155.

vide, and perhaps a more comfortable home and fewer hardships."[13] In still fewer words General de Trobriand expressed the same opinion when he wrote: "With a white man, they are better dressed, better cared for, better fed."[14]

Probably few Indian girls of prominent families had any real choice in the matter. Their Indian-style marriages to prosperous traders were arranged for them by their ambitious families. The case histories of both Medicine-Snake-Woman and Deer-Little-Woman illustrate how these women, as intermediaries and interpreters, aided in the realizing of their relatives' political ambitions, and at the same time helped to insure the success of their white husband's business enterprises. Also, such women, acting as intermediaries and interpreters, aided in the peaceful exploration of the West, the making of treaties, and the white man's quest for accurate knowledge of Indian life.

Marginal women also promoted cultural change among their own peoples—especially in the areas of arts and crafts and material culture. Elderly Blackfoot informants have attributed the introduction of seed beads and floral designs among their people to the Indian wives of white traders. These women also may have helped to introduce commercial dyes for coloring porcupine quills, commercial paints for decorating parfleche, a style of Indian dress resembling more closely that of white women, the braiding of hair by Indian women, greater use of trade cloth for clothing, such household utensils as metal frying pans and spoons, and perhaps even a lively demand for coffee and some white men's foods.

None of the roles practiced by an Indian woman was more important than was her biological role as a mother of the mixed bloods. Sacajawea's baby, whom she carried on the long trek to the Pacific, grew up to be one of the most remarkable men in western history. Educated by a Catholic priest or nun and by a Baptist minister at William Clark's expense, Baptiste Charbonneau was in a trader's village at the mouth of the Kansas River when the German Prince Paul of Württemberg met him in 1823. Prince Paul took him to

[13] Lewis Henry Morgan, *The Indian Journals*, 101.
[14] Philippe Regis de Trobriand, *Military Life in Dakota*, 84.

Europe, where he traveled widely. Returning to America in 1829, Baptiste spent the next fifteen years as a mountain man. In 1846 he helped to guide the Mormon Battalion from Santa Fe to San Diego. The next year he was a justice of the peace at Mission San Luis Rey, and in 1849 he was in the California gold fields. But in the early 1850's he returned to his mother's people, the Shoshonis, in Wyoming, where he lived until his death in 1885. This French-Indian man of the world spoke English, French, Italian, Spanish, several Indian languages, and could use the sign language. He could discuss—with almost equal ease—French philosophy, Spanish dances, the trapping of beaver, or the uses of Indian medicine bundles.[15]

In order to suggest the variety of achievements of the children of the marginal women of the Upper Missouri, I should like to mention just a few more of them. Joseph Kipp, son of James Kipp and Earth Woman of the Mandan tribe, was an interpreter and informant for Lewis Henry Morgan, a scout for the army, and a trader among the Blackfeet. Horse Guard, an outstanding warrior of Indian-white parentage, became a chief among the Crows. Helen P. Clark, daughter of Malcolm Clark and a Piegan woman, served as superintendent of public instruction for the state of Montana. And Senator James Gladstone, of Blood-Scottish ancestry, became the first Indian to occupy a seat in the upper house of the Canadian Parliament.

Grandchildren and great-grandchildren of the marginal women living on the reservations of the Upper Missouri Valley have carried on the tradition of distinguished service to their people and to their country. They have served as interpreters to a host of government officials and to a goodly number of anthropological field workers. As chairmen and members of tribal councils, as leaders of delegations to Washington, as officials of the National Congress of American Indians and other intertribal organizations, they have endeavored to safeguard the rights and to improve the economic and social conditions of their own tribes and of all Indians.

[15] A fine biographical sketch is by Anne W. Hafen, "Baptiste Charbonneau, Son of Bird Woman," *Westerners Brand Book*, 33–36.

PART TWO

DIPLOMATS, ARTISTS, AND DANDIES

FULLY A QUARTER OF A CENTURY after Lewis and Clark returned to St. Louis a new and exciting dimension was added to the white man's knowledge of the Indians of the Upper Missouri. It comprised the oil paintings and water colors created by two talented white artists who visited the tribes of this region and recorded in vivid detail what they saw with their own eyes.

St. Louis merchants had not been slow in seeking to reap the rich harvest of furs which Lewis and Clark had assured them would be found upriver—in the Missouri headwaters, far beyond the Mandan villages. But they made a costly mistake in employing white men to trap the streams in and near the country of the powerful Blackfeet. These Indians regarded the trappers as poachers on Indian lands. Repeatedly they attacked and killed members of large or small trapping parties, and twice (in 1811 and 1823) drove the whites out of present Montana. They did not permit a trading post to be built on the Missouri in the heart of their country until 1831, and then only when convinced that Indians would collect the furs and thus share in the profits of the trade. Not until the next year did the American Fur Company establish a trading post among the Crows on the Middle Yellowstone.

Thus a quarter of a century after Lewis and Clark the Americans were barely beginning to develop a stable Indian trade in the richest fur-yielding portion of the Upper Missouri. They were only beginning to compete with the strong Hudson's Bay Company for the trade of those tribes north of the Missouri who hunted on both

71

sides of the boundary between the United States and the British possessions.

In 1832 the largest firm engaged in the Upper Missouri Indian trade, the American Fur Company, inaugurated steamboat service to its posts as far upriver as four-year-old Fort Union at the mouth of the Yellowstone—nearly two thousand miles from St. Louis. It was as passengers on this company's steamboats and as guests at its trading posts that the artists George Catlin and Karl Bodmer came to meet the Indians of the Upper Missouri.

The American artist, Catlin, was aboard the steamer *Yellowstone* on its maiden voyage to Fort Union during the spring and early summer of 1832. Among his fellow passengers were the four members of a delegation of Indians, from tribes who traded at Fort Union, who were returning from a long trek to Washington—the first Indians from any tribes beyond the Mandans to visit the nation's capital. He drew their portraits. At Fort Pierre (mouth of the Teton) he saw and painted Western Sioux and two Cheyennes. At Fort Clark, near the Mandan and Hidatsa villages, he pictured visiting Crows and Arikaras as well as the resident Indians. He spent nearly a month at Fort Union painting the Assiniboins, Plains Crees, Plains Ojibways, some Blackfeet, and more Crows. On his return downstream he spent about three weeks among the Mandans.

The following summer Karl Bodmer, a young Swiss artist, accompanied the mature German scientist, Prince Maximilian of Wied-Neuwied, up the Missouri. From Fort Union they extended their journey by keelboat as far as Fort McKenzie, at the mouth of the Marias, in the heart of the Blackfoot country. And on their return downriver they spent the entire winter at Fort Clark.

Both artists were especially attracted to the Mandans, for in their time the Mandans still possessed the richest culture of any of the Upper Missouri tribes. Faithfully they pictured these Indians' palisaded villages, their earth lodges, their games and recreations, social dances, religious ceremonies, and nearby burial grounds. But they did not neglect the nomadic tribes, and pictured their homes of portable tipis and their methods of hunting buffalo.

Both artists painted many portraits of prominent chiefs, warriors, and Indian dandies dressed in their finest and most picturesque clothes. Carefully they delineated facial likenesses of each sitter. And so realistic were these pictures that they astonished the Indians, who had never seen a portrait. Their abilities to create living people in two dimensions won them reputations as medicine men of unusual powers among the Indians.

Nor did their influence end there. They also left an impression upon Indian art through the works of two Mandan artists who sought to imitate their realistic approach to painting Indians. At the same time, they created for the civilized world and for posterity a graphic record of the Indians of the Upper Missouri which remains a unique contribution to both art and ethnology.

CHAPTER SIX

When the Light Shone in Washington*

A QUARTER OF A CENTURY after Lewis and Clark the buffalo-hunting Indians who roamed the broad plains of the Upper Missouri Valley had little reason to be awed by the size or the power of the United States. They were independent, courageous people who tolerated rather than feared the few American citizens who dared to trespass on their beloved hunting grounds. Those Americans were traders eager to make friends among the Indians. They built posts on the Missouri and urged Indian hunters to bring their valuable furs and buffalo robes to them. That was no easy task. It meant luring the red men away from their old friends of the Hudson's Bay Company north of the international line in Canada. The powerful Blackfoot, Assiniboin, Cree, and Ojibway tribes had been trading with Hudson's Bay men for generations. In the year 1830 the enterprising Americans were finding it rough going trying to take the business away from their more experienced competitors across the border.

Then someone, quite possibly John Jacob Astor of New York, the cleverest of all fur traders, whose American Fur Company was the largest concern operating on the Upper Missouri, conceived the idea that the United States government should help its citizens to gain a larger share of the Indian trade in that area by employing a little tried and true diplomacy.

This proposal was quite simple. The Secretary of War should instruct the Indian agent for the Upper Missouri tribes to bring

* Reprinted in revised form from *Montana the Magazine of Western History*, Vol. VI, No. IV (Autumn, 1956).

some representative Indian leaders of those tribes to Washington to meet their Great White Father. These delegates would be impressed by the vastness of the United States, the great numbers of its citizens, the deadly weapons and the mechanical wonders of the white man's world. They would be touched by The Great White Father's interest in and liberality toward his red-skinned children. Surely, these Indians would return home with enthusiastic reports of the power and the kindness of Americans. In an atmosphere of interracial good will American business on the Upper Missouri would boom.

This formula was not new in Indian relations. Our government had sponsored many earlier delegations of Indian chiefs and headmen from eastern and middle western tribes to the seat of government, and with apparent success. Never before, however, had a party of red men from a region so remote been invited on this grand tour. Yet perhaps the very remoteness of the Upper Missouri tribes —more than two thousand miles upriver from St. Louis, over eleven hundred miles beyond the last Indian agency at Bellevue— was all the more reason some of these savages should be given a taste of civilization. Major John F. A. Sanford, subagent for the Upper Missouri Indians, had described his charges as "the most hostile and most remote of the Indians with whom our Citizens have intercourse, their trade the most valuable and constantly increasing—they are beyond the reach of punishment and with them influence is only to be acquired by fear of punishment or hope of presents."[1]

So it was that in the fall of 1831 young Major Sanford was authorized by the Secretary of War to conduct a selected group of Indian leaders from the several Upper Missouri tribes to the nation's capital. General William Clark, renowned co-leader of the Lewis and Clark overland expedition to the Pacific Ocean a quarter of a century earlier, and at this time superintendent of Indian Affairs in St. Louis, wrote Secretary of War Cass on September 3

[1] John F. A. Sanford to William Clark, June 20, 1830. National Archives, Indian Office Records, Letters Received, Upper Missouri Agency, 1824–35.

76

that he expected Sanford and his Indians to reach St. Louis about November 15.[2]

Meanwhile the Indian Agent was having his troubles rounding up members for his expedition. It wasn't easy to persuade young warriors that the attractions of a Washington they couldn't comprehend were sufficiently worth seeing to justify a whole year's absence from the known excitements of the buffalo hunt or the horse or scalp raids and the pleasures of their own firesides. Only really adventurous souls would join the Major's party. Even after they set out down river from Fort Union at the mouth of the Yellowstone (near the present Montana–North Dakota line) several volunteer delegates changed their minds and returned to their homes. They acted just like members of an Indian war party who, having received dream warnings that their expedition was ill starred, turned back long before they reached the enemy's camp.

Only four Indians and two interpreters remained with the Major on the Washington-bound mission as their mackinaw boat, manned by a crew of husky French-Canadians, neared the white settlements on the Lower Missouri in November. It was then (according to the story told George Catlin a few weeks later) that the Indians who had traveled more than fifteen hundred miles down river without seeing much evidence of the white man's vaunted civilization "commenced a register of the white men's houses (or cabins) by cutting a notch for each on the side of a pipestem in order to show when they got home how many white men's houses they saw on their journey. At first the cabins were scarce; but continually as they advanced down the river more and more rapidly increased in numbers, and they soon found their pipestem filled with marks, and they determined to put the rest of them on the handle of a war club, which they soon got marked all over likewise; and at length, while the boat was moored at the shore for the purpose of cooking the dinner of the party, (the Indians) stepped into the bushes and cut a long stick, from which they peeled the bark; and when the boat

---

[2] William Clark to Secretary of War Lewis Cass, Sept. 3, 1831. National Archives, Indian Office Records.

was again under way they sat down and with much labor copied the notches onto it from the pipestem and club, and also kept adding a notch for every house they passed. This stick was soon filled, and in a day or two several others, when at last they seemed much at a loss to know what to do with their troublesome records, until they came in sight of St. Louis, which is a town of fifteen thousand inhabitants, upon which, after consulting a little, they pitched their sticks overboard into the river."[3]

The *St. Louis Beacon* for December 15 briefly noted their arrival: "Major John Dougherty, Indian Agent for the Missouri, and Major J. F. A. Sandford, Sub-Agent for the upper Missouri, arrived at this place a short time since. Major S. is accompanied by several of the principal men of the Assiniboin, Cree and Soteau tribes of Indians, the first visit ever made by any of their bands to our settlements."

George Catlin, who had yet to gain his reputation as the most prolific painter of Indians in the pre-camera period, was in St. Louis at the time. With Major Sanford's help he persuaded these Indians to sit for him. Likenesses of two of the four Indian delegates are preserved in the collection of Catlin's original oil paintings in the Smithsonian Institution.[4]

First to pose was the Assiniboin delegate whom Catlin called "Wi-jun-jon, The Pigeon's Egg Head." However, Catlin was a painter, not a linguist. Some of his Indian names are more romantic sounding than exact. This Indian was "Ah-jon-jon," a name somewhat difficult to translate. Several of this man's descendants, elderly Indians living on Fort Peck and Fort Belknap Reservations, Montana, have told me the name refers to something transparent and bright. Probably the best short translation is "The Light," a rendering suggested more than a century ago by the Assiniboin-speaking fur trader, Edwin T. Denig.[5]

---

[3] Catlin, *Letters and Notes on the Manners, Customs and Condition of the North American Indians*, II, 195.

[4] "The Light" is Cat. No. 386,179, and "Broken Arm" is Cat. No. 386,176 in the Catlin Collection of the Smithsonian Institution.

[5] Denig, *Five Indian Tribes*, 86. Denig's Assiniboin wife, Deer Little Woman, was a sister of The Light.

PLATE 9   The Light, an Assiniboin leader, as painted by George Catlin
in St. Louis in the fall of 1831.

PLATE 10 Broken Arm, Cree Indian chief, as painted by George Catlin in St. Louis in the fall of 1831.

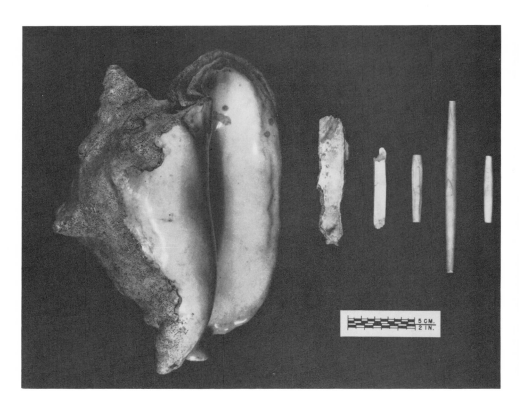

PLATE 12   Stages in the manufacture of a shell hair pipe. Left to right: shell of the *Strombus gigas*; piece of the lip broken away; two partially shaped hair pipes; shaped and bored hair pipes —one five inches and the other two inches long.

PLATE 13 A Mandan dandy wearing beaded hair bows, a beaded
choker, and other ornaments. Engraving from an original
water color by Karl Bodmer, 1834.

PLATE 14   Top: A beaded choker from the Upper Missouri.
Bottom: Front and back views of a beaded hair bow.

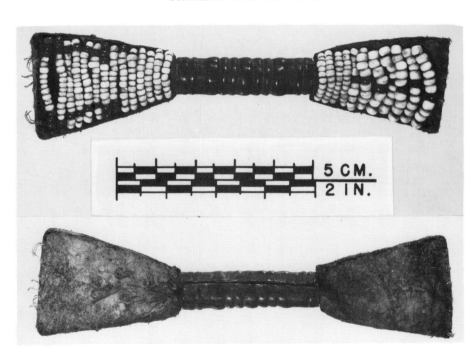

PLATE 15   Detail of a buffalo robe painted by a Mandan Indian and collected by Lewis and Clark in 1804–1805, showing style of rendering the human figure.

PLATE 16 Detail of a buffalo robe painted by a Mandan Indian and collected by Lewis and Clark in 1804–1805, showing style of rendering a horse and rider.

The Light was the outstanding personality, the star of the troupe. He was the eldest son of Iron Arrow Point, chief of the Stone Band, one of the major divisions of the large Assiniboin tribe. About thirty years of age, The Light had gained a high reputation among his people as a hunter and a warrior. He had become a great favorite of the American traders at Fort Union. They had recognized his qualities of leadership by appointing him to serve as a soldier at the fort, responsible for keeping order among the Indians when they came in to trade. He was also relied upon to recapture and bring back any horses that were stolen from the fort by brash young Assiniboin braves. The traders must have encouraged their good and influential friend, The Light, to leave his wife and children behind to make the long trek to Washington. Surely here was a savage Apollo who would make a striking impression in the drawing rooms of Washington.

Catlin's portrait emphasized the mongoloid features of this proud, handsome man—his large broad face, prominent cheekbones and nose; his firm lips, strong jaw, and straight, shining black hair. His powerful body was clothed in a shirt of finely dressed mountain-goat skin, tastefully embroidered with narrow bands and rosettes of delicately colored porcupine quills. (See Plate 9).

Catlin called one of The Light's fellow delegates "Eehtow-wees-ka-zeet, He who has Eyes behind him." Catlin erred less grievously in rendering this man's name. It was translated "Eyes on Both Sides" by both Denig and modern-day Indians. However, he was known to Catlin and even better known to the traders by the name of "Broken Arm." This name he had earned on the battlefield. In an intertribal fight this man's left arm was wounded, but with his one good arm he killed several of the enemy and counted coup repeatedly. Broken Arm, prominent warrior, was a delegate from the Plains Cree tribe.

Catlin portrayed Broken Arm as a good-looking young man of dignified bearing. The entire upper half of his face was painted vermilion. In addition to his decorated skin shirt he wore an elaborate choker covered with blue-and-white glass trade beads, ear drops of silver, and a frontlet made of large necklace beads and tubular white shell ornaments known to Indians and traders as "hair pipes." They were made from Bahama conch shells by white wampum makers in far-off New Jersey and were offered to western Indians by both Canadian and American traders. Broken Arm's portrait shows more clearly than The Light's the influence of the fur trade upon Indian ornamentation among the wild tribes of the Upper Missouri at that time.[6] (See Plate 10).

The other two Indian delegates made so little impression during their trip to Washington that even their names escaped recording. We know only that one of them was a Plains Ojibway (Soteau) and the other a Tête Coupe or Yanktonai Sioux. We know, too, that there were two Frenchmen in the party who served as interpreters for the Indians. One, Michel Gravil, interpreted for the two Algonquian-speaking Indians (Broken Arm and the nameless Ojibway). The other, Loupon Frenier, translated for the Siouan-speaking red men (The Light and the unnamed Yanktonai).

Soon after their arrival in St. Louis the party must have called upon "the red-head chief," General William Clark. In the large brick building attached to his residence on the corner of Vine and Main streets, Clark was accustomed to receive visiting Indians. He not only welcomed the red men with tact and dignity but took pains to show them the remarkable collection of Indian costumes, weapons, and utensils as well as the two-headed calf and the miscellaneous objects of natural history that adorned the walls of his council chamber. This room, in reality the first museum west of the Mississippi River, had become one of St. Louis' outstanding tourist attractions for both whites and Indians. Leading American scientists and members of European royalty traveling in this country had seen it and had written their praise of Clark's Indian Museum. Many of the most prominent Indian chiefs of the Mississippi Valley and not a few Plains Indian leaders had been formally received in that room. No doubt General Clark reminded the men of this first delegation from the Upper Missouri of his own travels in their country a quarter of a century before and expressed his appreciation of their returning his visit.

[6] See Plate 9.

In St. Louis, too, the Indians were examined by a doctor who vaccinated them against the dread smallpox. Every precaution was taken to insure their health and welfare. Nevertheless, the Indians became temporarily indisposed, it was thought because of changes in diet and climate. Major Sanford was compelled to delay in St. Louis longer than he had planned.

Not until New Year's Day of 1832 was the party ready to proceed on its way eastward. By then the Mississippi River was frozen over. Instead of continuing their travels by boat as originally planned, they had to take the more expensive stage route. The first leg of their overland journey took them to Maysville, Kentucky. From there they rode up the Ohio Valley to Wheeling (then in Virginia) in two hacks. They stopped over in Wheeling for two days (until January 10), then crossed the mountains to Frederick, Maryland, by stage.

The *Frederick Herald* reported the appearance of this strange party in that town on January 12, nearly two weeks after they left St. Louis:

INDIANS—Major John Sanford, the highly respectable and intelligent Indian Agent who has charge of the Indians in the vicinity of and beyond the Mandan villages, passed through this city on Thursday last, accompanied by the most distinguished braves or warriors of the Assynaboin, or Stone Indians, the Knisteneaux or Cree and Sotue tribes, which reside in remote sections of our territory in the vicinity of the Rocky Mountains, and are almost entire strangers to the arts of civilization—the only whites with whom they hold intercourse, with the exception of the agents of the Hudson Bay company, being a few of our own citizens engaged in the fur trade. We learn from Major Sanford that delegates from nine tribes would have accompanied him, but after having avoided their enemies and surmounted the greatest privations and difficulties, they became alarmed at reports of small pox, and five returned. These, however, by whom Maj. S. is accompanied, will fulfill the intention of the government, which is to impress them, and through them the warlike tribes which they represent, with an idea of the effects of civilization, and our ability to redress any injuries which they may inflict upon our citizens.

81

They will be under the direction of the agent, visit Washington, Baltimore, Philadelphia and New York, and take their departure for the West early in spring—and it is expected, so distant do they reside from the Atlantic seaboard, that nearly the balance of the year will be expended in returning them to their respective tribes.

This delegation is completely Ferae naturae, and an admirable specimen of those roving Indians of whose existence and feats we read more as romance than fact. In their native plains and forests they wear only a robe, carelessly thrown over the right shoulder, their limbs unfettered and free; and notwithstanding Major S. has provided them leggings and other clothing suitable to the season, they could not be prevailed upon to wear hats or caps; their only headdress being their enormous locks of hair.

The delegation is accompanied by two interpreters, and we have no doubt that the visit will prove of great benefit to our citizens engaged in the fur trade.

At Frederick the party boarded a train for Baltimore and Washington. The *Herald* reporter eagerly watched the wild Indians in order to catch some indication of their reactions to this new miracle of locomotion. He was, however, "struck by their philosophic demeanor, so eminently characteristic of the savage—they evinced no curiosity, no excitement, and seemed to think with him of old 'there is nothing new under the sun.' Even the rail road, that wonder of the world, could not arouse their phlegmatic temperment, and though the renowned 'Brokenarm' took an outside seat, it was more with a view to being near his friend Major S. than to look upon the mode by which the rails are travelled."

On their arrival in the capital city the party engaged lodgings at Brown's Hotel. On January 15, Major Sanford rendered an itemized bill listing the expenses encountered in bringing his delegation as far as Washington. This fascinating document, preserved in the National Archives, is a unique commentary on the complexity as well as the costliness of this undertaking. Transportation charges alone involved such diverse items as the purchase of a $49.00 mule used by the agent in his quest for potential delegates in the Indian country, the rental of a mackinaw boat from the American Fur Company, and payments for the services of five strong-backed oarsmen and boatmen to navigate the vessel down the Missouri; ferryage charges across the Mississippi, stage and hack fare from St. Louis to Frederick, and train fare from thence to Washington. Food items varied from the purchase of meat and pemmican on the Upper Missouri to the payment for individual meals as the party neared Washington. The pay of the interpreters and of the Major himself and lodging items were entered. This accounting also included such oddly interesting entries as: $42.00 paid to "Tous. Charbonneau" (well-known to western history as the undistinguished husband of the famous Indian girl, Sacajawea) for the hire of two horses to go from the Hidatsa villages toward the Rocky Mountains in a vain search for a Crow Indian delegate; $56.00 for the purchase of buffalo robes, which the Major justified by the explanation, "With the usual Indian improvidence they started unprovided and I was compelled to furnish them when the cold weather overtook us or run the risk of their attempting to return." In St. Louis there was an item of $35.25 for "vermilion, socks, mittens, etc." to keep the Indians' faces freshly painted and their appendages warm. There was also Dr. Tiffin's bill of $35.00 for "medical attendance and vaccinating Indians." Total expenditures to the date of the party's arrival in Washington were $2,402.04.[7]

Two days later Major Sanford submitted to the Secretary of War an estimate of the delegation's expenditures for the remainder of its trip, broken down into seven items:

$300 board and room while in Washington.
$500 to visit principal cities.
$700 return travel to St. Louis.
$700 travel from St. Louis to the Indians' homes (2,000 miles).
$500 pay of the two interpreters (15 January to August 1832).
$350 pay of Major Sanford for the same period.

[7] John F. A. Sanford to Secretary of War Lewis Cass, Jan. 15, 1832, National Archives, Indian Office Records.

$1000 presents to Indians consisting of "Guns, Swords, pistols, Suits of Clothes etc."[8]

Considering that there were only four Indians in the party, this item of $1,000 for presents seems to be rather steep. The Major justified it with the laconic notation, "Without presents they have no ears." By adding these seven items to the actual expenditures prior to January 15, we can see that this delegation must have cost in the neighborhood of $6,450. This was at a time when coffee was selling at eleven cents a pound, imported wine at thirty-seven cents a gallon, and when an ambitious young Indian agent was willing to risk his life for less than $700 a year. For the American taxpayer of 1832 this expedition from "the headwaters of the Missouri to Washington" and return was no joy ride.

In Washington, The Light really began to shine. His good looks, his straight, powerful physique, his tastefully decorated, spotless skin costume, his picturesque speeches, and his friendly disposition won him the smiles and admiration of fashionable ladies. The artist, Charles Bird King, painter of Washington society as well as many prominent Indian visitors to the nation's capital, asked The Light to pose for him. King's oil portrait, bearing the title "Assiniboin Indian from the Most Remote Tribe That Had ever Visited Washington previous to 1838" still hangs in the Redwood library and Athenaeum in Newport, Rhode Island. No doubt, the Indians visited the great council house (capitol) and met the country's lawmakers. They went to the White House where The Light made a particular hit with President Jackson. According to his Assiniboin descendants, The Light gave the President his name and his best skin suit. Andrew Jackson graciously reciprocated by presenting his name and general's uniform to The Light. Wherever they went, the other Indians tagged along, consistently outshone by The Light's magnetic personality and his superb showmanship.

The four Indians visited Baltimore, Philadelphia, and New York and observed in all these big cities the whites "as numerous as

[8] John F. A. Sanford to Secretary of War Lewis Cass, Jan. 17, 1832. National Archives, Indian Office Records.

84

blades of grass on the plains," so many, indeed, that "they had to build their tipis one on top of another" (two-story houses). They were shown the white men's forts, their shot towers, their great armories, and their loud-mouthed cannon, their ocean-going ships, their railroads, and their balloons—all the material wonders of the white man's civilization. Nor did they fail to notice many strange social customs among the whites.

By spring the Indians had seen the East and were back in St. Louis. Arrangements were made for them to return to their own country aboard the American Fur Company's new steamboat, the *Yellowstone*, on her maiden voyage upriver to Fort Union. It would be the first steamboat ever to sail so far up the Missouri.

George Catlin, a fellow passenger on the *Yellowstone*, was so impressed by the amazing transformation in The Light's appearance since he had seen him only a few months before in St. Louis that he painted a full-length two-figure oil portrait contrasting the handsome Indian in beautiful native dress who went to Washington with the grotesque and not a little ludicrous character he saw on his way home from there. As The Light strode on deck, he was wearing a military coat and trousers of fine blue broadcloth trimmed with gold lace. A pair of huge epaulettes covered his shoulders. A shining black stock wrapped round his neck and tight, high-heeled boots made him "step like a yoked hog." On his head sat a high beaver hat, banded with silver lace and surmounted by a red plume two feet tall. His long Indian locks flowed down his back hiding most of his high, stiff uniform collar. His hands were sheathed in white kid gloves. In one of them he held a blue umbrella; in the other, a large fan. Catlin added a couple of whisky bottles, partly concealed by his long coat, for good measure. The Light was whistling "Yankee Doodle."

For fully half an hour after The Light hobbled ashore at Fort Union, his wife and other relatives pretended not to know him in his strange garb. But gradually his white man's clothes were discarded. By the next day the lower part of his uniform coat had been converted into a pair of leggings for his wife. She held her new, blue leg coverings in place with garters made from the silver lace hat-band. One of The Light's brothers wore the top of the coat over a pair of Indian-made buckskin leggings. By noon of that first day the tight boots gave way to a pair of comfortable skin moccasins. By the close of the second day, after freely imbibing from the keg of whisky The Light had brought home, little remained of his new finery except his blue umbrella and his President Jackson medal.[9]

On August 1, Major Sanford, happy no doubt to have discharged his responsibility for the delegation, wrote to Elbert Herring, commissioner of Indian affairs in Washington: "The Indians I got back safe to their country and highly gratified with their trip and that it will be attended with great advantages to our traders, I don't hesitate to affirm positively."[10]

The next summer (1833), the traveling German scientist, Maximilian, Prince of Wied, met The Light at Fort Union. He had led his band of forty-two lodges (including about sixty warriors) to Fort Union to trade. The German Prince, like other white men before him, was charmed by this Indian; he described The Light in his published account of his travels: "He was a handsome man, in a fine dress; he wore a beautifully embroidered black leather shirt, a new scarlet blanket, and a great medal round his neck." The Prince also noted that this Indian commonly was called "General Jackson."

At Fort Union the Prince also saw Broken Arm, chief of a Cree band, "who had a medal with the effigy of the President hung round his neck, which he had received on a visit to Washington." So Major Sanford's confident prediction that the Indian delegation's journey to Washington would benefit the traders appeared on the surface to be borne out in the observations of a famous scientist a year later.[11]

But the traders knew better. Jackson, the erstwhile "Light," was becoming more and more of a problem to his own people, what with his continual, insistent talk about the strange miracles he had witnessed when he "was at Washington." To some of his fellow tribes-

[9] Catlin, *Letters and Notes*, II, 194–200.

[10] John F. A. Sanford to Commissioner Elbert Herring, Aug. 1, 1832. National Archives, Indian Office Records.

[11] Alexander Phillip Maximilian, *Travels*, vol. XXIII in Thwaites' *Early Western Travels*, 13, 20–21, 201.

men this fellow's "lying" was becoming unbearable. In fact, his accounts of the wonders of civilization had gotten him into more than one quarrel with former friends who dared to question his veracity. Nevertheless, the Assiniboins believed that Jackson led a charmed life—that he was impervious to death by lead bullets.

Then one evening (according to the intelligent fur trader, Edwin T. Denig) Jackson was amusing some of his friends by telling them about the shot tower he saw when "I was at Washington." A stranger in the group, unable to comprehend a structure made by man of such size and height as Jackson was describing, interrupted several times, challenging the teller's regard for the truth. This irked Jackson so that at the conclusion of his story he invited his friends to step outside his lodge into the moonlight while he convinced the stranger of the truth of his story.

Once outside, Jackson began to tell the stranger one more experience which had made an indelible impression upon him. "When I was at Washington in a private home, some gentleman was telling a strange story to the others. During the recital there was another man present who so far forgot himself as to call the other a liar. The gentleman said nothing at the time, but promised to convince him as soon as the company adjourned, which shortly afterward they did to a barroom of a public house, when the guest who told the story took the one who called him a liar by the arm thus and caned him most unmercifully." So saying, Jackson raised his own cane and broke it over the back of the disbelieving stranger.

The group dispersed. But later that night the stranger busied himself quietly filing down a piece of iron about an inch long to fit the caliber of his gun. He loaded it carefully into the muzzle of his firearm and went in search of the lead-proof Jackson, who was sitting at the back of his lodge smoking his pipe. The stranger placed the muzzle of his gun a few inches from the shadow of Jackson's head on the outside of the skin tipi cover and pulled the trigger. The iron slug tore away the upper part of Jackson's head.

All that was mortal of The Light, alias Jackson, was buried in a tree near the place the Assiniboins called "big white man's house," his beloved Fort Union. Next summer (according to Charles Larpenteur, the trader) some St. Louis doctors requested some Indian skulls. The Light's head was cut off, placed in a sack with several other Indian crania, and sent downriver to the civilization that had been the cause of his undoing.

Even after The Light's death his influence continued to plague the Assiniboins. One of his several brothers tracked his murderer to a Hidatsa village and killed him by shooting through the smoke-hole into the earth lodge where he was hiding. The feud continued over a period of several years until no fewer than six men of the contesting families were killed. The feud was not ended until a disastrous smallpox epidemic greatly reduced the numbers of the Assiniboins (in 1837).[12]

But what of The Light's traveling companion, Broken Arm? To be sure, he was no favorite of the traders. Larpenteur simply wrote that he "never amounted to anything." Denig claimed that Broken Arm, profiting from The Light's sad experience, "told all lies, represented the Americans as but a handful of people far inferior in every respect to his own." Denig termed him "a scheming, mean, beggerly Indian ... pretty generally despised by the traders." Yet in the year 1854, more than two decades after that fateful Indian delegation to Washington, Denig grudgingly admitted that Broken Arm had some influence among his own nation.[13]

Fortunately there are other data which may help us to appraise the character and status of Broken Arm. Larpenteur himself recognized "Broken Arm, the great chief of the Crees, who had been to Washington" as head of the Indian winter camp at Woody Mountain in January, 1844. Larpenteur had good reason to remember that camp; he obtained 180 buffalo robes from those Indians in exchange for a mere five gallons of diluted liquor. In 1851, Broken Arm was a tribal delegate to the Fort Laramie Treaty Council at which the first tribal boundaries in the Northern Plains were described and mapped. In the fall of 1855 he represented his people

---

[12] Denig, *Five Indian Tribes*, 86–88. Denig wrote a more detailed account of the events leading to the death of The Light, which was published in Pierre Jean De Smet, *Life, Letters, and Travels of Father Pierre Jean De Smet*, III, 1177–83.

[13] Denig, *Five Indian Tribes*, 114.

at the council on the Missouri River at the mouth of the Judith when the first treaty between the United States and the powerful Blackfoot tribes was negotiated.[14]

In January, 1848, the Canadian artist Paul Kane met this Indian near Fort Edmonton. Broken Arm, then chief of a band of forty lodges, was most hospitable, inviting Kane to supper and presenting his pipe to the white man as a gift. Kane's account of this visit reveals Broken Arm as both a practical philosopher and a homespun humorist:

> We sat up very late talking to the chief, who seemed to enjoy our society very much. Amongst the other topics of discourse, he began talking about the efforts of the missionaries amongst his people, and seemed to think that they would not be very successful; for though he did not interfere with the religious belief of any of his tribe, yet many thought as he did; and his idea was, that as Mr. Rundell had told him that what he preached was the only true road to heaven, and Mr. Hunter told him the same thing, and so did Mr. Thebo, and as all three said that the other two were wrong, and as he did not know which was right, he thought they ought to call a council among themselves, and that then he would go with them all three; but that until they agreed he would wait.
>
> He then told us that there was a tradition in his tribe of one of them having become a Christian, and was very good, and did all he ought; and that when he died he was taken up to the white man's heaven, where everything was very good and very beautiful, and all were happy amongst their friends and relatives who had gone before them, and where they had everything that the white man loves and longs for; but the Indian could not share their joy and pleasure, for all was strange to him, and he met none of the spirits of his ancestors, and there was none to welcome him, no hunting nor fishing, nor any of those joys in which he used to delight, and his spirit grew sad. Then the Great Manitou called him and asked him, "Why art thou sad in this beautiful heaven which I have made for your joy and happiness?" and the Indian told him that he sighed for the com-

[14] Charles Larpenteur, *Forty Years a Fur Trader on the Upper Missouri*, II, 412–31. Private Gustavus Sohon drew a pencil portrait of Broken Arm at the Blackfoot Treaty Council in October, 1855, which is now in the Washington State Historical Society, Tacoma.

pany of the spirits of his relations, and that he felt lone and sorrowful. So the Great Manitou told him that he could not send him to the Indian heaven, as he had, whilst on earth, chosen this one, but that as he had been a very good man, he would send him back to earth again, and give him another chance.[15]

This tradition is almost a parable of Broken Arm's own great adventure of some sixteen years earlier. He had traveled to the far-off white man's land. There he had seen and experienced many wonderful things which white men thought were good. But Broken Arm found that the white men's ways were not meant for him. He was happy to return home and pursue once again the old familiar life of a Cree Indian.

The Light, on the other hand, had been one of those Indians whom traders and Indian agents superficially termed "progressive." He was fascinated by the white men's ways. He enjoyed wearing the white man's collar. He thought he could interpret the wonders of the white man's world to unbelieving Indians who hadn't had this unusual opportunity to travel to far-off Washington. To his people he became something more distasteful than a mere bore or a chronic liar. He was a disturbing disciple of an alien way of life who had sold his Indian birthright for a mess of wild dreams. He was bad medicine. The Light had to be extinguished!

[15] Paul Kane, *Wanderings of an Artist Among the Indian Tribes of North America*, 275–77.

✖︎═══✖︎═══✖︎

CHAPTER SEVEN

Three Ornaments Worn by Upper Missouri Dandies in the 1830's*

IN THE YEARS 1831–34 two white artists created the earliest-known portraits of some of the most picturesque of all westerners—the Indians of the Upper Missouri. These field portraits by the self-taught American, George Catlin, and the thoroughly schooled Swiss, Karl Bodmer, are important sources of detailed information on the costumes worn by northern plainsmen a century and a quarter ago. Not only do they show the basic forms and methods of decoration of the larger garments but they also illustrate the ornamental accessories worn by prominent men and women among the tribes of the region to enhance their appearance on dress occasions.

Three types of ornaments worn by young men are of particular interest as examples of the ingenuity of the natives in combining trade articles with materials obtained by these Indians in their own country. These ornaments, the hair-pipe hair ornament, the beaded choker, and the beaded hair bow, are exceedingly rare in museum collections today.

As has been related, in the fall of 1831, George Catlin executed portraits of members of a small delegation of Indians from the Upper Missouri whom he met in St. Louis on their way to visit the Great White Father in Washington. One of them, Broken Arm, a band chief and renowned warrior of the Plains Cree, wore a particularly handsome costume. Across the frontal part of his head and dropping down each side of his face was a cord, probably of buckskin, on which were strung large glass trade beads and four long,

* Reprinted in revised form from *The New-York Historical Society Quarterly*, Vol. XLI, No. 1 (January, 1957).

white tubelike pendants. (See Plate 10.) The Six and Wolf Calf, representing two other tribes, were also depicted wearing similar ornaments. When Catlin visited the Upper Missouri tribes in the summer of 1832, he painted a portrait of The Six, a Plains Ojibway chief. The following summer, Karl Bodmer, among the Blackfeet near Fort McKenzie, made a fine water-color portrait of Wolf Calf, a young Piegan.

The most striking feature of these ornaments—the long, white tubes, tapering gradually from the centers toward each end—were known to Indian traders as hair pipes. They were fashioned in faraway New Jersey from the lip of the large conch shell, *Strombus gigas*. Thousands of these shells were carried to New York as ballast in ships returning from the West Indies. There they were bought by enterprising Bergen County wampum makers, who carted them home and with crude hand tools painstakingly worked them into ornaments for the Indian trade. Plate 12 illustrates the successive stages in the manufacture of a hair pipe. Starting with the unworked *Strombus gigas* shell, next a portion of the thick lip of a shell was broken off with a pick and chisel. A piece was then blocked out ready for drilling a hole through its center lengthwise. Finally the short pipe was drilled by hand with a metal drill which was passed halfway through the pipe. Then the pipe was reversed and drilled from the other end until the two holes met at the center. A long hair pipe would be shaped by holding it in wooden pinchers against a grindstone. A finished pipe's surface was carefully polished with Rockaway sand and water.

The Bergen County hair-pipe makers marketed their products through New York merchants who sold them to Indian traders in both Montreal and St. Louis as early as the first decade of the nineteenth century. Lewis and Clark are known to have purchased two dozen hair pipes from Auguste Chouteau, the leading Indian trader of St. Louis. They planned to distribute them sparingly, no more than two to each chief, among the tribes they met on their trip up the Missouri. Apparently hair pipes were rare and coveted Indian gifts at that time.

By the 1830's the American Fur Company in New York was

selling hair pipes in considerable quantities to Pratte, Chouteau and Company of St. Louis, the principal firm engaged in the Indian trade on the Upper Missouri. Records of these transactions appear in the American Fur Company papers in The New-York Historical Society. When an order for "6000 inches Wampum hair pipes" was received on December 12, 1834, it was accompanied by a complaint that some of the pipes in a previous order had not been bored through. Whereupon the American Fur Company wrote the manufacturer, Samuel Campbell, Franklin, Bergen County, New Jersey:

> We want 3250 inches Wampum Hair Pipes, none less than 5 inches long, and not many of them over 6 inches—You must have them here by the first day of February next, or say 4 weeks from this time, and we shall pay you the same price as last season—Some of those you furnished last winter were not bored entirely through—This will not do, and I hope such deception will never be practiced again.[1]

The hair pipes were shipped to St. Louis via New Orleans. Presumably they reached St. Louis in time to be sent to the upriver trading posts on the Missouri for the following summer and winter Indian trade. The natives were sharp traders who again refused to accept imperfectly drilled hair pipes. And again the St. Louis traders wrote to New York complaining that some of the holes didn't "meet in the middle."[2]

Catlin's portrait of Broken Arm discloses the appearance of a rarer ornament, a two-banded choker, worn around the subject's neck. (See Plate 10.) Catlin's portrait of The Six, Plains Ojibway chief, and Bodmer's likeness of a Mandan dandy (Plate 13) also illustrate this neck ornament.

At least two examples of this distinctive ornament are preserved in museum collections. Both specimens probably date from the 1830's or earlier. Neither is tribally identified. One of the chokers,[3] in the Peabody Museum of Archaeology and Ethnology, Harvard

[1] American Fur Company Papers, Orders Inward, Book 1, pp. 3, 29 (The New-York Historical Society).

[2] *Ibid.*, 154–55. I have described the various uses of hair pipes by western tribes in "Hair Pipes in Plains Indian Adornment: A Study in Indian and White Ingenuity," Anthropological Paper No. 50, Bureau of American Ethnology *Bulletin 164*, 1957.

[3] Peabody Museum of Archaeology and Ethnology, Cat. No. 53017.

University, Cambridge, Massachusetts, was formerly a part of the old Peale Museum Collection in Philadelphia. The other,[4] in the United States National Museum, was collected by John Varden, pioneer museum man of Washington, D.C., probably before 1840. It is identified merely by the regional designation "Missouri Valley." This choker (Plate 14) consists of a base of buckskin stuffed with some semisoft material. The two rolls measure one and seven-eighths inches in diameter and are ornamented on the outside with alternate bands of blue and white trade beads of large embroidering bead size, about one-eighth of an inch in diameter. The beads are sewn to the skin base with sinew thread. There are strings of the same type of beads pendant from the center of the front of this ornament. The choker was tied around the wearer's neck by two buckskin cords at the back of the specimen.

Another ornament which was more commonly depicted in Catlin's and Bodmer's portraits of Indian men among tribes on the Missouri north of the Teton Sioux was the beaded hair bow. Catlin shows this ornament in two portraits of Hidatsa Indians, two of Mandans, one each of an Assiniboin and a Crow Indian. Bodmer illustrated this ornament in nine portraits—six Mandans, a Hidatsa, a Crow, and a Yanktonai Sioux Indian.[5]

A tribally unidentified and undated example of the beaded hair bow is preserved in the United States National Museum. (See Plate 4.) This specimen clearly illustrates the details of hair-bow construction. The base is a bow-shaped piece of rawhide four and one-fourth inches long. A brass tube one and one-half inches in length is wrapped around the center of the piece. The front surface of each end section is embroidered with blue and white trade beads of one-eighth-inch diameter, sewn to the rawhide with sinew thread.

As indicated in the Bodmer portrait (Plate 23), these bows were worn in pairs, one over each temple, although the method of tying to the hair is not illustrated. Some of these ornaments were elaborated by a feather sewn upright to the top of the bow or by long

[4] United States National Museum, Cat. No. 5419.

[5] The original Catlin paintings are in the Smithsonian Institution. Bodmer's illustrations are reproduced in the *Atlas* accompanying Prince Maximilian's *Travels in the Interior of North America.*

PLATE 17   Four Bears, Mandan second chief, as painted by George
Catlin in 1832.

PLATE 18   Four Bears, Mandan second chief, from an engraving of an
original water color by Karl Bodmer, 1834.

COURTESY SMITHSONIAN INSTITUTION

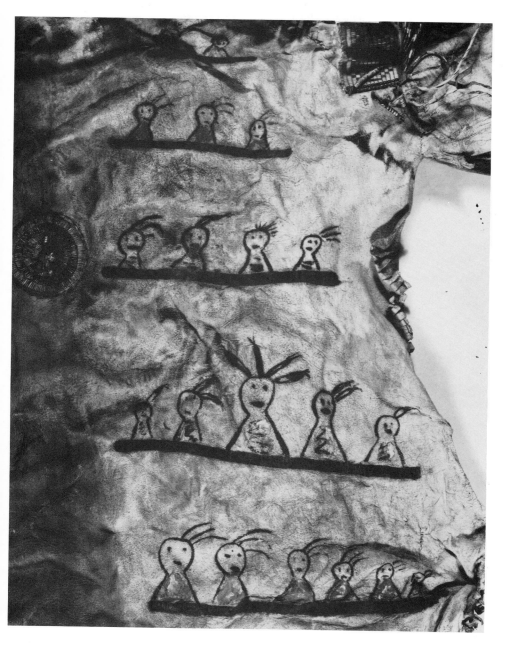

PLATE 19   Detail of coups counted by Four Bears—from painted representation on the front of shirt collected by George Catlin in 1832.

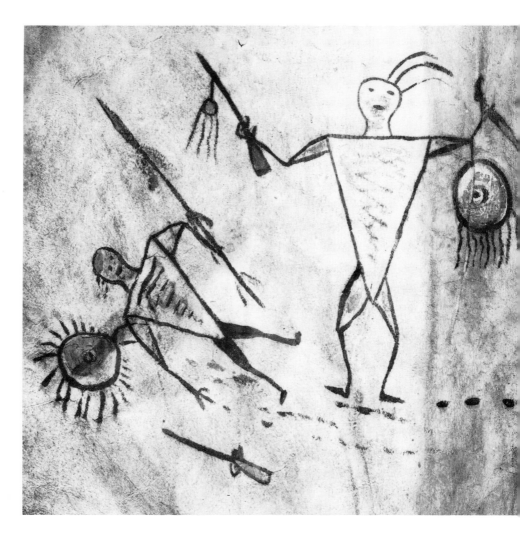

PLATE 20   Detail of painted record of counting a coup — on the back of
Four Bears' shirt collected by George Catlin in 1832.

PLATE 21   Four Bears' own water color of his killing a Cheyenne chief
with a knife in hand-to-hand combat, collected by Maximilian, Prince of Wied-Neuwied in 1834.

PLATE 22   Yellow Feather, Mandan artist, as painted by George Catlin
in 1832.

PLATE 23   Yellow Feather, Mandan artist (at left). Engraving from a
water color by Karl Bodmer in 1834.

PLATE 24   Water color drawing by the Mandan Indian Yellow Feather,
collected by Maximilian, Prince of Wied-Neuwied in 1834.

pendants from the bottom of the bow. Some pendants are lengths of braided hair or metal chain. Others are more elaborate, consisting of alternating elements of dentalium shells and large trade beads (Plate 23). The dentalium was obtained through intertribal trade from Indians living on the Pacific Coast. The trader, Alexander Henry, observed trade in these shells among the Chinooks on the Lower Columbia in 1813. "The best quality are two inches long. One fathom of these shells is valued at three blankets of 2½ points. They are gathered northward, somewhere about Woody point N. of Nootka, in the sand, at low water."[6]

Prince Maximilian, the German scientist whom Karl Bodmer accompanied to the Upper Missouri, learned that the Blackfoot Indians obtained dentalium shells from "the nations on the west side of the Rocky Mountains, especially the Kutanas."[7] Maximilian mentioned that the hair-bow ornaments worn by the Mandan men in 1833–34 were beaded with blue and white beads and had pendants of blue trade beads and white dentalium shells.[8] Probably the dentalium shells used by the Mandans and the Hidatsas were obtained from the Crow Indians who were intermediaries in the trade between the tribes west of the Rockies and the horticultural villages on the Missouri.

The large glass beads strung on pendants and the smaller ones sewn with sinew on chokers and hair bows are typical examples of the beads furnished in considerable quantities to the Upper Missouri tribes by American traders in the 1830's. The embroidering beads were of the larger size, known to older Indians in recent years as "big beads." They are about twice the size of the little seed beads commonly employed in Plains Indian beadwork of the late nineteenth century and still used in the beadwork of the western Indians.

The Indians selected their bead colors and sizes with great care. In the 1830's they had a definite preference for two colors—blue and white. These colors contrasted tastefully with the buckskin

---

[6] Henry and Thompson, *New Light*, II, 753.
[7] Maximilian, *Travels*, XXIII, 98.
[8] *Ibid.*, 259.

backgrounds of their dress clothing and the reddish-brown of their faces. The original Catlin paintings in the United States National Museum and the Bodmer water colors in the Joslyn Art Museum in Omaha clearly reveal the preference for blue and white beads among the Upper Missouri tribes. This preference also is indicated in the large orders for trade beads received by the American Fur Company in New York from Pratte, Chouteau and Company of St. Louis in the 1830's. On November 20, 1835, the St. Louis firm complained:

> With regard to the Glass Beads, blue and white pound Beads, all those received last year and this year . . . were entirely too large and unsaleable. You ought to have good samples with which we have furnished you for several years past besides Mr. Jacob Halsey has promised to assist you in the purchase of these articles. Have the goodness to see him on the subject and endeavor that so important an article should be furnished us of the color and size exactly suitable.[9]

Such complaints regarding unsalable beads in 1834 and 1835 and the failure of their Philadelphia importer to furnish beads in time for the 1836 trade caused the American Fur Company to place orders directly with Allesandre Bartolla of Venice, Italy, the great center for the manufacture of glass beads used in the Indian trade.[10]

Information now available on three types of ornaments worn by men among several tribes of the Upper Missouri at the time these Indians first were pictured by George Catlin and Karl Bodmer in the years 1831–34 reveals the ingenuity of these people in combining a few simple materials, native to their country and prepared with little difficulty (buckskin and hair cords, stuffed buckskin chokers, bow-shaped pieces of cut rawhide, and sinew thread), with trade materials to devise distinctive and attractive costume accessories. To the materials obtained through their own hunts they added dentalium shells secured in intertribal trade from the Pacific

[9] American Fur Company Papers, Orders Inward, Book 1, p. 164 (The New-York Historical Society).

[10] American Fur Company Papers, Letter Book No. 3, p. 222 (The New-York Historical Society).

Coast, hair pipes fashioned from West Indian conch shells by New Jersey wampum makers, brass tubes of undetermined origin, and glass beads from far-off Venice, Italy. New York City was the important distributing center for both hair pipes and trade beads.

While all three ornaments were portrayed in use among Upper Missouri tribes living northward of the Sioux, these ornaments appear to have had different tribal distributions, judging from the pictorial evidence now available. The hair-pipe hair pendant was worn by members of three Algonquian-speaking nomadic tribes, the Plains Crees, Plains Ojibways, and Blackfeet, all living north of the Missouri in present North Dakota, Montana, and adjacent areas of Canada. Beaded chokers were worn by young Mandans as well as by chiefs of the Plains Crees and Plains Ojibways. Beaded hair bows, apparently the most popular of the three ornaments, were worn by members of five Siouan-speaking tribes, the Assiniboins, Crows, Hidatsas, Mandans, and Yanktonais. However, the fact that more than half of the known wearers of this ornament were Mandan Indians suggests that the beaded hair bow may have been a Mandan invention.

CHAPTER EIGHT

Early White Influence Upon Plains Indian Painting: George Catlin and Karl Bodmer Among the Mandans, 1832-34*

During their visits to the Upper Missouri in the years 1832–34, the artists George Catlin and Karl Bodmer created some of the most authentic and best-known pictures of American Indians drawn or painted in the days before the development of photography. Their widely circulated originals and the published reproductions of their pictures have provided millions of viewers in this country and abroad, who never saw a Plains Indian, with a clear, accurate conception of the physical appearance and customs of those Indians early in the fourth decade of the nineteenth century.

Anthropologists, historians, and art critics have been accustomed to regard these artists as interpreters of Indian culture. Yet there is another point of view from which their contributions may be considered. While among the Indians they demonstrated their skill in handling an alien art style. They were, in effect, missionaries of the western European artistic tradition. To what extent was their example an influence upon native art? Might they not have been active as innovators in as well as observers of Indian culture?

Data are now available to demonstrate that Catlin's and Bodmer's artistic example did influence the development of the painting styles of at least two prominent Mandan artists who had rare opportunities to observe their artistic activity closely while these white artists were recording the native culture of the Mandan tribe.

From the time of the first known visit of white men to the Mandan villages in 1738 until the appearance of George Catlin among

---

* Reprinted in revised form from *Smithsonian Miscellaneous Collections*, Vol. CXXXIV, No. 7 (April 24, 1957).

them nearly a century later, the Mandans were repeatedly visited by white traders, explorers, and some government officials. Several traders are known to have lived among these Indians for a number of years during that period. But no one skilled in drawing or painting in the traditional, realistic, nineteenth-century style of western European culture is known to have practiced his art in the Mandan villages prior to the visit of George Catlin in the summer of 1832. Mandan Indian painting remained in the aboriginal tradition until that time.

The origin of the Mandan painting tradition is lost in antiquity. La Vérendrye, the French explorer-trader, observed, when he was in the Mandan villages on the Missouri in 1738, that these Indians traded painted buffalo robes to neighboring Assiniboin.[1] However, the oldest example of Mandan painting that has been preserved (which is also the earliest dated specimen of the figure painting of any Plains Indian tribe) is a painted buffalo robe collected by the American explorers Lewis and Clark in 1805. This robe is preserved in the collections of the Peabody Museum of Archaeology and Ethnology of Harvard University, Cambridge, Massachusetts. Lewis and Clark included it among the collection of ethnological materials which they sent to President Jefferson from the Mandan villages on April 5, 1805, before they embarked on their overland trek westward to the Pacific. They reported that the paintings on this robe portrayed a battle fought between Mandan warriors and enemy tribesmen about the year 1797. So this robe must have been painted within the period 1797–1805.[2]

This is a most interesting example of the aboriginal style of painting employed by men who were the delineators of heroic deeds of the tribe or of individual warriors on the inner surfaces of buffalo robes. The painting comprises a composition of forty-four foot warriors and twenty mounted men in combat. Their weapons include fifteen trade guns and a pistol in addition to a larger number of native-made offensive and defensive weapons—bows and arrows, lances, and shields. All the figures, human and animal, are

[1] La Vérendrye, *Journals*, 19.
[2] Lewis and Clark, *Original Journals*, I, 281, 288.

heavily outlined in a very dark brown, almost a black. Some of the outlined forms are filled in with dark brown, blue green, reddish brown, or yellow.

Careful examination of individual figures delineated on this specimen reveals some of the characteristics of the traditional native art style. An enlargement of one of the human figures on this robe clearly illustrates the characteristic style of human figure in this composition (see Plate 15). The head is a featureless, almost circular knob with pendent, conventionalized hair. The neck sits upon a separately rendered, elongated body which is geometric in character and drawn in outline only. The arms are lines extending outward from the shoulders and bent about midway of their length (*i.e.*, at the elbows). At the ends of these arms are solid ball-like hands with the five fingers extended as lines. The legs are relatively short, bent at the knees. The grossly shaped upper legs are connected to linear lower legs. The foot is merely a continuation of the line of the lower leg at an angle from it. There is no attempt to portray body clothing. Yet the conventionalized representation of the phallus and scrotum may be an indication that the Mandans and their neighbors wore no breechcloths at that period. Some contemporary descriptions of those Indians also suggest the absence of the breechcloth in the men's costume of the time.

The enlargement of one of the mounted figures painted on this robe shows the same style of rendering head, arms, and body of the human figure (see Plate 16). Notice that the man does not straddle the horse but merely sits atop it. There is no attempt to render the figure below the waist. The head and body of the horse are drawn in outline. The animal has neither eye nor mouth, but the ears are indicated one above the other and the mane is drawn in a conventionalized manner. The horse's neck and body are decorated in geometric fashion with lines forming angular patterns, some of which are partially filled with spots of color. As in the human figures, the upper legs of the horse are thick and the lower ones are mere lines. The hoofs are hook-shaped extensions of the legs.

This primitive Mandan painting accented the general characteristics of the human form—the roundness of the head, the straightness of the limbs, the bilateral symmetry of the body, qualities that Rudolf Arnheim has referred to as characteristics of the drawings of both primitives and children.[3]

Details of the human figure were unimportant to the primitive Mandan artist. In his drawings the head remained featureless. Bodies were crudely proportioned and appendages grossly generalized. Although his medium was paint, he used color sparingly. Heavy outlines gave to his work more the character of drawing than of painting. He had no knowledge of color modeling or such other sophisticated concepts as foreshortening and perspective. When one object overlapped another, he did not try to eliminate the outlines of the more distant one. Note the handling of the quiver carried by the warrior illustrated in Plate 15. But generally there was no overlapping of human or animal figures which were scattered over the surface of the robe, each being rendered individually beside, above, or below the others.

Anthropologists customarily refer to this primitive work as picture writing, a term which aptly expresses the major motive for its creation. The painter was more concerned with recording a memorable event by this pictorial shorthand than with the aesthetic appeal of his creation. He was more historian or biographer than artist.

George Catlin spent the summer of 1832 on the Upper Missouri. He traveled upriver on the first steamboat to ascend the Missouri to Fort Union, stopping briefly at Fort Clark, the American Fur Company's post at the Mandan villages. He returned downstream by skiff, stopping over at Fort Clark for a period of two or more weeks. During that period the amazingly energetic Catlin created more than forty pictures. Half this number were portraits of Mandan, Hidatsa, and Arikara Indians in the neighborhood of Fort Clark. The remainder were landscapes or scenes.

A self-taught artist whose forte was portraiture, Catlin possessed a remarkable ability to catch a likeness of his sitter with a few swift, bold strokes of his pencil or brush. His own account of his journey repeatedly referred to the Indians' delight and amazement

[3] Rudolf Arnheim, *Art as Perception*, 131.

101

at his ability to transfer their faces to canvas. They had seen nothing like this realistic portraiture before.[4]

No features of Catlin's lifelike portraits impressed the Indians quite so much as his rendering of his Indian sitters' eyes. Some Mandan viewers thought they could see these eyes move and follow them around Catlin's improvised studio. They pronounced Catlin a great "medicine white man" who possessed the power to make "living beings."[5]

Catlin was less skilled in rendering the human body. His interest in the details of Indian costume and ornamentation usually was secondary to his keen desire to record faithfully the heads and faces of his subjects. Not infrequently, he exaggerated or omitted important details of dress. Nevertheless, Catlin's very practice of painting from a model may have been a novelty in method of rendering the human figure that impressed some of his Indian sitters who had been familiar only with the generalized representations of humans created by native picture writers.

Karl Bodmer, on the other hand, was a meticulous draftsman thoroughly trained in the best European traditions of drawing from a model. The German scientist Prince Maximilian of Wied carefully picked young, Swiss-born Bodmer (he was only in his early twenties) to accompany him on his travels in America for the purpose of making drawings that would illustrate his own scientific observations. The exacting scientist expected his artist's records to be no less accurate in every detail than would be his own writings.

The Prince and Bodmer ascended the Missouri on an American Fur Company steamer in June, 1833. They met some of the Mandans briefly on their way upriver. In the fall of that year, after more than a month of observation and picture-making among the Blackfeet near Fort McKenzie, they returned to Fort Clark. There they remained from November 8, 1833, to April 18, 1834, during the colder months. James Kipp, the fur company's manager of Fort Clark, provided the German nobleman and his artist associate with a whitewashed room, which served as living quarters, studio, and

[4] Catlin, *Letters and Notes*, I, 105–109, 220–21.
[5] *Ibid.*, 106–110.

workroom, in a newly built wooden building within the fort. Throughout their stay, Bodmer worked assiduously, drawing and painting the likenesses of Mandans and other neighboring Indians in his studio, and scenes in the nearby Indian villages. He worked slowly and methodically, sometimes taking a full day or longer to complete a single portrait or view. During this period he created some of the most exact, realistic pictures of American Indians ever executed. These pictures possess a remarkable sharpness and depth of focus. Not only are the faces of the Indians truthful likenesses, but the minute details of costume and ornamentation are precisely delineated.[6]

Although Catlin introduced realistic portraiture to the Mandans, the superior draftsman, Karl Bodmer, showed them how every detail of a picture could be rendered with absolute truthfulness. Bodmer was the missionary par excellence of the white man's tradition of realism in art.

He was not content merely to exhibit his own work among the Indians. He furnished paper and water colors to some of them and encouraged them to make pictures for him and for Prince Maximilian. In the collections from the estate of Prince Maximilian of Wied, now preserved in the Joslyn Art Museum in Omaha, are no less than 10 original Indian drawings on paper, collected during Maximilian and Bodmer's trip to the Upper Missouri in 1833–34.

Both Catlin and Prince Maximilian considered Four Bears the most remarkable man in the Mandan tribe. Although he held the rank of second chief, he was his people's most popular leader. He was the son of a prominent warrior, Handsome Child. Four Bears himself, though of slight build and medium stature, claimed to have killed five enemy chiefs and to have taken fourteen scalps. Upon his return from a coup-counting session in the Mandan village of Ruhptare in January, 1834, Four Bears told his white friends "with great satisfaction and self-complacency, that he had enumerated all his exploits, and that no one had been able to surpass him."[7]

Four Bears was also a leader in Mandan ceremonies. Prince

[6] Ewers, *Artists of the Old West*, 95–117.
[7] Maximilian, *Travels*, XXIV, 58.

Maximilian saw him lead a dance of the Dog Society and learned that he had been selected as director of the great tribal religious festival, the Okipa, to be held the following summer (1834).

Four Bears' services to the traders and to visiting whites were many. Mr. Kipp relied upon him to protect the trading post at Fort Clark from the petty thievery of Mandan women and children. Maximilian found him to be his best authority on the language and religion of the Arikaras, a tribe the scientist had no opportunity to visit. He observed that Four Bears spoke Arikara "fluently."[8]

The active, versatile Four Bears was also an artist. This handsome, stout-hearted, friendly Mandan leader completely captivated George Catlin, as did no other Indian among the more than forty tribes Catlin visited. Catlin devoted a full chapter of his book to this warrior's exploits and frequently referred to him elsewhere. He painted two portraits of Four Bears (his Mah-to-toh-pa), both of which are preserved in the collections of the United States National Museum (Nos. 386128 and 386131). One portrait shows Four Bears in mourning, bare to the waist, with scars on his breast, arms, and legs evidencing his past submission to the excruciating self-torture of the Okipa. The other, painted in a day-long session, presents Four Bears at full length in his finest dress costume (see Plate 17). Catlin collected this costume and displayed it for many years in his traveling exhibition. The handsomely quilled and painted shirt is preserved in the United States National Museum (No. 386505). This shirt provides an excellent example of the art style Four Bears employed in depicting his war exploits in 1832 or earlier. On the left side of the shirt front he simply recorded his victims by painting their heads and upper bodies (see Plate 19). On the back of the shirt he portrayed one of his coups (see Plate 20). Note the very close similarity of this style to that of the painting on the buffalo robe collected by Lewis and Clark a quarter of a century earlier. Except for the crude representation of the features (two marks for eyes and one for the mouth), the rendering of the human figure is almost identical. It is definitely in the tradition of aboriginal Mandan picture writing.

[8] *Ibid.*, 73.

Shortly before Catlin left the Mandans, Four Bears invited him to a feast in his earth lodge and presented him with a robe bearing a representation of his most important coups. The chief had spent two weeks painting this robe during Catlin's residence in the village. Unfortunately, the original of this robe is lost, and Catlin's copy of the specimen, reproduced in his book and in one of his paintings in the American Museum of Natural History, appears to be an untrustworthy interpretation of the Indian artist's style. Catlin adopted conventions of his own for rapidly rendering his copies of Indian pictographs. They are more Catlin than Indian in style. Yet there is one detail in these paintings that Catlin surely did not invent—the hooklike hoofs of the horses, just like the horse hoofs portrayed by the unnamed Mandan artist prior to 1805.[9]

Prince Maximilian and Bodmer came to know Four Bears (their Mato-Tope) even better than Catlin knew him. They first met him at Fort Clark in June, 1833, on their way upriver, and the Prince bought from him "his painted buffalo dress," which suggests that the clever Indian was adept in dealing with white collectors. When Maximilian and Bodmer returned to Fort Clark in November, Four Bears came to visit them in their studio. Prince Maximilian's journal tells of Four Bears' repeated visits to their quarters during their long stay at Fort Clark. Sometimes he spent the night on the floor before their fire. He exhibited an unusual interest in Bodmer's art. He brought other Indians to the studio to be painted and remained to watch the proceedings. He himself posed for two portraits by the Swiss artist, one of which is reproduced as Plate 18. (The other, a full-length view in dress costume, is published as Plate 46 in Maximilian's *Atlas*.) He also prevailed upon Bodmer to paint for him a white-headed eagle holding a bloody scalp in its claws. In return Four Bears painted on a buffalo robe a representation of his principal coups and executed on paper a rendering of one of his exploits, the conquest of a Cheyenne chief in hand-to-hand combat.

The latter, a water color, is reproduced, as Plate 21 of this book, from the original in the Joslyn Art Museum. Comparison of this

[9] Catlin, *Letters and Notes*, I, 148–49, Plate 65.

picture with the paintings on Four Bears' shirt (Plates 19 and 20) clearly reveals the great changes in this Mandan artist's style during the period 1832–34. Gone were the knoblike heads, the stick figures, the crude proportions, the lack of detail. Heads were now painted in profile, the features sharply defined. Great care was taken in drawing a realistic human eye. The arms, legs, and bodies were well proportioned, and the details of headgear, ornaments, and body costume, and the moccasined feet were delineated with painstaking care. Some attempt at color modeling appears on the face and upper body of the warrior on the right. Can there be any doubt that this marked change in the painting style of Four Bears in the direction of a much more realistic treatment of the human figure should be attributed to the example of the white artists George Catlin and Karl Bodmer, whose artistic methods Four Bears had observed closely over a total period of several months?

Next to Four Bears, the most frequent Mandan Indian visitor to Bodmer's studio at Fort Clark during the winter of 1833–34 was a young warrior named Sih-Chida, The Yellow Feather. He was the son of a deceased Mandan head chief. Yellow Feather proudly showed Maximilian the Indians' copy of the first treaty between his tribe and the United States, signed by his father and General Atkinson in the year 1825.

Bodmer executed a full-length portrait of Yellow Feather in December, 1833 (see Plate 23, man on the left). Almost certainly this young man also posed for Catlin a year and a half earlier, although Catlin rendered his name "Seehk-hee-da, the Mouse-coloured Feather." (See Plate 22.) Not only are the facial features of the Bodmer and Catlin portraits similar, but the sitter wears long pendants of dentalium and large trade beads which appear to be identical.

Maximilian wrote:

> Sih-Chida, a tall, stout young man, the son of a celebrated chief now dead, was an Indian who might be depended on, who became one of our best friends and visited us almost daily. He was very polished in his manners, and possessed more delicacy of feeling than most of his countrymen. He never importuned us by asking for anything;

106

as soon as dinner was served he withdrew, though he was not rich, and did not even possess a horse. He came almost every evening, when his favorite employment was drawing, for which he had some talent, though his figures were no better than those drawn by our children.[10]

Yellow Feather spent several nights in Maximilian's quarters, sleeping on the ground before the fire. On one occasion he recovered Maximilian's thermometer which he found concealed under the robe of a woman who had stolen it. On April 10, Yellow Feather left to join a large Hidatsa and Mandan war party against an enemy tribe. But sometime before his leave-taking, Yellow Feather painted pictures in water colors on paper for the Prince's collection. One of these (Plate 24) is reproduced with the very kind permission of the Northern Natural Gas Company and the Joslyn Art Museum. The style of painting the human and animal figures exhibited by this picture, though crude, is vastly different from the simple figures of traditional Mandan picture writing. The rider sits astride his horse rather than on top of it. His face is shown in profile and considerable emphasis is given to a realistic representation of the human eye. The eye of the horse—both the white and the ball— is shown with an equal concern for detail. The ears, nostril, and mouth are delineated. There is some grace in the entire horse figure. The hoofs are realistically formed in contrast to the hooklike conventionalized hoofs of traditional Mandan pictography. The figures have some degree of roundness achieved by elementary color modeling, which is less apparent in the photographic reproduction than in the full-color original. Although we have no earlier example of Yellow Feather's art with which to compare this painting, the influence of the white artists Catlin and Bodmer is reflected in this example of the effort of a young Mandan artist to portray details and to achieve realism in his figure painting.

The foregoing data provide perhaps the best-documented case history of the influence of the European artistic tradition of realism upon the painting style of primitive American Indian artists. The details of this documentation are indeed remarkable. We know the

[10] Maximilian, *Travels*, XXIV, 15–16.

characteristics of traditional Mandan Indian picture writing, as it was practiced prior to and at the time of these Indians' introduction to the European art tradition. We know who the missionaries of the European tradition were (George Catlin and Karl Bodmer), and when they were active among the Mandans (1832–34). We know that these white men demonstrated the objectives and methods of realistic drawing and painting to the Mandans, and that they actively encouraged the efforts of native artists. We know who two of those native artists were—Four Bears and Yellow Feather. We know that these Indians posed for both white artists a total of six times and that they watched the white men paint many portraits of other Indians. We have examples of the painting of one native artist prior to the visits of Catlin and Bodmer, and examples of the work of both Four Bears and Yellow Feather, executed before Bodmer departed from Fort Clark, which clearly reveal the influence of European realism upon their painting styles.

It is not possible or necessary to distinguish the separate influences of Catlin and Bodmer upon the work of these artists. Probably the cumulative effect of the examples and the encouragement of these two white artists, who visited the Mandans within a period of a little over a year, was important in impressing upon the native artists' minds the possibilities of realistic representation of men and horses which found expression in their own later work.

Significant, too, were the character and position of the two Indian artists who fell under the spell of the white artists' realism. Both Four Bears and Yellow Feather were sons of prominent men in their tribe. They were not idle dreamers but active warriors, versatile and gregarious. Certainly Four Bears was a decided extrovert, who included painting among his many interests and accomplishments. He was the antithesis of the American artist James A. McNeill Whistler's imaginative conception of the primitive artist as a "man who took no joy in the ways of his brethren, who cared not for conquest, and fretted in the field—this designer of quaint patterns—this devisor of the beautiful—who perceived in Nature about curious curvings, as faces are seen in the fire—this dreamer apart, was the first artist."[11] Rather, the painting by Four Bears would suggest that the artist, living in a primitive hunting culture, was more likely to have been an active hunter and warrior, a fierce competitor, a wide-awake, keen participant in the affairs of his tribe—who enjoyed picturing the most exciting, heroic, and memorable of his rich experiences.

There remains the problem of determining the relative permanence of Catlin's and Bodmer's influence upon Mandan Indian art. This is difficult to solve. Examples of Mandan paintings of the late 1830's and the 1840's are lacking. Unfortunately, neither Four Bears nor Yellow Feather long survived Bodmer's sojourn among the Mandans. Catlin claimed that "Seehk-hee-da was killed by the Sioux, and scalped, two years after I painted his portrait."[12] The journal of François Chardon, who succeeded Kipp in charge of Fort Clark, repeatedly mentioned Four Bears' activity as a warrior during the middle 1830's, but said nothing of his artistic endeavors. In the summer of 1837, a disastrous smallpox epidemic decimated the Mandan tribe. Late in July of that year, Four Bears contracted that dread disease and died a few days later. But before his death he courageously delivered a speech to his people denouncing the whites as black-hearted dogs who had repaid his long and faithful friendship with a pestilence which was causing him to "die with my face rotten, that even the wolves will shrink with horror at seeing me." Chardon wrote Four Bears' brief obituary in his journal under the date Sunday, July 30, 1837: "One of our best friends of the Village (Four Bears), died today, regretted by all who knew him."[13]

[11] James A. McNeill Whistler, *"Ten O'Clock,"* 8.

[12] *A Descriptive Catalogue of Catlin's North American Indian Collection*, 19.

[13] François A. Chardon, *Chardon's Journal of Fort Clark, 1834–39*, 44–45, 50, 123–25.

PART THREE

::≡::≡::

CONSERVATISM, CHANGE, AND SURVIVAL

THE INDIANS that George Catlin saw on the Upper Missouri were not really living "in a state of nature" as he romantically stated in his writings. They relied upon the white man's horse and his manufactured trade goods—items their primitive ancestors of the early eighteenth century had never known. But, enriched by these additions to and substitutions for items in their aboriginal cultural inventory, the Indians appeared to be thriving.

Nevertheless, Catlin had known of the degradation of the once equally proud and independent Indian tribes east of the Mississippi who had been engulfed or displaced by an advancing white man's civilization. In 1832, he was conscious that he was picturing the Indians of the Upper Missouri before *they too* would be reduced in numbers and changed in character by the white man's diseases, his wars, and his vices. In his 1841 book Catlin made the melancholy prediction that the buffalo—the staff of life of the Plains Indians—would be exterminated. And as a voice crying in the wilderness this impractical artist called upon the American people to set aside the Great Plains as a national park in which both the Indians and the buffalo would be preserved.

No one in authority listened to Catlin. Another four decades passed before the last of the wild buffalo were exterminated on the plains of Montana. Nevertheless, even before 1841, a part of Catlin's gloomy prophecy was tragically fulfilled. In 1837 his beloved Mandans were more than decimated by a smallpox epidemic brought upriver from St. Louis on a fur company steamboat, and nearly all of the other tribes of the Upper Missouri lost many of their members in that same plague. The cultural superiority of the farming tribes was lost forever. By the early 1860's all of them—Arikaras, Hidatsas, and Mandans—were huddled together in the village Like-a-Fishhook (near Fort Berthold), where they lived in constant fear of the numerous and aggressive Sioux.

Actually the nomadic tribes had been growing in power since they acquired horses and guns during the eighteenth century. Their prowess as warriors was undergirded by a strong religious faith. And they shared many basic beliefs—such as a reverence for the sun, to which they vowed to undergo excruciating self-tortures in return for the sun's help, and a conviction that the supernatural powers of animals could be transferred to individual Indians through dreams and visions, power which would aid and protect active warriors in their engagements with their enemies.

Most of these enemies were Indians. For a longer time than any nineteenth-century Indians could remember these tribes had been fighting each other—Assiniboins, Blackfeet, Cheyennes, Crees, Crows, Gros Ventres, and Sioux—as well as the farming tribes of the Missouri and the tribes west of the Rockies. Peaceful alliances among tribes were loose and tended to be impermanent. Intertribal warfare, in the form of frequent horse-stealing raids by small parties and occasional revenge or scalp raids in force, continued after white immigrants, gold seekers, cattlemen, railroad builders, and hide hunters posed a more serious threat to the Indians' security than did their red enemies.

Few Upper Missouri tribes were among the hostiles in the bitter Indian Wars of the 1860's and 1870's in which the United States Army was engaged. They were most notably Sioux, Cheyenne, and Arapaho. Those tribes which had suffered most in the intertribal wars with the Sioux—Crow, Pawnee, and Shoshoni—sided with the whites.

Because these wars and individual dramatic engagements have been thoroughly treated in a host of recent books, they will not be summarized or described here. However, some neglected data on the last act of this tragedy—when the die-hard Sioux chief Sitting Bull returned from his Canadian exile in 1881 to surrender his

Winchester and to become a reservation Indian—will be included.

There were still wild buffalo in Montana then, but they were becoming scarce. During the winter of 1883–84 hundreds of Indians on the Blackfeet Reservation starved to death when "the tail of the last buffalo disappeared from the plain."

A goodly number of the veterans of the intertribal wars and of the buffalo hunt survived—on government rations. And they preserved some of their traditions, most notably ceremonies of their old-time religion. Those of us who have witnessed a sun dance or the opening of a medicine bundle know that the old culture did not completely disappear when buffalo were exterminated.

Only in recent years—since the end of World War II—have the last living members of the last generation of veterans of the intertribal wars and the Indian women who possessed vivid memories of tribal life in buffalo days passed away. Their passing has severed the living links with a way of life that is gone forever.

✂≡✂≡✂

CHAPTER NINE

The Blackfoot War Lodge:
Its Construction and Use*

IN THE LATE SPRING and early summer of 1805, members of the Lewis and Clark Expedition moved up the Missouri River across the present Montana plains on their way westward to the Pacific. They passed through the country of the powerful Blackfeet without meeting a single member of those tribes. Nevertheless, they frequently encountered Indian habitations, some of which appeared to them to have been occupied recently. Their journals for the period May 26 to June 13, 1805, covering the portion of their outward journey from the vicinity of the mouth of the Musselshell River to the Great Falls, contain several references to Indian lodges of sticks erected in timbered localities or to lodges of sticks and bark seen by the leaders of the party.[1] Reuben Gold Thwaites, editor of the Centennial Edition of the journals, assumes that these structures were abandoned tipis, the everyday homes of the nomadic Plains tribes.[2] Yet several factors suggest that these were no ordinary lodges. The nomadic Plains tribes did not abandon their tipi poles as a rule when they moved camp; they did not pitch their camps in small, isolated groups of lodges in heavy timber; nor did they cover them with bark. It seems much more likely that the explorers described another type of structure—the war lodge— much used by the tribes of the northwestern plains in later years and especially designed for the use of war parties.

If my identification is correct, this is the earliest reference to the

---

* Reprinted in revised form from *American Anthropologist*, Vol. XLVI, No. 2 (April–June, 1944).
[1] Lewis and Clark, *Original Journals*, II, 80, 84, 106, 108, 122, 124, 128, 152.
[2] *Ibid.*, 80 and n.

use of the war lodge in or near the country of the Blackfeet. The war lodge of the Blackfeet was a most ingenious example of Indian architecture. Its simplicity of design, ease in construction, ruggedness, and relative permanence made it a shelter admirably adapted to the peculiar needs of the many war parties, small mobile forces of footmen who traveled the war trails at all seasons of the year to capture horses from enemy camps. The structure was used by the Blackfeet until lack of wild game for subsistence on the trail, combined with the strong pressure brought to bear by both the Canadian and the United States governments, put an end to their intertribal warfare in 1885.

There are several brief references to the war lodges of the Blackfoot Indians in the earlier literature.[3] However, none of them furnish many details of either their construction or their use. The following account of the Blackfoot war lodge is based on information obtained from a number of elderly Piegans and one Blood Indian living on the Blackfeet Reservation in Montana in the winter of 1942–43, who made and used such lodges during the last decade of intertribal warfare.

Informants said that in the time of their youth there were a great many war lodges in the country of the Blackfeet and their enemies. The lodges were located in heavily timbered areas near rivers or streams, or on thickly wooded heights,[4] conveniently near well-known war trails. There were many along the Missouri River, and it was the business of leaders of Blackfoot war parties to know where they were located. Once constructed, the lodges were used over and over again by war parties for years. Old lodges were repaired or rebuilt when they became unfit for use.[5] But if no lodge

[3] Maximilian, *Travels*, XXIII, 42–43, refers to such a lodge seen on the Missouri near the mouth of Milk River in 1833, which may have been of Blackfoot make. George Bird Grinnell, *Blackfoot Lodge Tales*, 3–4, 252; James Willard Schultz, *My Life as an Indian*, 53; Clark Wissler, "Material Culture of the Blackfoot Indians," 155.

[4] In the late 1870's Schultz saw six war lodges on the summit of the Hairy Cap, a high butte east of the Little Rockies, the entire upper portion of which was covered with a dense stand of pine. Schultz, *My Life as an Indian*, 53.

[5] "They stood along war trails and were kept in repair from year to year." Wissler, "Material Culture," 155.

was available when needed a new lodge would be built if a suitable site was not far distant. Nevertheless, one Piegan, who led a number of war parties in his youth, stated that he never used the old lodges, because he believed the enemy knew their locations as well as the Blackfeet did, and it was safer to build a new lodge.

When a war lodge was to be built, the leader of the war party selected the site and served as foreman of construction. The site was usually well inside the edge of the timber, where a lodge could not be seen from the open plains. All members of the party went to work under his supervision, quickly collecting necessary materials. Windfalls usually were plentiful. The men used their sharp scalping knives to cut the timber if additional pieces were needed. Cottonwoods and willows were generally plentiful in the timbered river bottoms, and pines or aspens in the higher localities. But the builders were not overly particular about the species of wood employed. Size and usefulness were the important considerations.

When erecting a lodge in the lower altitudes, three or four heavy, forked trunks of cottonwood were locked together at the top to form the foundation. Their tops were not tied. These timbers were about twelve feet long for the average-sized lodge, which had an inside height of about seven feet. The butt ends of the pieces rested on top of the ground, held in place by their weight.[6] Then lighter red willow poles were leaned against the three stout foundation timbers at their top intersections to complete the steep-sided conical framework. The poles were set somewhat closer together than in the common skin-covered lodge. This framework was generally covered with long slabs of bark, stripped from large cottonwoods, and leaned on end over the outer side of the poles. The bark slabs either overlapped or were set close enough together to make the sides of the lodge virtually waterproof. As this part of the work progressed, the leader went inside the lodge and pointed out to his men working outside the spaces that remained to be covered to make the lodge weather tight. Sometimes brush was used instead of bark for the cover. It was not tied to the poles, but simply leaned

---

[6] All informants disagreed with Grinnell's statement that these pieces were lashed together like lodge poles with their butt ends up. Grinnell, *Blackfoot Lodge Tales*, 252.

against the framework as in the case of the brush walls of the Blackfoot medicine lodge. The bark cover was usually preferred. It was more difficult to make the brush cover snow, wind, or rain tight. Often sticks were propped against the brush or bark cover from the outside to hold it in place. An inverted-V-shaped opening was left on one side of the circular structure, affording an entrance to the lodge. Outward from this opening, for a distance of ten feet or more, was built a low, angling, covered entrance way, composed of rather heavy forked tree trunks.[7] The triangular passage thus formed was barely four feet high, making it necessary for a man to stoop low to enter the lodge. Usually, if not invariably, the entrance to the lodge was to the east, as was the case with the ordinary Blackfoot tipi. Finally, thick cottonwood logs or stones were piled around the base of the exterior to a height of about two feet. The interior was simply furnished. The fire for warmth and cooking was built in the center. Between the fireplace and the walls the floor was covered with pine boughs or brush over which dried grass was placed. The occupants wrapped themselves in their robes and slept on this prepared floor.

The construction of a war lodge was regarded as a co-operative venture in which every member of the war party worked. The lodge was commonly built within one or two days' journey from the enemy camps. It was on dangerous ground. All hands were needed to speed the work. A lazy fellow who refused to perform his share of labor for the party, who seemed content to let the others collect the materials and set up the lodge or who would not go after wood or water when asked to do so the leader, made himself very unpopular. Our oldest informant recalled that his father once told him that in his day other members of a party managed to make life very uncomfortable for the shirker. Sometimes they deliberately left a small hole in the side of the lodge over the place where he was to sleep to let the rain, snow, or breeze in on him. If the war party was to have a favorite dish of Crow guts (*i.e.*, buffalo intestines turned inside out over a stuffing of meat), the cook secretly would fill one

---

[7] ". . . the door . . . was protected by a curved covered way." Wissler, "Material Culture," 155.

end of the intestine with a piece of rawhide. While other members of the party were served the delicious meaty portion, the unpalatable rawhide-stuffed end was handed to the idle fellow. Such treatment sometimes made the indolent member so angry that he would leave the party and return home. If the others returned to camp from a successful horse raid, the lazy fellow became an object of ridicule.

It was stated that a war party of ten or more men, working industriously, could build a lodge of this kind in about two hours. The usual lodge would accommodate twelve warriors. Somewhat larger lodges occasionally were made which would house as many as eighteen men. If the war party was still larger, two or more lodges were erected a few feet apart.

A model of this type of Blackfoot war lodge was made by Reuben Black Boy, under the supervision of Weasel Tail, a Blood warrior in his middle eighties, in February, 1943, for the Museum of the Plains Indian. It is shown in Plate 25. Several elderly Piegan Indians, who had helped to make war lodges in their younger days, have voiced their approval of the design and construction.

Other forms of war shelter were sometimes used by the Blackfeet. "Sometimes a rectangular structure was made, the walls converging to the apex."[8] Weasel Head, a Piegan, said that once, while on a war party, a dilapidated structure "built like a house" was pointed out to him as an old-time war lodge. However, he himself had never made a rectangular one. Rectangular, houselike forts were built by some of the Plateau tribes.[9] Possibly the Blackfoot rectangular structure represents an influence from that direction. Two other less permanent forms were said to have been made when the party was small or in a great hurry. Rides-at-the-Door described a simple double lean-to which was made by leaning two sets of poles from opposite directions against a nearly horizontal outstretched limb of a strong tree and covering the outside with bark. A triangular-shaped interior resulted. Weasel Tail stated that a shelter was sometimes made of arched willow poles, "like a sweat lodge," and covered with brush. Both of these types of lodge were

[8] *Ibid.*
[9] James A. Teit, "The Salishan Tribes of the Western Plateaus," 118, 257.

too flimsily constructed to be of value for defense. The willow-pole lodge seems to have been employed during the early portions of a journey to the enemy when there was less danger of hostile attack. Parties used this structure nearer home, but built a conical war lodge after they penetrated deeper into the enemy country. It was necessary, of course, for war parties to camp on the plains when traversing an extended stretch of open country where no timber was available. This worked no real hardship in fair weather. But in stormy winter weather it was not unknown for members of war parties to freeze to death on the open plains. Weasel Tail said that sometimes in winter on the snow-covered plains, the men made crude beds by tramping down the snow and covering it with broken pieces of dried buffalo chips obtained from an exposed hillside. Wrapping themselves tightly in their buffalo robes, they tried to sleep and make the best of a difficult situation. According to Grinnell, "Sometimes when on the prairie, where there is no wood, in stormy weather they will build shelters of rocks."[10] However, no further information was given concerning such structures.

The relation of two war adventures of informants will help to explain the varied uses of the Blackfoot war lodge. The first, told by Weasel Tail, a Blood Indian, took place in the late 1870's:

> It was in winter when I helped to make my first war lodge. More than twenty of us went to steal horses from the Dakota.[11] The leader of our party was Eagle Child, a North Blackfoot. My wife's brother, Eagle Fly, was also in the party. I took my wife along.[12] The first night out we put up temporary shelters of bent willows

[10] Grinnell, *Blackfoot Lodge Tales*, 252.

[11] Probably the Dakotas, who were at that time in Canada, were followers of Sitting Bull.

[12] It was not uncommon for childless married couples among the Blackfoot tribes to join war parties together. Weasel Tail explained, "My wife said she loved me, and if I was to be killed on a war party she wanted to be killed too. I took her with me on five parties. Some of them I led and my wife was not required to perform the cooking or other chores. She carried a six shooter. On one occasion she stole a horse with saddle, ammunition bag and war club." He recalled three married women who had taken guns from the enemy on war expeditions with their husbands. This act ranked as the highest honor in the Blackfoot coup system. Two of the women were Piegan, one Blood. J. Willard Schultz has told the story of Running Eagle, the most famous Piegan woman warrior of the nineteenth century, in his book, *Running Eagle, the Warrior Girl*.

covered with grass, something like a sweat lodge in appearance. The second night we built the same kind of lodges. By the close of the third day's travel we were getting near the enemy. Our leader instructed us to build a conical lodge. He told us to build the lodge strong. We went into the thick brush, gathered long, heavy pieces of fallen timber for the framework, and covered the lodge with long pieces of bark from large cottonwoods. Other pieces of heavy timber were propped against the bark sections to hold them in place. By evening the lodge was completed except for the angling doorway and the outer circle of heavy logs. Our leader told us we would spend four days there hunting and getting in a supply of meat before proceeding to the enemy. That evening he sent out five men to scout ahead. They returned before morning reporting that the buffalo were at some distance back from the river ahead on either side, so there must have been people near the river to cause them to keep away from it. Our leader warned us that the enemy might be near. He told us to get timbers for the angling doorway. Then we got heavy pieces of cottonwood and placed them in two rows (horizontally) around the outside of the structure. Members of our party went out and killed buffalo to provide us with meat for the rest of the trip. Again our leader sent out five experienced men as scouts. He told them to travel farther than they had on their earlier trip, to be gone all day and return next morning. Meanwhile, the rest of us were kept busy cutting up the meat and drying it over frames of bent willows, the ends stuck in the ground like in a sweat lodge. The pieces of meat were laid on top of this framework and a wood fire made below its center to smoke-dry the meat. We made four of these drying frames, three outside and one inside the war lodge. While we worked at this, guards were posted on all sides of the camp to look out for the enemy.

Toward late afternoon the scouts returned. We saw them zigzagging and circling down a hill in the distance, a sign that they had seen the enemy. We piled up sticks at a place outside the lodge and all danced as the scouts approached. Our leader went out alone to meet them. They reported what they had seen to him. Then he led the scouts back to where the rest of us were around the pile of sticks. He kicked over the pile of sticks. All of us scrambled for them. We thought that whoever got the first stick would be the first to take a horse from the enemy. Then our leader told us what the scouts had seen.[13] They had gone on to a creek south of the Cypress Hills. With their glasses they saw a large camp of Dakota approaching from the other side of the creek after buffalo. The Dakota had lots of horses.

Toward evening our leader told us to start for the enemy. He instructed the scouts to proceed half way to where they had seen the enemy and wait for the rest of us there. At dusk we reached the scouts. We had taken some dried meat to eat on the way. We built a fire, made a smudge and had a medicine smoke. We sang our war songs. My wife's brother was fearful of her safety. He told us not to go on because she could not run as fast as the men if it became necessary to make a quick getaway afoot. But we did not listen to him. We continued with the others. The party moved faster then. The moon was bright and shining on the snow. We walked fast uphill and ran downhill. From a thick woods we saw the lights of the enemy camps. There were three camps of them. Our leader sent two scouts ahead to find out if the enemy had tied their horses or let them run loose. They soon returned to report that the enemy horses were corralled. We all started forward. When we came to a snow bank near a big tree my wife's brother told her to wait there, and for me to stay with her.

We waited what seemed to be a very long time. Toward morning I heard someone talking in the Sioux language. He was telling the people to let their horses out of the corral to feed, for it was almost morning. As soon as the Sioux released their horses, our party drove them away. My wife's brother got horses and started for home. In the excitement he had forgotten all about us. I decided to go myself to the first or nearest camp. I caught one of the horses, put my war

[13] Weasel Head gave a more detailed account of this custom: "If the scouts had seen the enemy, and had gone close enough to observe the number of their horses and the details of their camp, they halted before they came in sight of the war lodge party. They painted their faces, and put on the feathers or other small tokens of good luck given them by an old man in the camp before they left home. When they came in sight of the lodge they circled down the hill. We all knew they had gotten close to the enemy. As soon as we saw them we put all our weapons down and dared not touch them. We prayed that we might get horses without needing to fight the enemy. We danced and sang, circling about the war lodge as the scouts came nearer. Then we stopped dancing and quickly built a conical pile of sticks, like a very small tipi foundation, near the lodge. The leader of the party went out to meet the scouts. He returned with them and kicked over the pile of sticks. All the members of the party scrambled for them. Getting one meant that you would get a horse from the enemy. When a man picked up one of the sticks he held it in the air and shouted, 'Ah' hooey,' then he said a prayer for success."

bridle on it, and rode to where my wife was hiding, without being noticed. I told her to mount it and I would try to get another horse for myself. If I couldn't do that we would have to make our getaway by riding double on the one horse. I saw another, a fine horse with a feather on his head and another in his tail. I caught it. It was a good riding horse. I looked around and saw another horse that looked good to me, roped it and led it. As soon as I got back to my wife I told her, "Let's go." We hurried away. It was almost morning. We were so excited we left our little bundle of dry meat and a good knife behind where we had been told to wait by my wife's brother. When we reached our war lodge of the previous days, I stopped in and quickly got some of the dried meat we had left in the lodge. We continued on. . . . On the fourth day after we took the horses we reached the Blood camp.

The second account was obtained from Weasel Head, a few years younger than Weasel Tail, who, nevertheless, had a number of opportunities to go to war before horse-raiding parties were discontinued. On several occasions he led war parties:

Before I led my first war party I was a member of two other parties, one led by White Quiver, the other by Under Bull, on which we had made war lodges. The first time I led a war party, we went to the Crows to steal horses. There were 11 of us in the party. My grandfather had told me never to take too many men on a war party. They were apt to be difficult to manage, and be critical of their leader. South of the Missouri in the canyon of the river near the present town of Belt, Montana (Belt Creek), I ordered the construction of a war lodge of the kind illustrated by the museum model. It was in winter. All of the members of the party set to work, getting windfalls, using knives to cut the timber when necessary. We carried no axes on war parties. But our sharp scalping knives were as useful as any axe would be. Bark was used for covering. As the lodge neared completion, I went inside and pointed out to the others through my announcer, Moves Out, where to fill in to make the lodge tight.

We camped there at Belt to repair our moccasins and collect a supply of meat for the remainder of our journey. I sent out the two smartest of my men as scouts to look for the enemy, to be out all day and all the next night when they were to return whether or not they

125

had sighted the enemy. In the absence of the scouts the rest of us hunted buffalo, dried the meat and mixed it with peppermint to make fat back pemmican. Each member of the party except the leader carried his own meat from there on to the enemy camp. It was carried in a rectangular rawhide case, without side fringes, about a foot wide, by a rawhide strap over the man's shoulders, the bag hanging on his back. This bag was sometimes left at a distance from the enemy camp when the rush for enemy horses was made. The warrior expected to pick it up when he made his getaway. But in case he couldn't do that, he also carried a much smaller rawhide pouch at his waist, suspended from a rawhide cord over the right shoulder, which provided him with something to eat on the hurried trip home.[14]

Throughout the period of our stay at the war lodge it was guarded night and day by four members of the party, stationed on nearby hills, one in each direction. They took turns mounting guard.

From these two firsthand accounts it is obvious that the war lodges served many functions; at least five uses are enumerated:

1. *The war lodge provided protection against enemy attack.* A campfire in the open could have been seen easily by the enemy and would have either put them on their guard against attack or brought a party of their warriors to investigate. But inside the tight war lodge, a fire built of almost smokeless dry willow was concealed from the enemy.[15] In case the enemy did discover that the lodge was occupied by a hostile party, the war lodge became a strong defensive position. Night attacks on these lodges were not uncommon. Then, warned by their sentinels of the approach of the enemy, the little party in the lodge quickly tore holes in the sides of the structure for the use of their weapons, and protected their bodies behind the two-foot breastwork of logs or stones surrounding the lodge. The party did not leave the lodge but fought off the enemy attack from inside.[16]

2. *The war lodge provided protection from the weather.* Inside the tight little war lodge the party was able to cook, eat, repair

---

[14] This was known as *saskomiosina* war lunch, a veritable emergency ration.

[15] Schultz, *My Life as an Indian*, 53; Grinnell, *Blackfoot Lodge Tales*, 3–4, 252; and Wissler, "Material Culture," 155, stress its use for concealing the fire.

[16] Wissler, *ibid.*, also stresses its use as a defense against night attacks.

moccasins and weapons, rest and sleep out of the rain, snow, or wind.[17] In the winter season of sudden storms, quick drops in temperature, and intense cold on the northwestern plains, this function was particularly important. At times the war lodge meant the difference between comfort and severe frostbite or even death through freezing. Some Blackfeet preferred to go on horse raids in winter despite the treacherous weather. Weasel Tail said that he preferred winter war parties in his youth. Wrapped in a heavy Hudson's Bay blanket coat, fur cap, mittens, and hair-lined moccasins in winter, he felt more comfortable than in summer when severe sunburn and sore, aching feet were the warrior's lot. Moreover, there was less danger in winter of meeting hostile war parties, and the theft of horses from an enemy camp during a snowstorm made pursuit difficult, if not impossible, once he had made his getaway.

3. *The war lodge served as a base for scouting operations.* While the main body was active in other duties in preparing for the raid in comparative seclusion near the lodge, the leader sent out scouts to locate the enemy camp and report its size and wealth in horses. No time was lost in aimless wandering in enemy country on the part of the main body, nor did it expose itself needlessly to discovery by the enemy.

4. *The war lodge served as a supply base.* While the scouts were gone, the last hunting of the expedition was done by the rest of the party as near the war lodge as possible. At the war lodge the meat was dried and packed into rawhide containers, one for each member of the party. It was expected that each man would have enough to sustain him until he reached home. But in case any of the meat pouches should be lost near the enemy camp, a surplus was left at the lodge. It was hung on forked willow sticks, the long ends of which were tied with rawhide ropes to the lodge poles inside the lodge high enough to be out of reach of mice or bears or other carnivorous animals. Sometimes, after a good hunt, several of these hooks, each burdened with dried meat, were left in the lodge. Any member of the party who needed to replenish his supply on the way

[17] Grinnell, *Blackfoot Lodge Tales*, 252, also stresses its use as protection against rain, snow, and wind.

home could stop by the war lodge, unless too hotly pursued by the enemy, and quickly obtain enough food to supply nourishment on the long, tiresome, sleepless journey homeward.

5. *The war lodge served as an information station.* Since the location of the war lodge was well known to all members of the party, it served as an ideal location for the communication of intelligence among members of the party en route home after the theft of horses. If a man became separated from the rest of the party after the rush for horses, and he believed he had started home ahead of some of the others, he stopped by the war lodge (if it was not out of his way to do so) and picked up a buffalo shoulder blade or other flat bone and quickly drew his pictographic signature on it, together with other pictographs indicating the number of horses he had stolen, the enemy he had killed (if any), and added an arrow to show his direction of movement from the war lodge. When other members of the party arrived on the scene, they saw the marked bone propped against the entrance to the lodge. They knew that he was successful in taking horses and in making a getaway, and that they need not delay their own homeward movement on his account.

The Blackfeet were not alone in the construction of the conical war lodge here described.[18] According to informants, identical structures were made and used by the majority of their enemies—the Plains Crees, Crows,[19] Sioux, Gros Ventres, and Assiniboins. However, these informants had never heard of the Flatheads' using such a war lodge. Grinnell has written of its use by the Cheyennes,[20] and they may also have been used by the Arikaras as early as 1811, although we cannot be certain from Brackenridge's description that

[18] ". . . used by other tribes as well." Wissler, "Material Culture," 155.

[19] Richard Sanderville (Chief Bull) stated that the Crows on their last horse raid against the Piegan in 1884 built war lodges near Heart Butte on the Blackfeet Reservation within twenty miles of the Indian Agency (old agency). These lodges stood for a number of years after the end of intertribal warfare. Sanderville said they were like Blackfoot war lodges in every particular.

[20] "In the enemy's country, or when the weather was bad, that is, rainy, or snowy, or cold, a war-party usually built war lodges. They were conical shelters formed of poles, covered with boughs, grass, or bark, which kept out the weather and hid the light of the fire that burned within." George Bird Grinnell, *The Cheyenne Indians*, II, 14.

he had the conical war lodge in mind.[21] However, there can be no doubt that in 1850 Stansbury saw a number of these lodges on the North Platte in the southeastern part of present Wyoming. The structures were not occupied and might have been erected by any of several tribes who made war in that area.[22] It is apparent that the use of the war lodge was characteristic of northwestern plains war expeditions in the waning decades of intertribal warfare.

In architectural plan the conical war lodge of the Blackfeet suggests a tipi with elaboration in the way of an angling entrance and an encircling breastwork. As Weasel Tail's account states, the tipi was built first, the entrance and breastwork added. It, therefore, may be considered as a specialized form of tipi among a tipi-using people. The materials employed are suggestive of the conical bark-covered lodges of the Northern Woodlands. The foundation of four crotched poles, interlocked at the top without tying, was used by the Northern Saulteaux in their bark-covered conical lodges.[23] An eastern influence on the architecture of the war lodge of the northwestern plains is suggested.

The erection and various uses of the war lodges for defense, for protection against the weather, and as bases for scouting, supply, and pictographic intelligence indicate a degree of organization and co-operation within small war parties that has been ignored in many of the published descriptions of northern Plains Indian warfare which, in emphasizing the recruiting of parties, the counting of coup, and the return to camp, have stressed the individualistic aspects of warfare in this region.

The stereotyped conception of the nomadic Plains tribes as incessant wanderers on a sea of grass also is in need of some modification. The Plains Indians were more dependent on those little islands

[21] "To avoid surprise, they always encamp at the edge of a wood; and when a party is small they construct a kind of fortress, with wonderful expedition, of billets of wood, apparently piled up in a careless manner, but so arranged as to be very strong, and by this means to withstand an assault from a much superior force." H. M. Brackenridge, *Journal*, 124.

[22] Howard Stansbury, *An Expedition to the Valley of the Great Salt Lake, 1852.* Quoted in David I. Bushnell, Jr.'s "Villages of the Algonquian, Siouan, and Caddoan Tribes West of the Mississippi," 67.

[23] Alanson Skinner, *Notes on the Eastern Cree and Northern Saulteaux*, 119.

in the sea, the timbered areas, than is generally realized. In addition to furnishing wood for a wide variety of essential articles in their material culture, the timbered areas furnished protection both from the cold and from the enemy. With their lodges huddled close together in some timbered river bottom protected from the driving wind, these Indians, for the most part, remained relatively inactive through the four or five winter months. Also, when a Plains war party was confronted with a superior enemy force, its first reaction was to run for the timber, if any was near. Absence of timber rather than choice sometimes made it necessary for the Plains Indians to dig fox holes or hastily erect rude stone forts on the plains. Here again, in the case of the war lodge, we have another example of the dependence of the plainsman upon timber for protection. It is not suggested that the dependence on timber for defense is a survival from the warfare patterns of the woodlands, but it does indicate a keen awareness of the protective advantages of terrain, afforded by the wooded areas of their own country, on the part of the people of the plains.

⚬≡⚬≡⚬

CHAPTER TEN

The Bear Cult Among the Assiniboins and Their Neighbors of the Northern Plains*

ALICE C. FLETCHER has called attention to the prevalence of animal cults among the Siouan tribes of the Great Plains. She observed that each cult was composed of individuals who had obtained supernatural power from the same mammal or bird through a dream or vision and that each cult possessed a distinctive ritual and ceremonial regalia symbolic of the animal from which its power was derived.[1]

In the literature on the Indians of the northern Great Plains may be found a number of brief references to bear ceremonies among the Algonquian, Siouan, and Athapascan (Sarsi) tribes of that region in the nineteenth century. Although these references suggest the widespread occurrence of a Bear Cult among these tribes, they do not analyze the Bear Cult of any tribe sufficiently to provide a factual basis for comparative study.

During my field work among the Assiniboin Indians of Fort Peck Reservation, Montana, in the summer of 1953, Henry Black Tail, a full-blood member of that tribe (aged about seventy-eight years), imparted to me his recollections of the Assiniboin Bear Cult. He was not a cult member. It has been many years since that cult was active among his people. Nevertheless, Henry Black Tail's testimony sheds considerable light upon the complex of traits identified with the Assiniboin Bear Cult and renders more meaningful the

---

* Reprinted in revised form from *Southwestern Journal of Anthropology*, Vol. XI, No. 1 (Spring, 1955).

[1] Alice C. Fletcher, "The Elk Mystery of Festival. Ogallala Sioux," 276–82.

scattered references to bear ceremonies among neighboring tribes reported in the literature.

Black Tail recalled that the Assiniboin Bear Cult was composed of a small number of men who had obtained supernatural bear power through dreams. Their bear power was not transferred to fellow tribesmen during their lives nor was it inherited by relatives after their deaths. When a cult member died, "his power went with him."

Most Assiniboin Indians feared bears.[2] They knew bears to be powerful, vicious animals that had killed women and children when they were collecting wild fruits and berries. Most Assiniboins also feared members of the Bear Cult. It was thought that those who possessed bear power were touchy men who easily became angry. Bear Cult members also had the reputation for being unlucky. Even if they appeared to prosper for a time, their good fortune did not last.[3]

A distinctive shirt, hair dress, and face paint, the bear knife, the bear shield, and the bear-painted tipi were paraphernalia of the Assiniboin Bear Cult.

When participating in cult ceremonies, when doctoring the sick or fighting the enemy, cult members dressed in the manner illustrated in an adaptation of a drawing by Joshua Wetsit, an interpreter, executed from detailed information supplied by Henry Black Tail and under his critical eye (see Figure 1).

The cult member shaved the top of his head and rolled some of his hair at each side into a ball resembling a bear's ear. He painted his face red, then made vertical scratches, representing a bear's claw marks, on each side of his face by scraping away some of the paint with his fingernails. He then painted a black circle around each eye and around his mouth. He wore a bear-claw necklace over a yellow-painted skin shirt, which was perforated with many cut holes and was decorated with cut fringe along the bottom edge and the sleeve ends. A small, rectangular flap of skin, cut from the gar-

[2] Edwin Thompson Denig, "Indian Tribes of the Upper Missouri," 537–38.

[3] Fletcher ("The Elk Mystery," 281) reported an Oglala Sioux belief that bear power was unlucky "as the bear is slow and clumsy, and apt to be wounded; and although savage when cornered is not as likely as some animals to escape harm."

Figure 1.—*Distinctive dress of a member
of the Assiniboin Bear Cult.*

ment itself, hung down at the center of the wearer's chest. Black
Tail did not know the significance of this flap.

When going to war or participating in cult ceremonies, the member carried a distinctive knife, formed into a broad, flat, double-
edged metal blade, to the handle of which was attached a bear jaw.
This weapon was known to the Assiniboins as a "bear knife."

In combat a member might also carry a rawhide shield bearing
on its front surface a painted representation of a bear.

Black Tail also recalled having seen a bear-painted tipi formerly
owned by a Bear Cult member. It had been thirty or more years
since this tipi was set up. The greater part of the cover was painted
yellow. There was an area of black paint at the top. Two bears were
painted over the yellow background in a dark color. One stood on
hind legs at each side of the doorway.

Maximilian saw and described a similar tipi owned by an Assiniboin chief near Fort Union in 1833. It was "painted of the color of
yellow ochre, had a broad reddish-brown border below, and on each
of its sides, a large black bear was painted (something of a cari-
cature it must be confessed), to the head of which, just above the

133

nose, a piece of red cloth, that fluttered in the wind, was fastened, doubtless a medicine."[4]

Karl Bodmer, the talented Swiss artist who accompanied Prince Maximilian to the upper Missouri, made a drawing of this bear-painted tipi (see Plate 26).

It seems reasonable to infer that the owner of this tipi was a member of the Assiniboin Bear Cult, and that in 1833 the decorative pattern of the bear-painted tipi was very much like that of the cult tipi of Black Tail's memory.

Henry Black Tail recalled three major functions of the Assiniboin Bear Cult: (1) the conduct of ceremonies in honor of the bear (including the bear feast and the ceremonial bear hunt); (2) aggressive participation in war expeditions; (3) doctoring the sick.

When cult members gathered for the bear feast, they sang their distinctive bear songs. Each member was served a large bowl of berry soup. ("Bears love berries—their favorite food.") They vied with one another to see who first could consume his portion of soup. No meat was eaten at these cult feasts. Members observed a strict taboo against eating bear meat. Joshua Wetsit recalled that Pipe, a member of the Assiniboin Bear Cult, once ate some bear meat before he realized what it was. He appeared to throw a fit, but finally was calmed when other Indians induced him to smoke a pipe.

The ceremonial bear hunt was enacted by an individual cult member with the assistance of several boys at the summer Sun Dance encampment. The member erected his tipi inside the camp circle. He dressed in his bear outfit (previously described) and covered the upper part of his body with a buffalo robe which was tied over his head to resemble the head of a bear. He emerged from his tipi (symbolic den) carrying a bear knife in each hand. The boys on horseback shot at him with guns loaded only with powder. He would fall down as if wounded, then get up and chase the mounted boys until he had made a complete circuit of the camp circle and returned to his lodge.[5] Black Tail said that when he was

[4] Maximilian, *Travels*, XXIII, 19.
[5] Note the similarity of this action to that of the Assiniboin winter bear hunt

a boy he had peeped into a Bear Cult man's tipi shortly after the owner had returned from re-enacting this hunt. He saw the man "lying on his bed at the rear of the lodge, breathing heavily. His two bear knives were stuck in the ground beside him."

When a member of the Bear Cult went into action against the enemy he wore his distinctive bear outfit with accompanying hairdress and face paint and carried a bear knife. Bears were noted for their ferocious charges. When a cult member charged, he "made a noise like a bear" which was not a growl but a "huh, huh."

Cult members wore specialized garb again when they doctored sick people. However, they never performed curing ceremonies in public. Black Tail gave no details of the medicines or the procedures employed in curing rites.

Both Wetsit and Black Tail described the actions of Pipe preceding his death about 1920, aged about seventy years. For four nights prior to his death Pipe was heard to make strange noises like those of a young bear whining. He stuck out his tongue, which appeared to be pointed. All the Indians in attendance were frightened by these actions. They attributed them to Pipe's bear power exerting itself, aiding him in his struggle against death.

This fairly detailed description of Assiniboin Bear Cult organization, paraphernalia, and functions may be compared with what is known of bear ceremonies among other tribes of the region. The tribe most closely related to the Assiniboin is the Yanktonai. Not only are the Assiniboins traditionally considered an offshoot of the Yanktonais but these two tribes have shared the same reservation (Fort Peck) since the 1870's. Henry Black Tail had witnessed some Yanktonai Bear Cult ceremonies in his youth. He thought they were much like those of the Assiniboins, except that two or three Yanktonai cult members chased the mounted attackers in their ceremonial bear hunt and the Yanktonai cult performed curing ceremonies in public. He once saw them doctor a sick child. The

described by Denig prior to 1855: "When a den is discovered six or eight Indians go to attack it, approaching the hole so close as to see the foremost bear, there three of them fire, the others reserving their shots. They all run off some distance and if the animal, or any other pursue them, the rest fire." Denig, "Indian Tribes of the Upper Missouri," 538.

135

cult leader held a rawhide rattle in one hand and sagebrush in the other. He placed the sagebrush in his mouth and blew out a substance that resembled powdered yellow paint. Other cult members present at this curing rite carried bear knives.

The Eastern Dakotas greatly impressed many writers by their performance of the ceremonial bear hunt. Stephen Long heard of it in 1817, and Samuel Pond described it in 1834. No mention of the bear knife is found in their descriptions. "To lengthen his arms so that he could walk on all fours," the bear "carried hoops in his hands which he used as paws."[6] Yet the Santee informants of the writer Robert Lowie told him that the performer held a wooden knife in the same hand as the hoop. The ceremonial bear hunt was a prelude to the departure of a war party and to the belief that the first person to lay his hands upon the "bear" would kill an enemy.[7] Wallis repeatedly mentioned "bear feasts" given by those who had dreamed of bears, and one of his references to "members of the bear feast" suggests a degree of organization of those who possessed bear power among the Eastern Dakotas.[8]

Among the Teton Dakotas bear power was highly regarded as a curing agent. The Oglala Bear Cult was made up of men who had dreamed of bear power. When one of them gave a feast, all bear medicine men and those who had been cured by bear medicine were invited. Participants at this feast wore bear costumes, painted their bodies red, and danced mimicking the actions of bears.[9] One Teton informant of the writer Frances Densmore said, "The Bear is the only animal which is dreamed of as offering to give herbs for the healing of man." Another informant added, "We consider the bear as chief of all animals in regard to herb medicine, and therefore it is understood that if a man dreams of a bear he will be expert in the use of herbs for curing illness."[10]

[6] Stephen H. Long, "Voyage in a Six-oared Skiff to the Falls of Saint Anthony in 1817," 18–19; Samuel William Pond, "The Dakotas or Sioux in Minnesota as they were in 1834," 419.

[7] Robert H. Lowie, *Dance Associations of the Eastern Dakota*, 121–22.

[8] Wilson D. Wallis, *The Canadian Dakota*, 84, 89, 140, 181, 189.

[9] Clark Wissler, Societies and Ceremonial Associations in the Oglala Division of the Teton Dakota, 88–90.

Accordingly, Bowers' one-line characterization of the Mandan Bear Ceremony is significant as an indication of the purposes of it. Among the Mandans this rite was associated with "doctoring and warfare."[11]

After the death of the Mandan second chief, Four Bears, in the smallpox epidemic of 1837, George Catlin was sent the famous chief's bear knife and its scabbard, which was made from the skin of a grizzly bear's head. Catlin's illustration of this knife and sheath is reproduced here as Figure 2.[12]

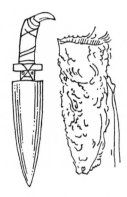

Figure 2.—*Bear knife and scabbard of Four Bears, Mandan chief.*

Other Siouan tribes of the Great Plains more remote from the Assiniboins had organized Bear Cults. The Iowa society known as Grizzly Bear Dance was composed of individuals who obtained their power from the grizzly bear. Functions of the society were directed toward curing the sick. In society dances the members feasted and imitated the actions of bears.[13]

Entrance into the Omahas' secret society known as Moⁿchu'-

[10] Frances Densmore, *Teton Sioux Music*, 195.

[11] Alfred W. Bowers, *Mandan Social and Ceremonial Organization*, 108.

[12] Catlin, *Letters and Notes*, I, 236–37, Plate 99.

[13] Alanson Skinner, "Societies of the Iowa, Kansa and Ponca Indians," 714–15, *Ethnology of the Iowa Indians*, 242.

ithaethe ("those to whom the bear has shown compassion") was gained by virtue of a dream of the bear. This society had been defunct for half a century prior to Fletcher and La Flesche's study of the Omahas, which offers no specific information regarding its functions or paraphernalia.[14] Nor does Skinner's reference to the Ponca Bear Dance provide detailed comparative material other than the statement that the shooting of a lone member with a gun was an episode in the ceremony.[15]

Still farther afield among the Siouan tribes, Radin found among the Winnebagos "a society possessing the powers of healing disease in which membership . . . is restricted to members of the Bear clan." The Bear clan was the second most important clan in the tribe.[16]

There does not appear to have been any strong Bear Cult organization among the Crow Indians, the southwestern neighbors of the Assiniboins. Lowie found that in their Bear Song Dance, "all those individuals who had in their bodies such animals as bears, eagles, horses, and the like would come together and display the supernatural presence within them, which was made to protrude part of its body from the performer's mouth." He likened this ceremony to the "dream cult performances of the Dakotas inasmuch as all who had similar religious experience joined in a demonstration of their mystic relations."[17]

Of the Algonquian tribes of the northern plains the Plains Cree were on the most consistently friendly terms with the Assiniboins. Mandelbaum briefly described the Plains Cree Bear Dance, which he found had been so long neglected that details of its performance were vague in the minds of his informants. They made no mention of distinctive paraphernalia. Nevertheless, their brief testimony revealed several functional parallels with the Assiniboin Bear Cult. There was feasting of those who had dreamed of bear power and the shooting of a gun was followed by the scattering of participants "as though they were fleeing from a hunter." The Plains Cree cere-

14 Alice C. Fletcher and Francis La Flesche, *The Omaha Tribe*, 486–87.

15 Skinner, "Societies of the Iowa, Kansa and Ponca Indians, 792.

16 Paul Radin, *The Winnebago Tribe*, 226–28.

17 Lowie, "Societies of the Crow, Hidatsa and Mandan Indians, 150.

mony was performed to bring about the recovery of a sick relative or to bring success in war.[18]

The nineteenth-century Blackfeet appeared to lack any Bear Cult group organization. Nevertheless, they employed cult paraphernalia and performed ceremonial functions characteristic of the Assiniboin Bear Cult. Particular emphasis was placed upon the bear knife, which was for them a distinct ceremonial bundle, subject to purchase and ceremonial transfer from one individual to another. In the transfer ceremony "the recipient must catch the knife thrown violently at him and is also cast naked upon thorns and held there while painted and beaten thoroughly with the flat of the knife."[19] My Blood and Piegan informants told me that there formerly were several bear knife bundles among the three Blackfoot tribes and that their owners carried these knives to war. In 1847 Father Point, a missionary to the Blackfeet, learned of a Frenchman who, in a fight with those Indians "brought back . . . a bear knife, which is for the Indians what a (captured) floating flag is for civilized man," which shows that the Blackfeet used bear knives in battle at that time.[20] Fourteen years earlier Maximilian saw and illustrated a bear knife of the Gros Ventres, a tribe then closely allied with the Blackfoot.[21]

Wissler and Duvall have published a myth explaining the origin of the bear knife. I obtained a very similar version of this myth from the Piegan, Fish Wolf Robe, in 1943. It recounts the transfer of the bear knife and other objects associated with bear power to a mixed Sarsi-Piegan by a family of bears. Not only did the male

[18] David G. Mandelbaum, *The Plains Cree*, 278.

[19] Wissler, *Ceremonial Bundles of the Blackfoot Indians*, 131–34.

[20] Father Nicholas Point, "A Journey on a Barge on the Missouri River from the Fort of the Blackfeet (Lewis) to that of the Assiniboine (Union) 1847," 247.

[21] Maximilian, *Travels*, XXIII, 105. A number of specimens of Blackfoot Indian bear knives are preserved in museum collections. Probably the oldest is Cat. No. IV B. 300 in the Museum für Volkerkunde in Berlin, which was collected by Prince Paul of Württemberg, and is illustrated on Plate 43b of Walter Krickeberg, *Altere Ethnographica aus Nordamerika im Berliner Museum für Volkerkunde*. A bear knife with an elaborate feather and skin pendant which was carried to war by Black Looks, a Piegan, is Cat. No. 835 in the Museum of the Plains Indian, Browning, Montana. Still another Blackfoot bear knife is Cat. No. 11/5086 in the Museum of the American Indian, Heye Foundation, New York City.

bear ceremonially transfer the bear knife to the young man, but he instructed him in the proper use of this knife in war, and the owner was obliged to paint the youth's face red with scratch (claw) marks on each cheek and add black marks "representing the bear-face." At the same time the bears gave the young man a bear spear and two bear-painted tipis.[22] The tipi transferred by the female bear had red bears painted on its cover. This painted lodge was purchased by the Museum of the Plains Indian in the fall of 1943. The tipi presented by the male bear bore representations of bears in black paint. I saw the male-bear-painted tipi at the Blood sun dance encampment in 1942. The background of the cover was solid yellow. A solid black bear, standing on its hind legs, was depicted at each side of the doorway. The similarity between this painted tipi and the bear-painted tipi of the Assiniboins is marked. That the bear-painted tipi may be of considerable age among the Blackfoot tribes is suggested by Alexander Henry's mention, in 1809,[23] of Blackfoot tipis with rude bear figures on their covers.

Some of the paraphernalia and functions of the Bear Cult were associated with ceremonies of three of the Piegan men's societies. There were two to four members of the Pigeons, Braves, and All-Brave Dogs Societies who wore bear costumes which included perforated shirts with cut-fringe edgings. The flap over the chest (mentioned in Black Tail's description of the Assiniboin bear shirt) is not a part of the Piegan shirts. Nevertheless, Wissler's illustration of the outfit of a bear member of the Braves shows a robe with a flap in it, which was worn in addition to the perforated shirt. During the ceremonies of these three societies the bear members drove the other dancers back four times, an action suggestive of the ceremonial bear hunt. They were also the first to partake of the ceremonial feast.[24]

Although later students of the Blackfoot tribes did not claim that these Indians emphasized the importance of bear power in curing rites, it is noteworthy that as early as 1832, George Catlin

[22] Clark Wissler and D. C. Duvall, *Mythology of the Blackfoot Indians*, 95–98.
[23] Henry and Thompson, *New Light*, II, 527.
[24] Clark Wissler, *Societies and Dance Associations of the Blackfoot Indians*, 371–75, 377–88, and Figure 5.

witnessed an attempt of a Blackfoot shaman to aid a dying man through his powers derived from the grizzly bear. This doctor wore a grizzly-bear skin over his head and upper body and bear bracelets and anklets. His bedside manner was featured by "grunts and snarls, and growls of the grizzly bear."[25]

The Blackfoot bear knife had its counterpart among the Sarsi, that small Athapascan tribe composed of friendly northern neighbors of the Blackfoot tribe. Sarsi bear knives were transferred ceremonially in the same fashion as those of the Blackfoot. The owner of a bear knife painted his face red and black before carrying the knife in war. One Sarsi bear knife bundle was said to have been made in consequence of a dream in which the bundle was given to the dreamer by a bear.[26]

The Cheyennes shared with other tribes of the northern plains the beliefs that bear power could be obtained by individuals in dreams and that bears possessed great healing powers. Nevertheless, Grinnell's monograph on that tribe gives no indication of an organized Bear Cult. In the Cheyenne Massaum Ceremony (Animal Dance) those who possessed bear power participated, but apparently they played no more prominent roles than did persons whose powers were derived from other animals. Grinnell mentioned several bear-painted shields owned by Cheyenne Indians.[27]

Likewise, the literature seems to indicate that bear power received little prominence in Arapaho culture. They did have a group of bear doctors whose powers were originally believed to have been derived from dreams of that animal. However, the Arapahoes had similar groups whose powers came from beavers, buffalo, foxes, horses, and lizards. Sister M. Inez Hilger found that an Arapaho might join one or several of these groups as an apprentice. "All groups were considered of equal value."[28]

Henry Black Tail's description of the defunct Bear Cult of the Assiniboins has provided a list of traits characterizing the organiza-

---

[25] Catlin, *Letters and Notes*, I, 38–40, Plate 19.

[26] Diamond Jenness, "The Sarcee Indians of Alberta," 89.

[27] Grinnell, *The Cheyenne Indians*, I, 198, 201; II, 105, 334.

[28] Sister M. Inez Hilger, "Arapaho Child Life and its Cultural Background," 124–27.

tion, concept of origin, functions, and distinctive paraphernalia of the cult in that tribe. Comparative study of the Bear Cult among Siouan, Algonquian, and Athapascan (Sarsi) tribes of the Great Plains is handicapped by the fragmentary nature of the data available in the literature on bear ceremonialism in these tribes. The fact that activities of the Bear Cult became decadent or disappeared entirely among them many years ago made difficult detailed analysis of the cult complex by field workers. Nevertheless, we now have sufficient information to demonstrate that the Bear Cult was widely diffused among the bison-hunting tribes of the northern and central plains in the nineteenth century.

Employing the traits of the Assiniboin Bear Cult as a basis for comparative study, our limited data are still sufficient to reveal widespread similarities in the cults of the different tribes. The accompanying table provides a comparative analysis of the distribution of traits of the cult as we now know them. It is especially noteworthy that no trait mentioned by Henry Black Tail as characteristic of the Assiniboin Bear Cult was peculiar to that tribe. Certain traits were common to many tribes and may formerly have been common to all tribes of the region. The belief that bear power could be obtained in dreams, the employment of bear power in curing sickness and as a potent war medicine may be regarded as basic traits of the Bear Cult among both Siouan and Algonquian tribes. The degree and nature of cult organization differed. The most common Bear Cult organization seems to have been the type known to the Assiniboins, *i.e.* membership composed of individuals who had obtained bear power through dreams. Yet among the Winnebago the membership was confined to the Bear clan, and therefore was of a hereditary nature. Among the Blackfoot and the Sarsi tribes there was no centralized Bear Cult organization. In these tribes, bear power was in the possession of individuals who were privileged to transfer it to others through ceremonies akin to those employed in other ceremonial bundle transactions typical of those tribes.

Some evidence of the ceremonial bear hunt and the bear feast has been found among both Siouan and Algonquian tribes. Their

Table 1

Distribution of Bear Cult Traits

Traits	Assiniboin	Yanktonai	Eastern Dakota	Teton Dakota	Crow	Mandan	Iowa	Omaha	Ponca	Winnebago	Plains Cree	Blackfoot	Cheyenne	Arapaho	Sarsi
	Siouan tribes										Algonquian				Athapascan
Organization:															
Members comprise organized ceremonial group	X	X	X	X		X	X	X	X	X	X			X	
Origin of bear power:															
In individual's dream	X	X	X	X	X	?	X	X	X		X		X	X	X
Through purchase												X			X
Functions:															
Bear power employed in curing sickness	X	X	X	X			X			X	X		X	X	
Bear power employed as war medicine	X	X	X			X	X				X	X	X		
Ceremonial bear hunt	X	X	X						X		X	X			X
The Bear Feast	X		X	X		X	X				X	X			
Paraphernalia:															
Bear shirt	X										X				
Bear face-painting	X										X				
Bear knife	X	X	X			X					X	X			X
Bear-painted lodge	X											X			X
Bear shield	X												X		

occurrence in attenuated form in Piegan men's societies may indicate the incorporation of old Bear Cult traits into the ceremonial context of age-graded societies among these Indians.

The literature affords little information on the distribution of distinctive paraphernalia of the Bear Cult. Had we more detailed comparative data we might find that the paraphernalia were more widely employed than we can demonstrate now. We know that the bear knife was known to Siouan tribes other than the Assiniboin (Yanktonai, Mandan, and Santee) and that it received particular emphasis among the Blackfoot and their friends the Sarsi. The striking resemblances between the bear shirt, bear face-painting, and the bear-painted lodge of the Assiniboins and the Blackfeet reveal historic connection between these traits even though the organization of the Bear Cults in these tribes was very different.

It is historically significant that concepts and practices typical of the Bear Cult among the Assiniboins and their neighbors of the northern plains in the nineteenth century were known to tribes of the Eastern Woodlands in earlier times. The belief that Indians could obtain supernatural bear power in dreams was current among tribes of the Great Lakes region in the Colonial period. Prior to 1700, Cadillac described the use of bear power as a war medicine by the leader of an Ottawa raiding party. A likeness of the bear was delineated on the prow of that leader's canoe.[29] Marquette, in 1763, described a bear dance organized by a Huron woman, who had dreamed of bear power, in the hope that it would cure her sickness. Feasting and bear mimicry (growling like bears and pretending "to Hide Like bears") were features of that ceremony.[30]

In the light of these resemblances and the known westward movements of Siouan and Algonquian tribes in protohistoric and early historic times it appears reasonable to suggest that basic elements in the Bear Cults of these tribes during the nineteenth century were survivals from the days when these Indians lived in the forests. These migrants did not leave bear country behind. On the plains they encountered the grizzly, a stronger, more ferocious, and more

[29] W. Vernon Kinietz, *The Indians of the Western Great Lakes, 1615–1760*, 251–53.
[30] *Ibid.*, 77–80.

awe-inspiring animal than any they or their ancestors had known in the forests. Contacts with the grizzly must have tended to encourage their traditional beliefs in the supernatural powers of bears. Such an hypothesis need not rule out the possibility of modifications in Bear Cult organization and functions nor the probability of considerable changes in cult paraphernalia among these tribes after they reached the open country. It does appear that in the case of the Bear Cult we have a basic complex linking the cultures of the bison-hunting tribes of the northern Great Plains with those of the tribes of the Eastern Woodlands.[31]

[31] Archaeologists are familiar with the occurrence of bear jaws and bear teeth (both black and grizzly bear) accompanying burials of the Hopewell culture and with the appearance of bear motives in Hopewell art. This may suggest the possibility that prehistoric Ohio Valley Indians possessed a Bear Cult, even though likenesses of many other mammals and birds appear in Hopewell art. Burials pertaining to that culture also yield disarticulated jaws and teeth of humans and of animals other than the bear.

※≡※≡※

CHAPTER ELEVEN

Self-torture in the Blood Indian Sun Dance*

WHEN GEORGE CATLIN, the artist and Indian enthusiast, published the first graphic account of the practice of self-torture in a Plains Indian ceremony, which he had witnessed in 1832, his description was termed fantastic by D. D. Mitchell, superintendent of Indian Affairs. Apparently shocked by Catlin's vivid portrayal of coolly premeditated self-sacrifice of human flesh and blood by participants in the Okipa ceremony of the Mandans, Mitchell declared, "The scenes described by Catlin, existed almost entirely in the fertile imagination of that gentleman."[1]

Catlin's description was substantiated, however, some years before Mitchell's accusations were made, by the independent Mandan investigations of Prince Maximilian in 1833–34. And Catlin was defended strongly by the intelligent fur trader James Kipp, who had been with Catlin when he witnessed the ceremony.[2]

Since the days of that historic controversy, the practice of self-torture in tribal sun-dance ceremonies has been reported, on reliable authority, as once characteristic of the Arapaho, Arikara, Assiniboin, Canadian Dakota, Cheyenne, Crow, Gros Ventre, Hidatsa, Oglala Dakota, Plains Cree, Plains Ojibway, Sarsi, Sisseton Dakota, and the three Blackfoot tribes. Furthermore, brief

---

* Reprinted in revised form from *Journal of the Washington Academy of Sciences*, Vol. XXXVIII, No. 5 (May 15, 1948).

[1] Henry Rowe Schoolcraft, *Historical and Statistical Information Respecting the History, Condition, and Prospects of the Indian Tribes of the United States*, III, 254; Catlin, *Letters and Notes*, I, 157–77.

[2] Maximilian, *Travels in the Interior of North America*, XXIII, 324; James Kipp, "On the Accuracy of Catlin's Account of the Mandan Ceremonies," Smithsonian Institution *Annual Report for 1872*, pp. 436–38.

accounts have been published of ceremonial self-torture, witnessed as early as 1805, among the Arikaras and Hidatsas by the fur traders Pierre-Antoine Tabeau and Charles Mackenzie.[3]

It seems most probable that some Plains tribes practiced forms of self-torture in the period before first white contact.

Among the Plains Indian tribes of the United States the practice of self-torture was prohibited during the 1880's. This ban resulted from the combined opposition of missionaries and the civil and military branches of the federal government to such self-imposed cruelties, which tended to excite the Indians, to perpetuate both Indian-white and intertribal hostilities, and to make difficult the process of civilization and Christianization of the Indians.

Published descriptions of self-torture among these tribes have been primarily of two kinds. Some were eye-witness accounts of interested but untrained white observers who not infrequently misinterpreted the purpose of the torture as a ceremony for "making braves." Others were based on the testimony of older Indians who had witnessed the tortures some years earlier but had not experienced torture themselves. Detailed case histories from the mouths of men who had submitted themselves to torture are few and fragmentary in the extensive literature on the sun dance.

Self-torture survived in the sun dances of the Blood and North Blackfoot Indians of southern Alberta for a few years after its discontinuance among the Plains tribes of this country. In the course of field work on the Blood Reserve in September, 1947, the writer met two elderly full bloods who had been tortured in the sun dance of their tribe. They were the last survivors of men of that tribe who had experienced this ordeal, and they were particularly desirous that their torture experiences should be recorded accurately. These narratives by Scraping White and Heavy Head, related to the writer through the interpreter Percy Creighton, provide new and significant information on the procedure of self-torture in the Blood sun-dance ceremony and its meaning to those who submitted to it. They help to round out the only published description of the Blood

[3] Leslie Spier, "The Sun Dance of the Plains Indians," 473–75; Tabeau, *Narrative*, 191–93; Mackenzie, "The Missouri Indians," 354–57.

self-torture, that of the missionary John McLean, who witnessed the ceremony prior to 1889.[4]

In the summer of 1889 the Blood medicine lodge was erected on the north bank of the Kootenay River, in southern Alberta. Three young men, Scraping White (then twenty-three years of age), Tough Bread (now deceased), and Heavy Head (then twenty years old), presented themselves to be tortured.

Scraping White described his experience thus:

> Three of us tortured ourselves in the sun dance that year—Tough Bread, Heavy Head, and I. I was the oldest of the three.
>
> I was on a war party to take horses from the Assiniboine when I made my vow to be tortured. Shortly before the sun went down, when we were in sight of the enemy camp, I turned to the sun and said, "I want good luck. Now I go to the enemy. I want to capture a good horse and go home safely. I'll be tortured this coming sun dance." As soon as it was dark I went into the enemy camp and took two fast horses out of their corral without any of them knowing it. I had good luck and reached home safely.
>
> Then I told my relatives of the vow I had made. Yellow Horn, an older relative, who had been through the torture before, told me, "Put up a sweat lodge for me and I shall look after you." I made the sweat lodge the very next day.
>
> Not long after that the sun dance was held. The torture took place the day after the center pole was raised for the medicine lodge. I was the first one to be tortured. The torture began about noon. Old Yellow Horn cut my breasts with an iron arrowhead and inserted a skewer through the cuts at each breast. These skewers were of serviceberry wood, flattened on both sides, thinned toward the ends but not sharpened, and about this long. [Scraping White indicated a distance of about 2 inches between his thumb and forefinger.] Then sinew was wrapped around the ends of the skewers and they were tied, each skewer to a 4-strand plaited rawhide rope. The two ropes were fastened at their far ends to the center pole at its forks.
>
> I stood up and Yellow Horn told me, "Now you walk up, put your arms around the center pole and pray. Tell sun, now your vow is

4 John McLean, "The Blackfoot Sun Dance," *Proceedings of the Canadian Institute,* Ser. 3, Vol. VI (1888).

being fulfilled." I did just as he told me. Then I stepped back. Yellow Horn pulled hard on the rawhide ropes attached to the skewers. Then I danced. I didn't dance long before my flesh gave way and the skewers pulled out. Yellow Horn came to me and cut the skin that had broken. He trimmed it off even. Then he gave me the pieces of skin he had cut away and told me to take them and stick them in the ground at the base of the center pole, saying, "Now sun, I have completed my vow."

Heavy Head's narrative of his torture experience was still more detailed:

There were only two of us, Buffalo Teeth, my partner, and I. We went to war together to take horses. At Medicine Hat we found a small camp of Cree half-breeds. It was night when we saw their camp. It was moonlight. I looked up at the moon and prayed to it, "I shall be tortured at the sun dance if I have good luck and get home safely." Then I stole up to the camp and got one bay that was tied in front of a lodge without any of the enemy waking or seeing me. Buffalo Teeth took a roan. We started back to the Blood camp, traveled three days and three nights with no food other than a black rabbit. We got awfully weak and hungry.

When I reached home I told my story to my father, Water Bull. The old man got up and sang his encouraging song. Then he told me, "My son, you have done something worth doing. You have made a vow that you will be tortured at the sun dance. You must do it this coming sun dance."

A few days later I went out to the east point of Belly Butte to fast. While I fasted I dreamed that a sacred person came to me and gave me a drum and certain herbs to use for doctoring. Then I returned to my home.

A short time after that the bands began to come together for the sun dance encampment. I prepared myself to go to an old man named Little Bear, a relative of mine, who had been through the torture himself, years before. I filled my pipe and took it to him. I gave him the pipe and a buckskin horse, and said, "Here is a horse for you. Keep this pipe too. I want you to look after me in the torture." When I gave him the pipe he put it down and went over to the next lodge. There were two old men there, Green Grass Bull and Red Bead. These men were not related to me, but they were both older than Little Bear, and both had been through the torture. Little Bear asked them to come to his lodge, to take my pipe and pray for me. After they prayed, they told me not to take any food or water the day I was to be tortured.

The day before the torture I ate or drank nothing. Next day I ate or drank nothing until after the torture. However, the three old men gave me some sagebrush to chew.

I was the last of the three Blood Indians to undergo the torture that day. Scraping White, who was the oldest, was first. Then Tough Bread, then I. I was the youngest. Inside the medicine lodge, on the west side of the center pole and north of the weather dancer's arbor, a shelter was built of sticks like a sweat lodge, covered with willow leaves. I went in there before noon of the day of the torture. I was laid on my back with my head pointed north. I was barefoot, and wore only a breechcloth made from a small, red, trade shawl purchased from the Hudson's Bay Company. There was a little bowl of white paint and another of black paint nearby. The three old men painted four black dots, one below the other, under each of my eyes. This was called "tear paint." If I cried the tears would run down there. Then they painted a double row of six black dots on each arm. They painted the symbol of the moon, points up, on my forehead in black. On the outside of each of my legs they painted a double row of six black dots. The rest of my body was painted white, also my face. They took some of the broad-leafed sagebrush from the ground inside the sweat lodge and bound it together, placed a wreath of it around my head, and bands of it around each wrist and ankle.

I was taken from the sweat lodge and laid upon a blanket on the ground at the north side of the center pole with my head to the north, my feet toward the center pole. Other people were told to keep back away from me. Then an old man named Low Horn was brought forward. He counted four of his coups. The three old men, Little Bear, Red Bead, and Green Grass Bull, held me—one at each arm, and one at my head. Red Bead took a sharp, iron arrowhead in his hand, and asked me, "How do you want me to cut them? Thick or thin?" I said, "Thin." (I learned later that this question was always asked of the man undergoing the torture before his breasts were pierced, and the one doing the cutting always did just the opposite of the young man's request. So when I said "thin," Red Bead knew to make his incisions deep.)[5] Red Bead gave four of his own war coups. He made no prayer. Then he pierced my breasts with the sharp arrowhead and inserted a serviceberry stick through each breast. The sticks were not sharp but flattened at the ends. The other two men held my arms as he cut and inserted the sticks. Blood flowed down my chest and legs over the white paint. Then Red Bead pressed the sticks against my body with his hands. They turned me around to face the sun and pierced my back. To the skewers on my back they hung an imitation shield, not so heavy as a war shield. The shield had feathers on it, but I don't remember how it was painted. It belonged to a man named Peninsula.

The ropes were brought out from the center pole and tied to the skewers in my breasts—right side first, then left side. Red Bead then grabbed the ropes and jerked them hard twice. Then he told me, "Now you go to the center pole and pray that your vow will come true." I walked up there. I knew I was supposed to pretend to cry. But oh! I really cried. It hurt so much. Coming back from the center pole I was shouting. Then, before I started to dance, I jerked the shield off my back.

I leaned back and began dancing, facing the center pole. It felt just like the center pole was pulling me toward it. I began to dance from the west toward the doorway of the sun lodge and back. Then, when the skewers did not break loose, the old men realized that the incisions had been made too deep. Red Bead came up and cut the outside of the incisions again so they would break loose. As I started dancing again the left side gave way and I had to continue dancing with only my right side holding. An old man named Strangling Wolf jumped up from the crowd and came toward me shouting. He called out four coups he had counted and jumped on me. The last rope gave way and I fell to the ground.

The three old men came to me and cut the rough pieces of flesh hanging from my breasts off even. They told me to take this flesh that had been trimmed off, and the sagebrush from my head, wrists, and ankles, and place them at the base of the center pole. I did as they told me.

[5] Diamond Jenness, *The Sarcee Indians of Alberta,* 54–55, reported the same contrariness of action on the part of the Sarcee surgeon when the suppliant pleaded for a "thin" cutting.

151

Then I took my robe and walked out of the medicine lodge alone. I went to a lonely place and fasted for a night. I wanted to dream. But I couldn't sleep at all because of the pain. At sunrise I prayed to the sun.

Some time after that I saw a man approaching on horseback. He said, "I'm going to take you home right away." He took me up behind him his horse and rode me slowly back to camp. My breasts were swollen and hurt. The rider's name was Red Crane. He told me of a mix-up that took place at the sun dance over horses stolen from the Gros Ventres.

When I got to my lodge, my mother gave me something to eat. She and my father told me what had happened at the sun dance gathering —a mix-up between the Mounted Police and Indians. I had to stay in the lodge several days. My breasts were so swollen I could hardly move. Indian doctors used herb medicines to take the swelling away and cure my wounds.[6]

The common elements in these two accounts reveal the pattern of the self-torture experience among the Blood Indians more clearly and completely than the brief description of the ordeal previously published by McLean. This experience was initiated by a warrior through a vow to the celestial deities, sun or moon (the latter in Blackfoot belief was sun's wife), very shortly before the man exposed himself to danger. The vow was a simple, direct appeal to the deity for protection and success in the immediate, hazardous undertaking. In return for such aid the petitioner promised to make the self-torture sacrifice in the sun-dance lodge of his people. On return home after the successful exploit the pledger made known his vow to his relatives. They helped him to obtain the services of one or more older men who had been through the ordeal and were qualified, therefore, to instruct and care for the young man in the ceremonial fulfillment of his vow. The public ceremony took place in the sun-dance lodge, about midday of the day following the erection

---

[6] In the summer of 1889, the Mounted Police sought to apprehend Calf Robe, a Blood horse thief, who sought sanctuary in the medicine lodge of his people. The Indians overpowered the police and set Calf Robe free, but there was no bloodshed. See S. B. Steele, *Forty Years in Canada*, 252–60.

of the center pole. One man was tortured at a time. Each young man's experienced helper or helpers prepared him for the ordeal, pierced his breasts, inserted the wooden skewers, and attached the thongs leading from the crotch of the center pole. They guided his actions by telling him first to embrace the center pole and pray for successful fulfillment of his vow, watched him closely until he freed himself from the ropes, trimmed off the ragged edges of flesh from his breasts and instructed him to place them at the base of the center pole as an offering to the sun. With this act the vow was fulfilled.

Both informants stated that the helpers were always men well advanced in years, rather than men who had been through the torture only a few years earlier. The number of helpers depended primarily on the age of the victim and his relative's confidence in his ability to take the punishment. Younger men generally had more helpers to hold them as the incisions were made. Fasting was not considered obligatory. Scraping White said he was not required to abstain from food on the day prior to the torture. Scraping White's narrative omits mention of the painting of his body in preparation for the torture. However, Heavy Head asserted that all who under-went the torture were painted just as he had been.

Neither Scraping White nor Heavy Head took any active part in the tortures at the sun dance of 1891, the last occurrence of self-torture in the Blood ceremony. They said that four men, Calf Tail, Buckskin Tom, Old Man Owl, and Takes Paint, all now deceased, were tortured in that year. R. N. Wilson, a trader on the Blood Reserve, photographed these torture ceremonies. One of his photographs is reproduced here, through the courtesy of Arch-deacon S. H. Middleton, principal of St. Paul's Residential School, on the Blood Reserve, owner of a print from the original glass-plate negative. Percy Creighton believed that the Indian shown in the act of torture was Takes Paint. (See Plate 28).

The Blood Indians were the last Blackfoot tribe, and probably the last tribe of Plains Indians to observe the self-torture cere-mony. After their 1891 performance of the torture it was prohibited by the Indian Department and the Mounted Police. A year earlier the North Blackfeet had been persuaded to abandon torture.[7] The Piegans eliminated torture from their sun dances at least twenty years earlier. Weasel Head (born about 1860), for many years a prominent weather dancer in the South Piegan sun dance, before his death in 1943, told the writer that he had never seen the torture performed in the sun dance of his tribe, although he recalled that as a youth he had seen older men who bore the scars of torture. Red Plume (born before 1850) informed Curtis that he had seen the torture rites in the Piegan sun dance only four times, thrice when a small boy and once when a young man. Each time a single man had submitted to the torture. Red Plume attributed the discontinuance of self-torture in the Piegan sun dance to the warning of a North Piegan weather dancer that "they would die if they gave their bodies to the sun."[8] Clark Wissler and Walter McClintock reported the persistence of this belief among the Piegan in the first decade of the present century.[9]

Wissler believed that self-torture had not become thoroughly adjusted to its place in the Piegan sun-dance ceremony at the time it was abandoned. On the other hand, the torture appears to have found much more favor among the neighboring Blood Indians. McLean stated that from two to five men underwent this torture every year in the Blood sun dance. Whereas the Piegans seem to have abandoned torture as a result of native fear and distaste for the ceremony, the Bloods continued to practice it until they were compelled by government authorities to give it up.[10]

Wissler was inclined to credit a Piegan tradition that the Blackfoot tribes borrowed the torture ceremony from the Arapahoes.[11] There still exist among the Piegans vague but persistent traditions of a group of Blood Indians who sojourned for a number of years with the Arapahoes in the early part of the nineteenth century.

[7] *Annual Report* of the Department of Indian Affairs for 1891, Canada, 83–84.

[8] Edward S. Curtis, *The North American Indian*, VI, 55.

[9] Clark Wissler, "The Sun Dance of the Blackfoot Indians," 262; Walter McClintock, *The Old North Trail*, 320.

[10] Wissler, *ibid*. McLean, "The Blackfoot Sun Dance," 236.

[11] Wissler, "The Sun Dance of the Blackfoot Indians," 263–64.

Cheyenne traditions, obtained from elderly men of the Southern Cheyennes nearly half a century ago by George Bird Grinnell and George E. Hyde, tell of a group of Gros Ventres and "Blackfeet" (division not indicated) who joined the Cheyennes and Arapahoes in the Black Hills or on the Platte about the year 1826. According to one version of this tradition, the "Blackfeet" returned north a few years later.[12] Major Culbertson, who was married to a Blood woman, is reported to have found ten lodges of Blood Indians living with the Arapahoes, when he attended the Fort Laramie Treaty Council in 1851. "They were unknown to him, and he did not learn how long they had been there or whether they ever returned." These data and the fact that the Piegan were relatively indifferent to the torture in later years suggest the possibility that the torture feature was introduced among the Blackfoot tribes by Blood Indians, who may have borrowed it from the Arapahoes no earlier than the second quarter of the nineteenth century.[13]

Spier regarded the self-torture as a nonessential element in the sun-dance ceremony of most Plains tribes.[14] Our evidence certainly supports this conclusion insofar as the Blood sun dance is concerned. Neither the torture pledger nor his helpers played a necessary part in the sun-dance ceremony. They entered the medicine lodge for the sole purpose of fulfilling the pledger's vow. The Blackfoot tribes have continued their annual sun dances to the present day, with no apparent sense of loss of any essential feature. Now, as formerly, the sun dance centers about the elaborate ritual prescribed for the fulfillment of the vow of the medicine woman who pledged the ceremony. Her objective was reached upon completion of the medicine lodge the day before the tortures took place.

The Blackfoot tribes regarded the torture, such as was endured by Scraping White and Heavy Head, as the most dangerous and severe form of physical sacrifice to the sun. The mutilation of the body by offerings of a finger or bits of flesh from the arms and legs

[12] Grinnell, *The Cheyenne Indians*, I, 39–40.

[13] James H. Bradley, "The Bradley Manuscript," Montana Historical Society Library, Book A, p. 184.

[14] Spier, "The Sun Dance of the Plains Indians," 491.

were considered lesser ordeals.[15] Scraping White showed the writer scars on his legs resulting from the sacrifice of pieces of flesh to the sun prior to the year of his torture experience. Nevertheless, the belief of the Piegans that men who submitted to the torture would not live long after they had given their bodies to the sun seems to have been based upon religious fear rather than the life histories of men who had been tortured. Several of our elderly South Piegan informants recalled having seen older men of the tribe who bore the scars of the torture. The severity of the torture varied with the depth of the incisions. Older men watched the suppliant carefully, and did not permit the torture to be prolonged indefinitely. Even in the case of Heavy Head, whose experience was described by other elderly Blood Indians as the most severe punishment they had witnessed in sun-dance tortures, the performance lasted only a few minutes. His narrative indicates that the pain and nervous shock must have been intense. But in most cases it probably did no permanent damage to the individual. Although Scraping White and Heavy Head still bore the scars of their torture, these men appeared to be in fair health and mentally and physically active nearly six decades after they expiated their vows to the sun in the Blood medicine lodge in the summer of 1889.

[15] Wissler, "The Sun Dance of the Blackfoot Indians," 263–65.

✂══✂══✂

CHAPTER TWELVE

The Last Bison Drive
of the Blackfoot Indians*

AT THE HEIGHT of their power, before the middle of the nineteenth century, the three Blackfoot tribes (Piegan, Blood, and North Blackfoot) and their culturally related allies, Gros Ventre and Sarsi, laid claim to a vast area of grassland immediately east of the Rocky Mountains, extending from the North Saskatchewan River in present Alberta southward to present Yellowstone Park. At its greatest eastward extension Blackfoot territory reached the mouth of Milk River on the Missouri.

That this region formerly was a well-stocked bison hunting ground is proved not only by the testimony of early white explorers and traders but also by the large number of remains of old bison-drive sites still observable in the region. A bison-drive site generally is now recognized by low piles of rocks placed at intervals of several hundred feet in two lines extending for hundreds of yards over flat or gently rolling plains and converging at the top of a cliff into a great V shape. At the base of the cliff, under soil and talus accumulations, is a bed of bison bones. At such sites groups of Indian hunters, working in co-operation, lured or drove herds of bison into the stone-bordered funnels and over the cliffs to destruction in the valleys below. These sites have been variously referred to as "drives," "pounds," "parks," "traps," "falls," and "kills." The Blackfoot Indians term such a site "piskun," which Grinnell translated "deep-blood-kettle."[1]

* Reprinted in revised form from *Journal of the Washington Academy of Sciences*, Vol. XXXIX, No. 11 (November 15, 1949).

[1] Grinnell, *Blackfoot Lodge Tales*, 228.

Although the existence of a number of these sites has been known to anthropologists for many years, no comprehensive effort has been made to locate and enumerate all such sites within the former Blackfoot territory. With the exception of two sites in the valley of the Yellowstone River near the town of Emigrant in Park County, Montana, partially excavated by Barnum Brown, of the American Museum of Natural History, and briefly reported by him in an article in *Natural History Magazine* in 1932, none of the bison-drive sites of this area has been systematically explored by scientifically trained persons. However, the sites have attracted many relic hunters, both Indian and white, searching for arrowheads. Some sites also have been despoiled by enterprising individuals who have used both hand and power equipment to gather bison bones for sale to commercial fertilizer manufacturers. A few seriously interested amateur archaeologists have dug into the bone pits. One of them, the late H. P. Lewis, of Conrad, Montana, located some twenty-four bison-drive sites in the neighborhood of the Sun, Madison, Teton, and Marias rivers and their tributaries in Montana. Yet Mr. Lewis himself recognized that he had recorded only a portion of the total number of these sites remaining within the area of his search.[2]

Stone arrowheads of a variety of sizes, shapes, and materials are the artifacts most commonly found at these sites. Mr. Lewis was impressed by the fact that he had found no objects of metal and no materials suggesting Indian contact with the horse in the bone beds. The findings of the relic hunters and bone collectors appear to have been similar to those of Lewis. During three and one-half years' residence within the area, at Browning, Montana, we heard only one vague and doubtful claim that trade materials (a few blue beads) had been found in a bone bed at a bison-drive site. The apparent absence of metal arrowheads or other objects of white manufacture in these sites has caused local enthusiasts to look upon them as prehistoric and possibly of considerable antiquity.

[2] H. P. Lewis, "Manuscript on Bison Kills in Montana." (Copy in Missouri River Basin Archaeological Survey Offices, Lincoln, Nebraska.)

PLATE 25   Two views of an Indian-made model of a Blackfoot Indian
war lodge.

PLATE 26   An Assiniboin bear tipi, 1833. Engraved from an original
water color by Karl Bodmer.

PLATE 27   Scraping White (left) and Heavy Head (right), two Blood
Indians who underwent the self-torture in the sun dance
of 1889.

PHOTOGRAPHS BY JOHN C. EWERS, 1947

PLATE 28   Young man undergoing the self-torture in the Blood Indian
sun dance, 1891.

PHOTOGRAPH BY R. N. WILSON
COURTESY AMERICAN MUSEUM OF NATURAL HISTORY

PLATE 29   Piegan Indians watching the slaughter of beef for rations on the Blackfeet Reservation, Montana, in 1889.

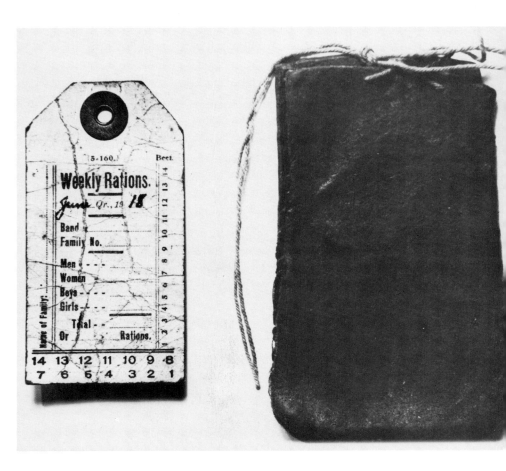

PLATE 30   Blackfoot ration ticket and case.

PLATE 31   Sitting Bull and the Winchester rifle he surrendered to
Major Brotherton, July 20, 1881.

PLATE 32   Sitting Bull's son, Crow Foot, through whom he surrendered
his Winchester to Major Brotherton.

COURTESY SMITHSONIAN INSTITUTION

That projectile points of Folsom, Yuma, and other apparently early types have been found in association with extinct as well as modern bison species at other sites on or near the western portion of the plains to the southeast of the region under consideration is well known. However, Brown said of the bison-drive sites near Emigrant, "There is no evidence of great antiquity in this discovery for the Bison were the living species, but the form of the arrows indicated that they were not made by the Indians who inhabited that region at the time of white settlement. Several implements were found by other people on the camp sites, among them a steatite bowl (found and owned by the proprietor of the Wanagen Store, a few miles from the buffalo jumpoff site). Such vessels were used by the Shoshone Indians, but not by the Blackfoot tribe who recently inhabited this region. The arrows were probably not more than two or three hundred years old."[3] Obviously the age of each bison-drive site within the former Blackfoot area must be determined on its own merits after careful investigation by trained and experienced archaeologists.

Brown's statement that an artifact of Shoshonean type was found in the vicinity of the Emigrant buffalo drives may have particular significance. Other tribes than the Blackfeet and their allies are known to have hunted bison in the area both before and during Blackfoot occupancy. The Blackfoot tribes probably did not move southwestward from the present province of Saskatchewan into this area until the middle or late eighteenth century.[4] Prior to the Blackfoot push into the area, it was held by the Kutenais, Salish (Flatheads and Pend d'Oreilles), and Shoshonis.[5] As late as 1800 the southern boundary of Blackfoot territory extended but a few miles below the present Montana-Alberta boundary.[6] The Salishan tribes as well as the Kutenais and Nez Percés dwelling west of the moun-

---

[3] Barnum Brown, "The Buffalo Drive," *Natural History*, Vol. 32, No. 1 (1932), 81.

[4] Thompson, *Narrative*, 348.

[5] *Ibid.*, 327, 328; James A. Teit, "The Salishan Tribes," 45th *Annual Report*, Bureau of American Ethnology, 303, 307.

[6] Thompson, *Narrative*, 345–46; Wissler, "The Material Culture of the Blackfoot Indians," 12.

tains continued to cross the Rockies on periodic bison-hunting excursions into the area claimed by the Blackfoot tribes until bison were exterminated in that region.

What limited ethnological data have been obtained from those tribes regarding their use of bison drives are somewhat contradictory and largely negative. We have found no contemporary description of the use of bison drives by any of those tribes. Lemhi Shoshoni informants stated in 1906 that the Blackfoot method of driving a herd down a ledge was unknown to their people.[7] Teit obtained information to the effect that the Flatheads and Coeur d'Alênes formerly stampeded bison over cliffs, but he could not determine whether they used that hunting method before the advent of the horse.[8] Turney-High's Flathead informants denied that their ancestors drove bison over cliffs or into pounds. The modern Kutenais denied that members of that tribe drove bison over cliffs in the period before the acquisition of horses, even though that method was mentioned in tribal folklore.[9]

The use of buffalo drives by the Blackfoot tribes and their allies, on the other hand, can be proved by many references in the literature, even from the writings of firsthand observers. Blackfoot use of drives can be traced through the historic period until a relatively short time before the extermination of the bison in their territory. Our field notes, based on the testimony of elderly Indians on the Blackfeet Reservation in Montana, obtained during the 1940's, help to establish the terminal dates of the use of bison drives by the Blackfeet.

The earliest historic reference to the use of bison drives by the tribes of the northwestern plains appears in the Journal of Mathew Cocking, a Hudson's Bay Company trader, who visited a Gros Ventre "beast pound" in the western part of the present province of Saskatchewan in the fall of 1772. He described this pound as "a circle fenced round with trees laid one upon another, at the foot of an Hill about 7 feet high & an hundred yards in Circumference;

[7] Lowie, "The Northern Shoshoni," 185.
[8] Teit, "The Salishan Tribes," 103, 347.
[9] Harry H. Turney-High, "The Flathead Indians of Montana," 36, 115.

the entrance on the Hill-side where the Animals can easily go over; but when in, cannot return: From this entrance small sticks are laid on each side like a fence, in form of an angle extending from the pound; beyond these to about 1½ mile distant. Buffalo dung, or old roots are laid in heaps, in the same direction as the fence: This pound was made by our Archithinue friends last spring, who had great success, Many Skulls & Bones lying in the pound." Although Cocking spent a month and a half near this pound, during which many attempts were made to drive bison into it, both by members of his party and by some twenty-eight lodges of Gros Ventres, very few animals were driven into the corral. On December 6, he reported "no success in pounding; the Strangers say the season is past."[10]

On their journey up the Missouri across present Montana in the spring of 1805, the Lewis and Clark party observed a drive site of a different kind on the north side of the Missouri between the mouths of the Musselshell and the Marias rivers. Under date of May 29, 1805, Captain Lewis reported, "Today we passed on the Star'd side the remains of a vast many mangled carcases of Buffalow which had been driven over a precipice of 120 feet by the Indians & perished; the water appeared to have washed away a part of this immence pile of slaughter and still there remained the fragments of at least a hundred carcases, they created a most horrid stench."[11]

The fur trader Alexander Henry visited a North Blackfoot pound at the elbow of the Vermilion River in present Alberta, December 20–22, 1809. He did not describe the construction of that pound but commented upon the mangled carcases left in it from a previous drive. "The bulls were mostly entire, none but the good cows having been cut up."

During Henry's stay at the site the Indians were unsuccessful in luring buffalo into the pound, giving as the reason for their failure that the wind was from the wrong direction and the "smell of the

[10] Mathew Cocking, *An Adventurer from Hudson Bay; Journal of Mathew Cocking from York Factory to the Blackfoot Country, 1772–1773*, 109–13.
[11] Lewis and Clark, *Original Journals*, II, 94.

smoke from the camps turned buffalo back before they approached, as soon as they scented the smoke." Yet the day after Henry left the site he received word that he had "scarcely left when a large herd was brought in."[12]

Writing of the Piegans in 1811, the same author stated: "In winter . . . they disperse in small camps of 10 to 20 tents, make pounds for buffalo, and hunt wolves and kits. . . . So much do these people abhor work that, to avoid the trouble of making proper pounds, they seek some precipice along the bank of the river, to which they extend their ranks and drive the buffalo over it. If not killed or entirely disabled from the fall, the animals are generally so much bruised as to be easily dispatched with the bow and arrow."[13]

While at Fort McKenzie on the Missouri in the fall of 1833, Prince Maximilian of Wied was told by the Blackfeet of their methods of hunting bison, "for which they make in the winter season, large parks into which they are driven."[14]

When writing of the bison during his visit to Fort Union on the upper Missouri in 1843, the naturalist Audubon stated, "The animal is pounded, especially by the Gros Ventres, Black Feet and Assiniboins."[15] This is the last contemporary mention of the practice by the Blackfeet and their allies. When Edwin T. Denig described the use of bison pounds by the Assiniboins in 1854, he said, "We know of no nation now except the Assiniboin and Cree who practice it, because all the rest are well supplied with horses that can catch the buffalo, therefore, they are not compelled to resort to these means to entrap them."[16] When Lieutenant Bradley wrote briefly of Blackfoot bison hunting in the mid-seventies he used the past tense in referring to this method. "The usual manner of hunting buffalo was by making pens at the edge of a precipice and

[12] Henry and Thompson, *New Light*, II, 576–77.

[13] *Ibid.*, 723–25.

[14] Maximilian, *Travels*, XXIII, 108.

[15] Maria R. Audubon, *Audubon and his Journals*, II, 145–46.

[16] Denig, "Indian Tribes of the Upper Missouri," 582.

driving the animals over, sometimes killing them by hundreds and even thousands. The Indians were very expert in driving them long distances by means of mounted warriors."[17]

The most complete descriptions of Blackfoot Indian use of the piskun were based upon the testimony of informants obtained by George Bird Grinnell and Clark Wissler after bison were exterminated. Grinnell distinguished three types of piskun, each adopted to a particular hunting terrain. The North Blackfeet, who hunted to a considerable extent on relatively level ground, built their piskun like that of the Cree Indians in the form of a corral with a rising timbered causeway leading up to the entrance of the corral from which there was a sheer drop of about four feet into the corral. The Piegan and Blood, living in more broken country nearer the mountains, drove the bison over cliffs. If the cliff was not a high one, they built a corral at its base to prevent the animals' escape. But if the cliff was a sufficient height to insure the death or serious injury of the bison as result of their fall, no corral was necessary.[18]

The descriptions previously quoted indicate that in historic times, after they obtained horses, the Blackfeet employed the piskun primarily late in fall and early in winter. At that season the Blackfoot tribes were divided into hunting bands, comprising small fractions of the total tribal populations, engaged in collecting adequate supplies of meat for subsistence through the prolonged winter of snow and ice and bitter cold. In the Blackfoot country the severe winter period usually does not begin until the last week of December or early in January. The dated references to the use of drives in the early contemporary accounts of Cocking and Henry refer to its employment no later than December. Cocking was told on December 6 that the season for pounding was already past. This seems to confirm the testimony of Piegan informants to S. A. Barrett that "the Indians had certain spots where the fixed winter camps were established in the fall of the year. At this season the

[17] Bradley, "Characteristics, Habits and Customs of the Blackfoot Indians," 256.
[18] Grinnell, *Blackfoot Lodge Tales*, 228–32; Wissler, "The Material Culture of the Blackfoot Indians," 34–38.

buffalo were fat and prime and the drives to secure a winter's food supply were usually held immediately after this fixed camp was established."[19]

The survival of the use of the piskun among the Piegans can be dated with considerable accuracy. Grinnell stated that in 1892 "many men were still living who have seen the buffalo driven over the cliff." He estimated that "the piskun was in use up to within thirty five or forty years ago" among the Piegans.[20] That would have been until about 1852–57. Wissler said that none of the Piegan informants who described the use of the piskun to him had taken part in a drive.[21] However, Barrett found in 1921 that "two of the oldest men on the reservation claimed that they had themselves, when very young men, participated in buffalo drives."[22] In 1943 there was no Piegan living on the Blackfeet Reservation in Montana who had witnessed a buffalo drive. Nevertheless, the story of the destruction of the last Piegan piskun was known to a number of the older Indians. The following account of this event was obtained from Lazy Boy (born about 1855; died 1948) in 1943. At that time Lazy Boy was the oldest member of the Piegan tribe.

This happened when I was a baby. My father told me about it, and I have heard the story many times since from the old people.

The Piegan band called Never Laughs was camped on the Teton River a few miles north of the present town of Choteau. Their chief announced, "Now we are going to make a buffalo fall." They built a corral below the cliff and piled rocks in a great V shape on the slope above the fall. They chose the man who was to lead the buffalo to the fall. But each time he lured them in between the lines of rocks they broke away before they reached the cliff edge. After this had happened three times, young Many Tail Feathers became angry. That night he made a fire and burned the corral.

That same night a war party started from camp. Many Tail Feathers followed it. When he caught up with the war party the

[19] S. A. Barrett, "Collecting Among the Blackfoot Indians," *Year Book*, Public Museum of the City of Milwaukee, for 1921," 23.

[20] Grinnell, *Blackfoot Lodge Tales*, 230.

[21] Wissler, "The Material Culture of the Blackfoot Indians, 36.

[22] Barrett, "Collecting Among the Blackfoot Indians," 27.

leader told him, "You go back home. Everybody is against you because you burned the corral."

Many Tail Feathers returned to the Teton River, to Harm Hill. He slept on top of it that night seeking a vision, but no dream came to him. A second night he slept there. In his dream he saw two young boys coming toward him. They asked him, "Are you the man who saved all the women and children?" He answered, "Yes." As the two boys walked away he saw them turn into buffalo. On the third night he saw in his dream a group of people, men, women, and children, dancing toward him. Their leader wore a handsome red war bonnet. When he came near, the leader asked, "Are you the man who saved all the buffalo by tearing up the corral?" Many Tail Feathers replied, "Yes." Then the leader said, "We are the buffalo. For saving all our men, women and children we thank you. I give you my bonnet—the red war bonnet." The group turned away. Before they disappeared they turned into buffalo. Two scabby bulls, running behind the rest, turned back and gave Many Tail Feathers their power too.

After Many Tail Feathers returned to camp he set about collecting material to make up the bonnet he had been given in his dream. Every bird gave him one of his feathers to put on the bonnet. It was a straight-up bonnet, decorated with weasel hides, red flannel and brass tacks as well as feathers. It looked so pretty all the men wanted it. But Many Tail Feathers kept it for his own. He wore it to war many times before he transferred it to another man.

Many Tail Feathers, the son of the second chief of the Never Laughs band, was a young man at the time he burned the corral near Choteau. He had a fine war record. According to Richard Sanderville, he died about 1888. His red war bonnet, one of the most respected sacred headdresses of the Piegans, was transferred to another Piegan before the end of intertribal warfare. It proved unlucky to its later wearers. One owner was killed by the Crows while wearing it, and the enemy took the bonnet from his head. The bonnet was remade by the dead man's father and brother, Calf Tail. Calf Tail was accidentally killed while hunting buffalo, and the bonnet was buried with him. Still later in the nineteenth century the bonnet was again remade. This bonnet is now in the collections of the Museum of the Plains Indians, Browning Montana (Catalog No. 176). Doubtless the interest of the Piegans in the origin and history of the sacred red war bonnet has helped to fix in their memory the last bison drive of their tribe.

Elderly Piegan informants acknowledged that the North Blackfeet of Canada continued to make use of the piskun for a number of years after the Piegans abandoned it. During the summer of 1947, Weasel Tail, an aged Blood Indian, then living on the Blackfeet Reservation in Montana, related his own experiences as a participant in these later bison drives. His account is of value for its detailed description of the drive as well as for the light it sheds on the survival of piskun use among the Canadian Blackfeet:

> Twice I have seen buffalo corralled. The first time I was a small boy about four years old. We were camped near the North Piegan in the Porcupine Hills west of the present town of Macleod (Alberta). I don't remember anything about it except that I saw the dead buffalo in the corral and that I fell over one of the pointed stakes projecting into the corral and cut a bad gash in my forehead just over my right eye. You can still see the scar.
>
> The second time I was about 15 years old. I killed one of the buffalo in that corral with a gun. I remember it well.
>
> I was then among the North Blackfoot near present Gleichen (Alberta). It was in winter. We didn't drive the buffalo over a cliff. We built a corral near the edge of timber toward the bottom of a downhill slope. We made the corral of cottonwood posts set upright in the ground to a height of about 7 feet, and connected by crosspoles of cottonwood or birch tied to the posts with rawhide ropes. All around the corral stakes of cottonwood or birch were laid over the lowest crosspoles. Their butt ends were firmly braced in the ground outside the corral. Their other ends projected about 3 feet or more inside the corral at an angle so that the ends were about the height of a buffalo's body. These ends were sharpened to points, so that if the buffalo tried to break through the corral, after they had been driven into it, they would be impaled on the stakes. From the open side of the corral the fence of poles extended in two wings outward and up the hill. These lines were further extended by piles of cut willows in the shape of little lodges tied together at the tops. These piles were about half as high as a man and were spaced at intervals of several

166

feet. On the hill just above the opening of the corral a number of poles were placed on the ground crosswise of the slope and parallel to each other. The buffalo had to cross these poles to enter the corral. These poles were covered with manure and water which froze and became slippery so that once the buffalo were in the corral they couldn't escape by climbing back up the hill.

Before the drive began a beaver bundle owner handled the sacred buffalo stones in his bundle and prayed. He sang a song, "Give me one head of buffalo or more. Help me to fall the buffalo."

Then the men of the camp rode out on horseback, got around behind a herd of buffalo and drove it toward the corral. A man stood at the top of the hill and gave a signal to the women and children, who were hiding behind the willow piles, when the buffalo were coming. As the buffalo passed them the women and children ran out from their hiding places.

Once inside the corral, the buffalo were killed by men and boys with guns. I believe we killed 33 buffalo that time. Then the camp chief went into the corral to take charge of the butchering and division of the meat. While butchering in the corral the people ate buffalo liver, kidneys, and slices of brisket raw. Two young men took kidneys, liver, brisket, tripe, and manifold to the beaver bundle owner who had prayed for the success of the fall and who had remained in his lodge. Each man who had killed a buffalo in the corral was given its hide and ribs. Then the rest was cut into quarters and the chief divided the quarters among the families in the camp. Each family got the same share, whether the family was large or small. After the buffalo were divided the corral was broken up for fire wood.

I have never heard of a buffalo corral made by any of the Blackfoot tribes since the time of this fall in which I participated. Of course we had plenty of guns then. There were already less buffalo than there had been. We could hunt them on horseback.

Since Weasel Tail, born about 1859, was about fifteen years of age at the time of this event, we can date the last bison drive of the Blackfeet at about the year 1874. This was a full century after Mathew Cocking's first description of the use of the piskun by Indians of the northwestern plains. It was only a decade before the bison were exterminated in the Blackfoot country.

167

In the use of bison drives by the Blackfoot tribes we observe the survival of traditional, prehistoric bison-hunting techniques among the historic peoples. Undoubtedly the drive was devised in pre-historic times as a method of co-operative hunting by pedestrian Indians armed with bows and arrows or lances which were most effective at short range. After the Blackfeet acquired firearms and horses in the eighteenth century, they possessed more efficient and surer means of killing bison. Nevertheless, they rarely used guns in hunting bison on horseback. They employed the surround and individual chase on horseback in bison hunting during the spring and summer seasons. However, all the Blackfoot tribes continued to make use of the traditional drives in collecting their winter meat supply late in fall. The Piegans abandoned the use of drives in the middle of the nineteenth century. The North Blackfeet, poorest in horses of the three Blackfoot tribes, continued to engage in drives until bison were nearly exterminated in their territory.

✠══✠══✠

CHAPTER THIRTEEN

Food Rationing—From Buffalo to Beef*

MOST AMERICANS think of food rationing as a wartime necessity. In peaceful days we carry no ration books on our periodic trips to the corner grocery. We fill our baskets with whatever foods our needs and tastes dictate and our pocketbooks permit. But to many an elderly resident of the Indian reservations of the Great Plains, food rationing is an old, familiar story.

It is said that in buffalo days the Blackfeet employed a rationing system of their own to tide them over periods of food scarcity. In autumn, during the "month of falling leaves," they made a great buffalo hunt. Hunters packed the meat into camp. The women were kept busy pounding much of it into small pieces, and mixing it with mashed berries and marrow grease to form a concentrated, nourishing food known as pemmican. This was put up for winter use in bags made from the skins of unborn buffalo. After the fall hunt each band group selected a winter camping place in the valley of a river or stream, sheltered from the driving winds by high, steep-cut banks. During the bitter winter cold they ate pemmican, augmented by whatever fresh meat they could obtain at no great distance from their camp. But sometimes the buffalo drifted away from their camp, and other game was difficult to find. If this condition continued for some little time, the pemmican supply of the poorer households became exhausted. They were forced to boil the grease-soaked buffalo-calf skins in which they had kept their pemmican, and eat them, or to depend upon the charity of their better-supplied

* Reprinted in revised form from *The Masterkey*, The Southwest Museum, Vol. XVIII, No. 3 (May, 1944).

friends and relatives. If hunger became general, they ate but one meal a day to conserve their food supplies as long as possible. The chief encouraged men of his camp to hunt and bring in any animals they could secure that might furnish food. If they succeeded in killing one or two buffalo or a few smaller animals, they brought the meat to their chief. It was his responsibility to see that this meat was cut up and divided in such a way that each family in the camp got its fair share. Each family head received very nearly the same amount, regardless of the number of persons in his household. When buffalo again became more plentiful, this primitive form of rationing was discontinued. The chief relinquished his authority in the distribution of food. Each family procured its own meat according to its ability and its needs.

When buffalo were numerous, the Blackfeet ate incredibly large amounts. A successful hunt was often followed by a round of feasting from lodge to lodge. Early white traders were sometimes invited to these feasts. They have remarked on the seemingly unlimited capacities of the Indians and their ability to attend six or eight feasts in succession in which they ate almost constantly for hours on end. Yet in time of food scarcity, these same ravenous eaters could manage for days on little or no food.

Although their country abounded in other game animals—elk, deer, antelope, bighorn sheep, bear, and moose—buffalo meat was their favorite food year in and year out. Vegetal foods served primarily as secondary elements in meat dishes. Buffalo meat was appetizing and healthful. Infants were given small pieces of it to suck even before they acquired any teeth. It was not unusual for a man to consume eight or ten pounds of it in a day. Old Blackfeet say their people had preferred certain cuts—tongue, boss ribs (*i.e.*, hump), and ribs. Nevertheless, in times of food scarcity very few parts of the buffalo were not eaten, even to the white, second scrapings of the hide itself. Truly the buffalo was their staff of life in primitive times.

Few Blackfeet were familiar with white men's foods before their first treaty with the United States in the fall of 1855. At the conclusion of that treaty the government commissioners distributed

170

presents among the large body of Indians in attendance. A quantity of sugar, coffee, rice, and flour was dispensed. Many of them had no idea how this strange food should be used. They threw flour into the air and were amused to see it fall to the ground and cover the grass with its fine powder. They emptied quantities of their sugar into a stream, and eagerly drank the sweetened water. They cooked huge batches of rice, until their kettles overflowed with the curious, sticky foodstuff. Under the terms of the treaty, the government was to furnish annuities to the Indians for a period of ten years. The annuities included a variety of dry goods and hardware, as well as some food. The goods were transported up the Missouri River by steamboat to Fort Union, on the present Montana–North Dakota border, a distance of more than 1,750 miles, that required more than a month's journey. There they were transferred to a keelboat for the second leg of their trip to Fort Benton in the heart of the Blackfoot country, 500 miles farther upstream. This took another month. Agent Vaughan described his method of distributing annuities to the Indians in 1858:

> Having first ascertained the exact number of lodges by a bundle of sticks given me at my own request by the headmen of the band, each stick indicating a lodge or family, I placed the representatives of the various lodges in a large circle, the presents to be distributed forming the centre. To each individual in this circle or ring was given in turn his just and due proportion, as nearly as the nature of the goods would permit, of every article of merchandise sent to this agency.[1]

In this annual distribution there was some food, including bread —which in two months' travel up the Missouri had become something less than edible—and coffee. In his report Vaughan recommended that flour be substituted for the bread and that the coffee supply be reduced by one-half because the Indians did not care very much for it. As the years passed, the Blackfeet became fonder of coffee. By the seventies they were drinking it in large quantities. They also made much use of sugar and flour.

Three Calf, an elderly Piegan, said the government began to

[1] *Annual Report* of the Commissioner of Indian Affairs for 1858, p. 429.

furnish rations to the Blackfeet regularly some years before the buffalo were exterminated in their country. One item in the Appropriation Act of March 3, 1875, for the Indian Service, stated:

> It is made the duty of each agent in charge of Indians and having supplies to distribute, to make out, at the commencement of each fiscal year, rolls of the Indians entitled to supplies at the agency, with the number of the Indians and of the heads of families or lodges, with the number in each family or lodge, and to give out supplies to the heads of the families, and not the heads of tribes or bands, and not to give out supplies for a greater length of time than one week in advance.

In the Museum of the Plains Indian is the ration roll at the Blackfeet Agency on Badger Creek (now known as Old Agency) for the week ending March 19, 1881. The native name of the head of each family is given, together with its English translation. The number of persons in each family is designated, and the quantity of rations received by the family head for his household during the week is given. One ration was considered a day's supply for one person, adult or child. Thus each family head was entitled to receive foodstuff totaling seven rations for each member of his household each week. A table of ration values is printed on the back of the form, as follows:

TABLE OF QUANTITY ALLOWED TO 100 RATIONS

Bacon	10 lbs.	Coffee	4 lbs.	Salt	1 lb.
Beans	3 lbs.	Corn	50 lbs.	Soda	1 lb.
Beef (net)	150 lbs.	Flour	50 lbs.	Sugar	8 lbs.
				Tobacco	½ lb.

The Blackfeet were primarily meat eaters. Their allowance of meat was liberal, but it did not equal their per capita consumption of meat under primitive conditions, which has been estimated at three pounds daily. In 1881 each Indian was allowed a pound and a half of beef a day.

The printed ration roll indicates that only a small proportion of the heads of families on the reservation called for their rations during that week in March, 1881. Three Calf said this was usual in the days when buffalo and other wild game were obtainable. In those days some of the Indians left quantities of their rations with white men married into the tribe while they went off on a buffalo hunt. From time to time a few of them would come in to pick up some of their rations from their white friends and take heavy packs of flour, sugar, coffee, corn, and beans back to their hunting camps. He said the Blackfeet received their first rations of beef from the government in 1874 or 1875. The Indians did not like the taste of it. They gave it to white men, and promptly rode off in pursuit of more buffalo.

In the early 1880's, Indians, half-bloods, and white hide-hunters combined to cause the extermination of the buffalo in the Blackfoot country. By 1883 the buffalo were nearly gone. During the next winter government rations were woefully deficient to care for the 2,300 Blackfeet in the United States. More than a quarter of them died of starvation.

In 1884 a party of Piegans found and killed four lone buffalo near the Sweetgrass Hills. They were the last buffalo in the Blackfoot country. The tribe then became entirely dependent upon government rations for subsistence. During the next decade the government helped to give the Blackfeet a start in cattle raising. In 1895, the agent reported that the issue of government rations furnished 70 per cent of the subsistence of the Blackfeet. This figure had been estimated at 84 per cent two years earlier.

For a few more years rations were issued weekly to every family, regardless of need. Each family head carried a ration ticket. The Indians were warned not to lose their tickets. Women made fancy pouches to hold them; some people carried them tied around their necks. Beef was butchered every Friday. Saturday was ration day, when the men stood in line and presented their tickets to be punched as they received their rations. An unused ration ticket of this type, issued at a more recent date (1918), is shown in Plate 30. Each ticket bore the dates of usefulness, the name of the head of the family, his band affiliation, and the number of persons in his household. Meat was procured from a different place from other rationed

173

commodities, hence two sets of figures are included. Figures at the right side of the card were punched on receipt of the beef; those at the bottom were used for other commodities. The ticket was good for fourteen weeks.

In subsequent years Blackfoot ration rolls lengthened or shortened in accordance with the changing economic status of the tribe. In times of depression ration rolls gained in length. In prosperous years relatively few people received rations. Officials commonly insisted that able-bodied Indians perform some labor in return for rations.

The Blackfeet were subject to the wartime food rationing regulations of the United States government, as were all other citizens during World War II. Most of them found it most difficult to become adjusted to meat rationing. Before the war, most full bloods, and others of a high degree of Indian blood, considered tea or coffee, bread, and plenty of meat the necessary components of a good meal. The war made it necessary for them to find meat substitutes, such as eggs or macaroni, for many meals. They were intensely patriotic. They realized the necessity of being rationed once again. In 1943, Short Face, an elderly full blood, summed up his personal reactions to rationing in a few words: "I can't complain. Everyone is treated the same way. But I really suffer. I get very little meat. It gives me heartburn to have so little. I'm used to lots of meat and I suffer without it. . . . But let's not talk about it. It makes me hungry."

PLATE 33   Petalesharro, Pawnee hero of 1821. Lithograph in McKenney
and Hall's *History of the Indian Tribes of North America*,
1836.

PLATE 34   The first published illustration of a Plains Indian tipi, an engraving from Titian Peale's water color of Sioux lodges executed on the Long Expedition to the Rocky Mountains in 1819–20 (1823).

COURTESY SMITHSONIAN INSTITUTION

PLATE 35   Titian Peale's view of a buffalo chase—a lithograph in *The Cabinet of Natural History and American Rural Sports* in 1832.

PLATE 36   John Neagle's 1821 portrait of Big Elk, Omaha chief—the
frontispiece in Samuel Morton's *Crania Americana*, 1839.

PLATE 37 "Return from the Hunt," a popular lithograph by the famous
American illustrator Felix O. C. Darley, 1885.

PLATE 38   George Catlin's influence upon middle nineteenth-century
            illustrators is apparent in this portrait of "Pontiac" (left)
            from William V. Moore's *Indian Wars of the United States*,
            1856, and the one of "Paw-puk-keewis" (right) from Long-
            fellow's *The Song of Hiawatha*, 1856. Both are variations of
            Catlin's portrait of Four Bears, the Mandan second chief.

A CREEK WARRIOR.

PLATE 39   George Catlin's engraving (1841) of a Crow warrior on
horseback (top) became "A Creek Warrior" from Alabama
(bottom) in William V. Moore's *Indian Wars of the United
States*, 1856.

PLATE 40   "Indians Attacking Butterfield's Overland Dispatch Coach,"
from a field sketch by Theodore R. Davis. (*Harper's Weekly,*
April 21, 1866.)

※≡※≡※

CHAPTER FOURTEEN

When Sitting Bull Surrendered
His Winchester*

AT HIGH NOON, July 19, 1881, a tired, hungry, sullen Indian rode into Fort Buford on the Missouri River at the head of 186 faithful followers to give himself up to the authority of the United States. It must have been difficult for soldiers at that frontier post to realize that this quiet, shabbily dressed little man was the most notorious hostile Indian in the West—Sitting Bull. Five years earlier he had been a leader in the great camp of thousands of Indians whose warriors overwhelmed Custer and his men on the Little Big Horn. In the spring of 1877 he had crossed the medicine line into Canada to seek protection from the "Grandmother" (Queen Victoria). For four more years Sitting Bull, the perennial hostile, remained a threat to the peaceful development of the northwestern plains and a source of embarrassment to authorities in both Canada and the United States. His very presence at the head of a large force of veteran fighters just north of the international line discouraged settlement in neighboring areas on both sides of the boundary.

Until the winter of 1880, Sitting Bull held more than a thousand of his followers together. Then, when scarcity of buffalo brought pangs of hunger to their women and children, his fellow chiefs with their personal followers began to turn south to make their peace with the United States. Sitting Bull and his most loyal friends continued to hold out. Not until they came face to face with starvation did they grudgingly return to their own country to give up their

* Reprinted in revised form from *The Beaver* (Magazine of the North), Outfit 287 (Winter, 1956).

guns and ponies and settle down to the monotonous, beef-eating existence of agency Indians.

The day after Sitting Bull's arrival at Fort Buford, Major David H. Brotherton, commanding officer, called a formal council to accept the chief's surrender. Those who attended this historic meeting at eleven o'clock on the morning of July 20, 1881, in Brotherton's office, included the commanding officer and officers of his staff, Inspector Macdonell of the North West Mounted Police who had arrived the preceding evening from Wood Mountain, Sitting Bull, his young son Crowfoot, and thirty-two of the leading men of Sitting Bull's camp. Also present was a single reporter who scooped the big city press by obtaining an on-the-spot description of the council for his paper, *The Daily Pioneer Press* of St. Paul. He described the chief's appearance thus:

> Sitting Bull as he entered the council seated himself at the left hand of Major Brotherton, placed his rifle, which he had not yet been required to give up, between his feet, and with a sullen, bull dog expression upon his countenance, relapsed into perfect silence. His dress consisted of a cheap calico shirt, considerably worn in appearance, from dirt and long use, a pair of black leggings, a blanket dirty and worn, and a calico handkerchief was tied turban-like around his head so as to partly conceal his eyes, which are quite sore, from the view of spectators. So long as he maintained silence there was nothing about the man to indicate the strength of will which has made his name so famous.

He remained silent while Major Brotherton opened the council with an explanation of the government's policy toward Sitting Bull and his people and its plans for their future. Then Sitting Bull arose. According to the reporter:

> He remained perfectly silent for at least five minutes, as if making a review of his past life, then addressing himself in a short speech to the Indians present, which speech was not interpreted, he finally turned to his little son, and directed him to take up his rifle and present it to Maj. Brotherton.

This being done the chief said:

176

"I surrender this rifle to you through my son, whom I now desire to teach in this manner that he has become a friend of the Americans. I wish him to learn the habits of the whites and to be educated as their sons are educated. *I wish it to be remembered that I was the last man of my tribe to surrender my rifle!*"

The reporter acknowledged that Sitting Bull's speech may have been somewhat mangled by the interpreter, but he said he recorded it just as it was interpreted. Many decades later Indians who claimed to have been present at that council said these were not Sitting Bull's exact words. Nevertheless, there can be no doubt that Sitting Bull surrendered his gun to Major Brotherton during the historic meeting.

There is no contemporary record of the make or model of this weapon in either official or unofficial records of the event. As a symbol of the final capitulation of the fighting Sioux and as the personal weapon of the most famous warrior chief in the history of the West, this gun certainly would be a most desirable museum piece. What happened to it after it dropped out of sight that hot July day at Fort Buford on the Upper Missouri? Has it been preserved? How? Where?

Most museum specialists in American Indian objects have become very wary of so-called Sitting Bull relics. So many collectors bring in pipes, tobacco pouches, knives, war clubs, moccasins, or feather headdresses with the unsupported verbal claim that these articles once belonged to the great chief Sitting Bull that experienced curators have become suspicious of all such objects. Surely there must be almost enough so-called Sitting Bull relics in circulation to rearm and reclothe the Sioux.

Yet, curiously enough, there may be a truthful basis for a number of these claims. Even before Sitting Bull returned to the United States from his exile in Canada, Sitting Bull relics passed into the hands of white men. In the Royal Canadian Mounted Police Museum at Regina, Saskatchewan, are preserved six items attributed to Sitting Bull or his followers. Five of these—an arrow, gun case, tobacco pouch, knife sheath, and war club—had been given to Superintendent J. M. Walsh of the Mounted Police, who had responsibility for Sitting Bull and his people while they were in Canada and whose just treatment of these Indians was appreciated by the Sioux chief.

On June 26, 1880, the *Yellowstone Journal* of Miles City, Montana, stated that a Mr. Hoeingsberger of Chicago had been at Wolf Point and Poplar purchasing buffalo robes. "He succeeded in purchasing the headdress or war bonnet used by Sitting Bull not only in the Custer fight, but in all excursions during the past three years. It is considered by the hostiles as the most beautiful war bonnet ever worn by an Indian. There have been several of these bonnets paraded through the country, but this one is certified to by Major Walch [Walsh] of the Canadian mounted police as the original, he having received it in person soon after the memorable fight."

After his surrender, Sitting Bull, the public enemy, was transformed into a hero in the eyes of the public. Newspaper men went west to interview him. People begged him for autographs and souvenirs. And Sitting Bull was smart enough to try to meet the demand. Ten days after his formal surrender, he was copying his name on a piece of paper and selling it to men and boys for three dollars an autograph. On August 1, he sold his smoked-glass goggles for five dollars, his pipe for one hundred dollars. The *Chicago Tribune* reporter, who noted these transactions, concluded, "he has a keen eye for business."

Doubtless Sitting Bull's market for souvenirs expanded in succeeding years when he appeared in local and traveling exhibitions and when he toured with Buffalo Bill's Wild West Show in 1885. Hundreds of Indian relics may have been distributed, at a good price, by the one and only Sitting Bull himself. However, it is improbable that rifles were among the articles passed out by the wily chief before or after performances.

Museum curators and experienced collectors have come to insist upon proof of authenticity of Sitting Bull relics. Granted, such proof is very difficult to furnish. In the case of the surrender gun this proof would have to be of such nature as to reasonably place the weapon in Sitting Bull's hands at the surrender site on that memorable day of July 20, 1881.

178

Thirteen years after the surrender, Major James L. Bell deposited a collection of Plains Indian materials in the United States National Museum, a division of the Smithsonian Institution in Washington, D.C. As a captain in 1881, Bell had been one of the officers present when Sitting Bull surrendered at Fort Buford. His collection contained a number of items obtained from the Hunkpapa Sioux of Sitting Bull's band. One of them was a gun identified by Bell briefly as "surrendered by Sitting Bull." This was not a rifle (as the reporter had referred to the surrender weapon) but a smoothbore flintlock bearing the lockplate imprint "Barnett, London, 1876."

In spite of Major Bell's claim, it seems highly improbable that Sitting Bull, proud leader of the hostiles, would have carried such an antique type of weapon in 1881. Official records of the surrender of Crow King, Sitting Bull's lieutenant, and his immediate followers five months earlier stated that nearly all the firearms given up by them were Winchester or Henry rifles. Indians who knew Sitting Bull well have said that he owned repeating rifles prior to 1881. It would appear most likely, then, that this flintlock, a good example of the trade gun in common use among western Indians before the development of repeating arms, may have been one of the guns surrendered by one of Sitting Bull's followers at Fort Buford.

Then, in the year 1946, a Winchester turned up in a fine collection of Sioux Indian artifacts collected in the early 1880's. The initials "S.B." carved in the stock were not particularly significant, but the records accompanying it were. This gun was part of the personal collection of the late Colonel David H. Brotherton, who had been the commanding officer at Fort Buford to whom Sitting Bull surrendered. Brotherton's written record designated this as the weapon Sitting Bull turned over to him at that time.

Upon receipt of this gun's serial number, the manufacturers wrote me that the number, 124,335 F.S., was given to a Winchester, Model 1866, Caliber .44 rimfire, in carbine form. The magazine held thirteen cartridges and the gun was nickel finished before it left the factory. It was manufactured in 1875 and shipped on November 5, 1875. The letters "F.S." after the number may have stood for "Fancy Stock," a stock of very fine wood. This piece was not priced in the 1875 Winchester catalog, but in 1873 its list price was forty dollars plus two dollars for the nickel plating. The company had no record of the purchaser of this weapon.

This firearm was a far cry from the muzzle-loading flintlock. In range, accuracy, and rapidity of fire it ranked with the most efficient military weapons of its time. In fact the Swiss government found it the finest gun for arming its sharpshooters. The Model '66 also saw action in the Russo-Turkish War of 1877. Henry M. Stanley carried one of these guns when he searched for Dr. Livingstone in Africa.

In the absence of records we can only speculate about how Sitting Bull could have acquired this efficient and expensive weapon. Certainly the manufacturers were not selling Winchester repeaters to hostile Indians in 1875. It is equally certain that Sitting Bull did not buy this gun over the counter in a licensed trader's store on one of the Sioux reservations. Three years before this piece was made, the sale of repeating arms and fixed ammunition to the Sioux by reservation traders was prohibited by the United States. Yet, as the Indian agent at Fort Peck pointed out in 1874, there was no law to prevent avaricious traders from selling guns to Indians, no matter how hostile, provided the transaction occurred off the reservation.

The Indians themselves were very secretive about their acquisition of guns and ammunition. Mrs. Spotted Horn Bull, wife of one of Sitting Bull's staunchest supporters, recalled that the men sometimes went on long trips with buffalo robes and tanned deer and elk hides. They returned with bright new guns and many rounds of ammunition. Their wives knew the men's movements were secret ones, so they never asked questions about them.

We do know that, as early as the summer of 1873, soldiers who bested the Hunkpapa Sioux, Sitting Bull's people, in a skirmish on the Yellowstone River, found two new Winchesters left on the field by retreating Indians. They thought these arms came from "that center of iniquity in Indian affairs," Fort Peck. However, it is more probable that these guns came from unlicensed American or Canadian traders farther north. In the summer of 1874, trade in breech-loaders and fixed ammunition from a post on the Canadian boundary was known to the United States Army. In mid-April, 1876, only two months before the Custer debacle on the Little Big Horn, daring Red River half-bloods were trading ammunition to the Sioux in the Black Hills.

Probably through an unlicensed trader operating off reservation, or on a portion of a reservation remote from headquarters, Sitting Bull's nickeled Winchester first passed into Indian hands. Possibly one of his younger followers obtained it from the trader as a gift for the chief.

It would be interesting to know more about the part this gun may have played in the frontier warfare of the late 1870's. Did Sitting Bull receive it before the Custer battle? Did it see action in that most debated engagement in the history of the United States Army? Was it employed in later skirmishes with whites or enemy Indians? These things we may never know. Yet, even if this gun was never fired in anger, it should be remembered as a symbol of the final capitulation of the last tired and hungry remnant of the hostile Sioux and their renowned leader. The surrender of this weapon marked the end of a dramatic era in the colorful history of the Great Plains.

PART FOUR

THE PERSISTENT IMAGE

NEARLY NINE DECADES have passed since Sitting Bull surrendered his Winchester. He was killed in 1890 during the Ghost Dance excitement among the Sioux at a time when many of those Indians believed they could cause the buffalo to return and bring back their lost relatives and their old way of life by observing the rituals of that messianic doctrine.

Since 1891, descendants of the old-time Plains Indian warriors have served beside non-Indian comrades in their country's wars in Europe, in the Pacific, in Korea, and in Vietnam. Meanwhile the Indians of the Upper Missouri have become a small minority in their own region—even though tribal populations have increased during the twentieth century. Many of these Indians have found work in towns and cities far from their reservations. Those who remain at home dress, go to school and to church, travel by automobile, and shop in town like their non-Indian neighbors.

But it is not as contemporaries that most Americans and Europeans think of these Indians of the Great Plains. When they think of Indians—of any North American Indians—they tend to picture in their minds a romantic and heroic figure of an earlier time—the wearer of a picturesque, flowing feather bonnet, the hard-riding warrior and big game hunter of buffalo days—when the Plains Indians were literally riding high.

We should neither credit nor blame the motion pictures and television for the creation of this popular image of the Indian. They have merely perpetuated it. Its development began early in the nineteenth century—even before George Catlin and Karl Bodmer went West to immortalize the Plains Indians through their vivid pictures. Many other artists, writers, and showmen have contributed to the formation and preservation of this image. And it is most probable that the Plains Indian of nineteenth-century buffalo days will remain the widely recognized symbol of primitive man par excellence—and the persistent image of the North American Indian.

⚙══⚙══⚙

CHAPTER FIFTEEN

The Emergence of the Plains Indian as the Symbol of the North American Indian*

ONE SUMMER'S DAY in 1941, I stood on the North Montana Fairground in Great Falls. From a stand in front of me a fast-talking patent medicine salesman was vigorously extolling the curative powers of his bottled wares. From time to time he pointed to the living advertisement standing beside him—a tall, erect, young white man whose paint-streaked face was framed by a beautiful, flowing feather bonnet. The young man's body was clothed in a cloth shirt, leggings, and a breechclout dyed to resemble buckskin. His feet were clad in beaded moccasins. The audience, for the most part, was composed of Indians from Montana reservations wearing common white men's clothes—shirts and trousers. I was intrigued by the fact that this pale-faced symbol of an American Indian standing before us was wearing a close approximation of the same costume the Blackfeet, Crees, and Crows in the audience would put on when they staged an Indian show for the enjoyment of tourists.

How did this picturesque costume come to symbolize "Indianness" to the minds of Indians and whites alike? How did the popular image of the Indian come to be formed in a Plains Indian mold? Why do people in Europe and America, when they think of Indians, tend to think of them as wearers of backswept feather bonnets, as dwellers in conical tipis, as mounted warriors and buffalo hunters? Surely our founding fathers had no such conception of the Indian in the days when the frontier of settlement extended only a short distance west of the Alleghenies, and the only Indians the remote

* Reprinted in revised form from *The Smithsonian Report for 1964* (pages 531–44), Publication 4636 (1965).

frontiersmen knew were forest dwellers who lived in bark-covered houses, traveled in bark canoes or dugouts, hunted and fought on foot, and wore no flowing feather bonnets. Nor was the prevailing popular image of the Indian an original creation of the motion pictures during the twentieth century. How and when, then, did this image emerge?

Probing into history we find that the creation and clarification of this image was a prolonged process to which many factors contributed. Let us try to trace the development of this image from what appear to be its earliest beginnings.

Obviously, before non-Indians could begin to picture Indians in Plains Indian terms, they had to have fairly clear ideas of the appearance of the Indians of the Great Plains and of those aspects of their culture that typified their way of life. European explorers and traders traversed considerable portions of the Plains in the two and one-half centuries between Coronado's quest for the fabled city of Quivira on the grasslands of Kansas in 1541 and the purchase of Louisiana by the United States in 1803. Nevertheless, those Spaniards, French, and Englishmen produced no popular literature about and no known pictures of Plains Indians—either portraits or scenes of Indian life. At the time of the Louisiana Purchase these Indians remained virtually unknown to the peoples of Europe and of the United States (although a number of earlier explorers' and traders' accounts have been published since that time).

The earliest-known portraits of Plains Indians were made in the cities of the East during the first decade of the nineteenth century. They were likenesses of Indians whom President Jefferson urged Lewis and Clark to send to the seat of government in Washington. They were profiles executed by two very competent artists, who both employed versions of a mechanical device, known as a "physiognotrace," to delineate accurately the outlines of their sitters' heads. The French refugee artist Charles Balthazer Fevret de Saint-Mémin made portraits of some of the twelve men and two boys of the Osages who comprised the first delegation of Indians from beyond the Mississippi. Thomas Jefferson welcomed these Indians to the Presidential Mansion in the summer of 1804, and

188

enthusiastically termed them "the most gigantic" and "the finest men we have ever seen."[1]

Charles Willson Peale, prominent Philadelphia artist and museum proprietor, cut miniature silhouettes of ten members of a second Indian delegation from the West. He sent a set of these profiles to President Jefferson on February 8, 1806, with the comment, "Some of those Indians have interesting characters by the lines of their faces."[2]

After his return from the Pacific Coast, Meriwether Lewis purchased several originals or copies of Saint-Mémin's Indian portraits. Undoubtedly he intended to reproduce them in an elaborately illustrated account of the Lewis and Clark explorations which he proposed but never produced because of his untimely death in 1809. Peale also was to have furnished illustrations for this ill-fated work. Doubtless they would have included accurate drawings of the Plains Indian costumes and other artifacts sent or brought back by Lewis and Clark, which Peale exhibited in his popular Philadelphia Museum.

More significant factors in the early diffusion of the Plains Indian image were the oil portraits of several members of an Indian delegation from the Lower Missouri and Platte Valley tribes who arrived in Washington late in the year 1821. Although Charles Bird King painted these Indians for Thomas McKenney, superintendent of Indian trade, he executed several replicas of these paintings that were diffused more widely—one set being sent to Denmark, another to London. The original portraits formed the nucleus of the National Indian Portrait Gallery, which became one of Washington's popular tourist attractions before it was almost completely destroyed in the Smithsonian Institution fire of 1865.[3]

The most popular Indian in that 1821 delegation was Petale-

[1] Donald Jackson, *Letters of the Lewis and Clark Expedition*, 199; Ewers, *Artists of the Old West*, 10–16 includes full-page reproductions of Saint-Mémin's portraits of three of these Indians.

[2] Ewers, "Chiefs from the Missouri and Mississippi," including Peale's Silhouettes of 1806, *The Smithsonian Journal of History*, Vol. I, No. 1 (1966), 1–26. Peale's silhouettes of these Indians are reproduced in this article.

[3] Ewers, "Charles Bird King, painter of Indian Visitors to the Nation's Capital," Smithsonian Institution *Annual Report for 1953*, pp. 436–73.

sharro, a young Pawnee warrior. He was hailed as a hero during his eastern tour because he had courageously rescued a Comanche girl captive just as her life was to be taken in the traditional human sacrifice to the morning star, an annual Pawnee ceremony. Petale-sharro's portrait was painted by John Neagle in Philadelphia, as well as by King, and Samuel F. B. Morse placed him in front of the visitors' gallery in his well-known painting of "The Old House of Representatives," executed in 1822. All three paintings show this Indian hero wearing a flowing feather bonnet. They are, to the best of my knowledge, the first of the millions of pictorial renderings of this picturesque Indian headgear produced by artists and photographers. (See Plate 33.)[4]

The popular novelist James Fenimore Cooper met Petalesharro during that Indian's eastern tour. This meeting was a source of inspiration to the author in writing *The Prairie*, the only one of the *Leatherstocking Tales* to have a Great Plains setting. In the living Indians of the Plains, Cooper recognized the virtues he had imputed to his Woodland Indian heroes of an earlier period in *The Last of the Mohicans*. Writing of the Indians two years after that popular novel was published, he observed: "The majority of them, in or near the settlements, are an humbled and much degraded race. As you recede from the Mississippi, the finer traits of savage life become visible."

Cooper thought that Plains Indian chiefs possessed a "loftiness of spirit, of bearing and of savage heroism . . . that might embarrass the fertility of the richest inventor to equal," and he cited Petale-sharro as a prime example.[5]

Some of the distinctive traits of the Plains Indians were pictured in illustrated books and magazines prior to 1840. The first published picture of the conical skin-covered tipis of the nomadic Plains tribes was a crude engraving after Titian Peale's field sketch on

---

[4] Ewers, *Artists of the Old West*, 38–52. King's portrait of Petalesharro was first published as a small engraving as the frontispiece to Jedidiah Morse, *A Report to the Secretary of War of the United States on Indian Affairs*.

[5] James Fenimore Cooper, *Notions of the Americans; Picked Up by a Traveling Bachelor*, II, 287–88.

PLATE 41 "Custer's Last Fight," lithograph by Otto Becker for Anheuser Busch Brewing Association—a very popular decoration for barrooms.

PLATE 42   The Indian attack on the Deadwood stage coach was featured
on the cover of the program for Buffalo Bill's Wild West
Show.

PLATE 43   "The Medicine Man," by Cyrus E. Dallin, now stands in
Fairmount Park, Philadelphia.

PLATE 44 A Cherokee Indian "chiefing" in front of a curio shop in
Cherokee, North Carolina, 1962.

PHOTOGRAPH BY JOHN C. EWERS

PLATE 45   The Jeannie Brownscombe painting (about 1919) "The First
Thanksgiving" depicts war-bonneted Plains Indians sitting
at the feast.

COURTESY PILGRIM HALL, PLYMOUTH, MASSACHUSETTS

PLATE 46   Iron Tail, Sioux Indian model for the buffalo nickel, and the
buffalo nickel.

PLATE 47   Hollow Horn Bear, Sioux Indian model for the fourteen-cent
stamp (insert) honoring the American Indian.

COURTESY SMITHSONIAN INSTITUTION

PLATE 48   Plenty Coups, Crow Indian chief, standing beside the Tomb
of the Unknown Soldier in Arlington Cemetery, November
11, 1921, wearing the war bonnet and carrying the coup
stick which he placed on the casket as a tribute from all
American Indians.

Major Long's expedition of 1819–20, which appeared in Edwin James's account of those explorations.[6] (See Plate 34.)

Titian Peale may also be credited with the first published picture of a Plains Indian on horseback killing a buffalo with a bow and arrow. It appeared as a colored lithograph in *Cabinet of Natural History and American Rural Sports*, in Philadelphia in 1832 (see Plate 35).

The first reproduction of a Plains Indian warrior on horseback appears to have been the lithograph of Peter Rindisbacher's drawing, "Sioux Warrior Charging," which was published in the October, 1829, issue of *The American Turf Register and Sporting Magazine* to accompany an article on "Horsemanship of the North American Indians." Rindisbacher had ample opportunities to observe Plains Indian warriors and buffalo hunters during nearly five years' residence in Lord Selkirk's settlement on the Red River of the North, 1821–26.[7] Undoubtedly both Peale and Rindisbacher were helping to encourage a growing interest among army officers, horsemen, and sportsmen in the remarkable skill of the Indians of the Great Plains as mounted warriors and big game hunters.

Rindisbacher's portrayal of mounted Indians chasing buffalo was offered as a colored lithographic frontispiece in the second volume of Thomas McKenney and James Hall's classic *History of the Indian Tribes of North America* (1836–44). Yet only a small proportion of the 120 finely printed colored lithographs of Indians in that handsome work portray Plains Indians. And nearly all of these were portraits of members of western delegations to Washington, the originals of which had been executed by Saint-Mémin, King, or the latter's pupil George Cooke.

In 1839, Samuel George Morton of Philadelphia, now known as the father of physical anthropology in America, published his major work, *Crania Americana*. Its frontispiece is a lithographic reproduction of John Neagle's portrait of the Omaha head chief Big Elk, a prominent member of the 1821 deputation from the

[6] Edwin James, *Account of an Expedition from Pittsburgh to the Rocky Mountains Performed in the Years 1819 and 1820.*

[7] Ewers, *Artists of the Old West*, 53–64.

Great Plains. Morton explained this selection: "Among the multitude of Indian portraits which have come under my notice, I know of no one that embraces more characteristic traits than this, as seen in the retreating forehead, the low brow, the dull and seemingly unobservant eye, the large aquiline nose, the high cheek bones, full mouth and chin and angular face."[8] (See Plate 36.)

The first illustrated schoolbook on American history was Rev. Charles A. Goodrich's *History of the United States*. First published in 1823, it went through 150 printings by 1847. However, Noah Webster's *History of the United States* was a popular competitor from its first appearance in 1832. The small and sometimes indistinct woodcuts in these books are not numerous. Nevertheless, some of them include Indians. A few scenes in Webster's history were adopted from John White's sixteenth-century drawings of Indian life in coastal North Carolina. But the scenes depicting early explorers' meetings with Indians, the making of Indian treaties, and the conduct of Indian wars seem to be based largely upon the imaginations of their anonymous creators. Plains Indians are conspicuously absent. They had yet to make an indelible mark upon American history in their determined resistance to the expansion of white settlement onto and across their grassy homeland.

No other mid-nineteenth-century factors had such stimulating influence on both the projection of the Plains Indian image and the acceptance of this image as the American Indian par excellence as did the writings of the American artist George Catlin and the German scientist Alexander Philipp Maximilian, prince of Wied-Neuwied, and the pictures by Catlin and by the Swiss artist Karl Bodmer, who accompanied the prince on his exploration of the Upper Missouri in 1833–34.

Inspired by the sight of a delegation of western Indians passing through Philadelphia on their way to Washington and his own conviction that the picturesque Plains Indians were doomed to cultural extinction as the frontier expanded westward, Catlin determined to rescue these Indians from oblivion and to "become their

[8] Samuel George Morton, *Crania Americana*, 292.

192

historian" before it was too late. During the summers of 1832 and 1834 he traveled among the tribes of the Upper Missouri and the Southern Plains gathering information and preparing pictures for an Indian Gallery, which he exhibited to enthusiastic audiences in the larger American cities. In 1840, he took the exhibition to England for a four-year display in London; this was followed by a Paris exhibition that included a special showing for King Louis Philippe in the Louvre. In addition to his paintings, this exhibition included costumed mannequins, a pitched Crow tipi, and enactments of Indian dances and ceremonies by Chippewa or Iowa Indians. No one brought the "Wild West" to civilization as did Catlin, and his exhibition must have made a lasting impression upon all Americans and Europeans who saw it.

Nevertheless, Catlin's books must have had a still wider influence. His two-volume *Manners, Customs, and Condition of the North American Indians*, published in London in 1841, combined a vivid description of his travels and observations with 312 steel-engraved reproductions of his paintings. The work was enthusiastically reviewed in America and abroad, and was reprinted five times in as many years. Although Catlin included brief descriptions and illustrations, primarily portraits, of a number of the semi-civilized Woodland tribes, he concentrated primarily upon the wild tribes of the Great Plains. There could be no mistaking either from his text or from his pictures that the Plains Indians were his favorites. Repeatedly, if not consistently, Catlin sang their praises. He declared that the tribes of the Upper Missouri were the "finest specimens of Indians on the Continent . . . all entirely in the state of primitive rudeness and wildness, and consequently are picturesque and handsome, almost beyond description." The Crows were as "handsome and well-formed set of men as can be seen in any part of the world"; the Assiniboins "a fine and noble looking race." There were no "finer looking men than the Sioux"; and Catlin used almost the same words to describe the Cheyennes.[9] He devoted several chapters of his book to Four Bears, the second chief of the

[9] Catlin, *Letters and Notes*, I, 22, 23, 49, 54, 210; II, 2.

Mandans, whom he called the "most extraordinary man, perhaps, who lives to this day, in the atmosphere of Nature's noblemen." (See Plate 17.)

Prince Maximilian's *Reise in das Innere Nord-America in den Jahren 1832 bis 1834*, first published in Coblenz (1839–41), offered a more restrained, scientific description of the Indians of the Upper Missouri. Nevertheless, it was reprinted in Paris and London within three years, and the demand for it soon exceeded the supply. Its great popularity was due largely to the excellent reproductions of Karl Bodmer's incomparable field sketches of Plains Indians that appeared in the accompanying *Atlas*.[10]

Together the works of Catlin and Maximilian-Bodmer, appearing almost simultaneously, greatly stimulated popular interest in the Plains Indians in this country and abroad and had a strong influence on the work of many other artists.

They influenced the pictorial representation of Indians during the mid-nineteenth century in three important ways. First, the Catlin-Maximilian-Bodmer example encouraged other artists to go West and draw and paint the Indians of the Plains in the field. Among the best known of these artists were the American John Mix Stanley, the German-American Charles Wimar, the Canadian Paul Kane, and the Swiss Rudolph Friedrich Kurz.

Secondly, they encouraged some of the most able illustrators of the period, who had not visited the western Indian country, to help meet the popular demand for pictures of Plains Indians by using the works of Catlin and Bodmer for reference. In 1843, two years after the first publication of Catlin's popular book, an enterprising Philadelphia publisher offered *Scenes in Indian Life: A Series of Original Designs Portraying Events in the Life of an Indian Chief. Drawn and Etched on Stone by Felix O. C. Darley*. The work pictured episodes in the life history of a fictional Sioux chief. The artist was then an almost unknown "local boy," twenty years of age; but he possessed remarkable skill as a draftsman. Darley became the outstanding American book and magazine illustrator of

10 In the United States *Graham's Magazine* reprinted some of Bodmer's most interesting Plains Indian pictures as small engravings in 1844.

the century. Even though most of his finely drawn illustrations are of non-Indian subjects, he repeatedly pictured buffalo hunts and other Plains Indian activities. He prepared the frontispiece and illustrated title page for the first edition of Francis Parkman's classic, *The California and Oregon Trail* (1849), and toward the end of his life designed a colored lithograph, "Return from the Hunt," which has the qualities of spurious realism that only a highly skilled artist who does not know his subject can impart to his work. The picture shows a birchbark canoe in the foreground, a village of tipis in the middle ground, and a background of high mountains. Darley appears to have produced a handsome geographical and cultural monstrosity in which characteristics of the region from the Great Lakes to the Rocky Mountains are compressed into a single scene (see Plate 37).

Darley was on firmer ground when he followed Catlin and Bodmer more closely. A few of his book illustrations are frankly acknowledged as "after Catlin."[11]

Some of the most popular Currier and Ives prints of the 1850's and 1860's were western scenes, lithographed from very realistic drawings executed jointly by German-born Louis Maurer and English-born Arthur Fitzwilliam Tait, neither of whom had any firsthand knowledge of Plains Indians. Maurer acknowledged that they learned about Indians from the reproductions of Bodmer's and Catlin's works in the Astor Library in New York City.[12]

Finally Catlin and Bodmer powerfully influenced those lesser, poorly paid artists who anonymously illustrated a number of popular books on Indians as well as school histories; these began to appear within a very few years after the books of Catlin and Bodmer were published. One can trace the progressive degeneration of truthfulness in illustration in the copies of these once popular books preserved in the Rare Book Room of the Library of Congress.

A prolific writer of popular books of the 1840–60 period was Samuel Griswold Goodrich, who commonly used the pen name

[11] This was particularly true of Darley's illustrations of buffalo hunts for John Frost's *The Book of the Indians of North America*.
[12] Harry T. Peters, *America on Stone*, 21.

Peter Parley, and who claimed in 1856 that he had written 170 books, of which seven million copies had been sold. Goodrich had discovered Catlin by 1844, when he published *History of the Indians of North and South America;* he quoted Catlin in the text and copied Catlin's "Four Bears" in one illustration. Two years later Goodrich's *The Manners, Customs, and Antiquities of the Indians of North America* derived all of its thirty-five illustrations of North American Indians from Catlin—twenty-eight of these being Plains Indian subjects. Finally, in Goodrich's *The American Child's Pictorial History of the United States,* first published in 1860 and adopted as a textbook for the public schools of Maryland five years later, the Indians of New England, Virginia, and Roanoke Island are pictured living in tipis and wearing flowing feather bonnets of Plains Indian type, while seventeenth-century Indians of Virginia are shown wrapped in painted buffalo robes and performing a buffalo dance in front of their tipis.

Impressionable young readers of popular histories of the Indian wars published in the 1850's also saw the common traits of Plains Indian culture applied to the Woodland tribes. John Frost's *Indian Wars of the United States from the Earliest Period to the Present Time* pictures a buffalo hunt on horseback in the chapter on the French and Indian Wars, Catlin's Crow warrior on horseback in the one on the War of 1812, and the same artist's portrait of Eagle Ribs, a Blackfoot warrior, in the Creek war chapter.

Catlin's and Bodmer's representations of Plains Indians underwent even more miraculous changes in identity in William V. Moore's *Indian Wars of the United States from the Discovery to the Present Time.* In that book Catlin's "Four Bears" became "Pontiac" (see Plate 38), his Crow Indian on horseback, "A Creek Warrior" (see Plate 39), and a ceremonial in a Mandan setting emerged as "Village of the Seminoles." Bodmer's well-identified portraits of Mandan, Hidatsa, and Sioux leaders became "Saturiouva," a sixteenth-century Florida chief, and two leaders in the Indian wars of colonial New England.

The first illustrated edition of Henry Wadsworth Longfellow's popular *Song of Hiawatha* was published in England in 1856. John

196

Gilbert, its illustrator, did not copy Catlin slavishly, but leaned heavily upon him in representing the poet's ancient Ojibways of the southern shore of Lake Superior as typical Indians of the Upper Missouri. His portrait of "Paw-puk-keewis," for example, is but a slightly altered version of Catlin's Mandan hero, "Four Bears" (see Plate 38).

Nor were these Woodland Indians in Plains Indian clothing limited to the works of artists who had had no firsthand knowledge of Indians. John Mix Stanley had known the Plains tribes well, yet when he attempted a portrait of "Young Uncas" (the seventeenth-century Mohegan) or "The Trial of Red Jacket" (the Seneca), he tended to clothe his Indians in the dress costume of the tribes of the western grasslands. And when Karl Bodmer collaborated with the French artist Jean François Millet to produce a series of realistic but imaginative scenes of the border warfare of the Ohio Valley during the Revolutionary War, the war-bonneted Plains Indian was clearly portrayed.[13]

In 1860 a new medium appeared to exploit the American boy's fascination for the Indian's prowess as a warrior. Dime novels increased very rapidly in both numbers and sales. A favorite theme in this lurid literature was Indian fighting on the Western Plains in which many a wild Comanche, Kiowa, Blackfoot, or Sioux "bit the dust" before the hero ended his perilous adventures. Bales of these cheap paperbacks were sent to the soldiers in camp or in the field during the Civil War, and reading them helped the boys in blue or gray to forget, for a time at least, their own hardships and sufferings.[14]

The horrors of Plains Indian warfare became very real as emigrants, prospectors, stage, and telegraph and railroad lines pushed across the Plains after the Civil War, and the Sioux, Cheyennes, Arapahoes, Kiowas, and Comanches resisted white invasion of their buffalo-hunting grounds. Newspaper and magazine reporters were

[13] De Cost Smith, "Jean François Millet's Drawings of American Indians," *The Century Illustrated Monthly Magazine*, Vol. LXXX, No. 1 (1910), 78–84.

[14] Albert Johannsen, *The House of Beadle and Adams and Its Dime and Nickel Novels*, I, 39.

sent West to report the resultant Indian wars. Theodore R. Davis, artist-reporter for *Harper's Weekly*, was riding in a Butterfield Overland Dispatch coach when it was attacked by Cheyennes near the Smoky Hill Spring stage station on November 24, 1865. His vivid picture of this real-life experience, published in *Harper's Weekly*, April 21, 1866, was the prototype of one of the most enduring symbols of the Wild West—the Indian attack on the overland stage (see Plate 40).

In their attempt to keep the civilized world informed of the character and conduct of the Plains Indian wars, the popular illustrated magazines of the day sent pictorial reporters into the field to picture Indian life, treaty councils, and as much of the swift-moving armed conflict as they could witness or learn about from participants. Theodore R. Davis covered General Hancock's campaign against hostile Cheyennes, Sioux, and Kiowas in Kansas in 1867 for *Harper's*, and James E. Taylor pictured the Medicine Lodge Treaty in October of that year for *Frank Leslie's Illustrated Weekly Newspaper*. Artists and reporters came from as far away as Germany, and our western Indian wars were followed in Canada and England through such pictorial journals as the *Canadian Illustrated News* and the *Illustrated London News*.[15]

As the Indians of the Plains made their desperate last stand against the Army of the United States, they again and again demonstrated their courage and skill as warriors. On the Little Big Horn, June 26, 1876, they wiped out Custer's immediate command in the most decisive defeat for American arms in our long history. Many artists, largely upon the basis of their imaginations, sought to picture that dramatic action. One pictorial reconstruction of a closing stage of this battle, Otto Becker's lithograph, "Custer's Last Fight," after Cassilly Adams' painting, has become one of the best-known American pictures. More than 150,000 copies of this large print, copyrighted by Anheuser-Busch in 1896, have been distributed. It has provided a lively conversation piece for millions

[15] See Ewers, *Artists of the Old West*, chap. 12, and Robert Taft, *Artists and Illustrators of the Old West*.

of customers in thousands of barrooms throughout the country.[16]
(See Plate 41.)

Four years before his death, George Armstrong Custer published
serially in *Galaxy*, a respectable middle-class magazine, *My Life on
the Plains*, in which he expressed his admiration for "the fearless
hunter, matchless horseman and warrior of the Plains." Many
army officers who had fought against these Indians expressed
similar opinions in widely read books on their experiences, some of
which were profusely illustrated with reproductions of drawings
and photographs, including portraits of many of the leading chiefs
and warriors among the hostiles—Red Cloud, Satanta, Gaul, Sitting Bull, and others. The exploits of these leaders on the warpath
became better known to late nineteenth-century readers than those
of such earlier Indian heroes of the forest as King Philip, Pontiac,
Tecumseh, Osceola, and Black Hawk.

On July 20, 1881, Sitting Bull, the last of the prominent Indian
leaders in the Plains Indian wars to surrender his rifle, returned
from his Canadian exile and gave himself up to the authorities of
the United States. But within two years William F. Cody, pony
express rider, scout, Indian fighter, and hero of hundreds of dime
novels, whose hunting skill had earned him the name "Buffalo Bill,"
organized a re-enactment of exciting episodes of the Old West that
was so realistic no one who ever saw it could forget it. Buffalo Bill's
Wild West Show opened in Omaha, Nebraska on May 17, 1883. It
ran for more than three decades, before millions of wide-eyed
viewers in the cities and towns of the United States, Canada, England, and the Continent. Sitting Bull himself traveled with the show
in 1885. It always included a series of performances staged in the
open by genuine Plains Indians—Pawnees, Sioux, Cheyennes, and
Arapahoes—chasing a small herd of buffalo, war dancing, horse
racing, attacking a settler's cabin or an emigrant train crossing the
Plains. A highlight of every performance was the Indian attack on
the Deadwood mail coach, whose passengers were rescued in the
nick of time by "Buffalo Bill" himself and his hard-riding cowboys.

[16] Taft, *Artists and Illustrators of the Old West*, 142–48.

This scene was commonly portrayed on the program covers and the posters advertising the show. (See Plate 42.)

In 1887 this show was the hit of the American Exhibition at the celebration of Queen Victoria's Golden Jubilee in England, playing to packed audiences in a large arena that held forty thousand spectators. The *Illustrated London News* for April 16, 1887, tried to explain its fascination:

> This remarkable exhibition, the "Wild West," has created a furore in America, and the reason is easy to understand. It is not a circus, nor indeed is it acting at all, in a theatrical sense, but an exact reproduction of daily scenes in frontier life, as experienced and enacted by the very people who now form the "Wild West" Company.

Except in Spain, where no outdoor drama could quite replace the bull fight, Buffalo Bill's Wild West Show met with almost equal success on the Continent. During its seven months' stand at the Paris Exposition of 1889, it attracted many artists. The famous French animal painter Rosa Bonheur pictured the show's Indians chasing buffalo. What is more, the Indians inspired Cyrus Dallin, a gifted American sculptor then studying in Paris, to create the first of a series of heroic statues of Plains Indians. "The Signal of Peace," completed in time to win a medal at the Paris Salon of 1890, now stands in Lincoln Park, Chicago. A second work, "The Medicine Man" (1899), is in Fairmount Park, Philadelphia. The famous sculptor Lorado Taft considered it Dallin's "greatest achievement" and "one of the most notable and significant products of American sculpture." (See Plate 43.) In "The Appeal" (to the Great Spirit), winner of a gold medal at the Paris Salon of 1909, an Indian sits astride his horse in front of the Museum of Fine Arts in Boston. And still a fourth work, "The Scout," may be seen atop a hill in Kansas City. Taft termed Dallin's realistic equestrian Plains Indians "among the most interesting public monuments in the country."[17]

The phenomenal success of Buffalo Bill's Wild West Show encouraged others to organize similar shows, which, together with

---

[17] Lorado Taft, *The History of American Sculpture*, 476–78, 576.

the small-scale Indian "medicine" shows, toured the country and the Canadian provinces in the early years of the present century, giving employment to many Indians who were not members of the Plains tribes. These shows played a definite role in diffusing such Plains Indian traits as the flowing feather bonnet, the tipi, and the war dances of the Plains tribes to Indians who lived at very considerable distances from the Great Plains. A Cheyenne Indian who traveled with a medicine show is reputed to have introduced the "war bonnet" among the Indians of Cape Breton Island as early as the 1890's.[18] Contacts with Plains Indian showmen at the Pan-American Exposition in Buffalo during 1901 encouraged New York State Seneca Indians to substitute the Plains type of feather bonnet for their traditional crown of upright feathers, and to learn to ride and dance like the Plains Indians so that they could obtain employment with the popular Indian shows of the period. Carl Standing Deer, a professional sideshow and circus Indian, is credited with introducing the Plains Indian feather bonnet among his people, the Cherokees of North Carolina, in the fall of 1911.[19]

The acceptance of the typical Plains Indian costume, of the tipi, and some other traits of Plains Indian culture as standard "show Indian" equipment by Indians of other culture areas is revealed through study of twentieth-century pictures. My collection of photographic prints, post cards, and newspaper clippings, dating from the turn of the century, shows Penobscot Indians of Maine (women as well as men) wearing typical Plains Indian garb, dancing in front of their tipis at an Indian celebration in Bangor; a Yuma Indian brass band in Arizona, every member of which wears a complete Plains Indian costume; dancing Zia Pueblo Indians of New Mexico wearing flowing feather bonnets; Cayuse Indians of Oregon posing in typical Plains Indian garb in front of a tipi; and a young Indian standing in front of a tipi in the town of Cherokee, North Carolina, to attract picture-taking tourists and to lure them into an adjacent curio shop. (See Plate 44.)

[18] Avery Shaw, *A Micmac Glengarry*, iv.

[19] Communications from William N. Fenton, New York State Museum, June 12, 1964 (re Seneca), and John Witthoft, Pennsylvania Historical and Museum Commission, August 2, 1964 (re Cherokee).

In 1958, I talked to a Mattapony Indian in tidewater Virginia about the handsome Sioux-type feather bonnet he was wearing as he welcomed visitors to the little Indian museum on his reservation. He was proud of the fact that he had made it himself, even to beading the browband. With that simple and irrefutable logic which so often appears in Indian comments on American culture, he explained, "Your women copy their hats from Paris because they like them. We Indians use the styles of other tribes because we like them too."

The trend toward standardization in Indian costume based upon Plains Indian models has also been reflected in the art of some of the able painters of the Taos, New Mexico, art colony, for whom a sensitive interpretation of "Indianness" was more important than tribal consistency in detail. Likewise, it appears in prominently placed paintings purporting to commemorate significant historic events of the Colonial period in the East. It is not difficult to recognize the Plains Indian costumes in Robert Reid's mural, "Boston Tea Party," in the State House, Boston, or in Edward Trumbull's "William Penn's Treaty with the Indians" in the capitol at Harrisburg, both of which were executed in the first quarter of this century. So perhaps it should not seem strange to see nineteenth-century Plains Indians sitting at the feast in Jennie Brownscombe's appealing painting, "The First Thanksgiving," which hangs in Pilgrim Hall, Plymouth, Massachusetts (see Plate 45).

Every American coin bearing any resemblance to a representation of an Indian has strong Plains Indian associations. Both the Indian-head penny, first minted in 1859, and the ten-dollar gold piece, designed by Augustus Saint-Gaudens for issue in 1907, represent the artists' conceptions of the Goddess of Liberty wearing a feathered bonnet. A number of Indians have claimed they were the models for the fine Indian head on the famous "buffalo nickel." However, its designer, James Earle Fraser, in a letter to the Commissioner of Indian Affairs, dated June 10, 1931, stated: "I used three different heads: I remember two of the men, one was Irontail, the best Indian head I can remember; the other one was Two Moons, and the third I cannot recall."

202

Significantly, the two models remembered by the artist were Plains Indians. Two Moons, the Cheyenne chief, had helped to "rub out" Custer's force on the Little Big Horn. Strong-featured Iron Tail had repeatedly led the Sioux attack on the Deadwood coach in Buffalo Bill's Wild West Show (see Plate 46). For twenty-five years after this coin was first minted in 1913—during the days when a nickel would purchase a ride on the New York subway, a cigar, or an ice-cream cone—this striking Indian head, in association with the buffalo on the opposite side of the coin, served to remind Americans of the Plains Indians.

The only regular-issue United States stamp to bear the portrait of an Indian is the fourteen-cent stamp issued May 30, 1923. Titled "American Indian," it bears the likeness of Hollow Horn Bear, a handsome Sioux from the Rosebud Reservation, South Dakota, who died in Washington after participating in the parade following President Woodrow Wilson's inauguration (see Plate 47).

In the solemn ceremonies marking the burial of the Unknown Soldier of World War I in Arlington Cemetery on November 11, 1921, one man was selected to place a magnificent feather bonnet upon the casket as a tribute from all American Indians to their country's unknown dead. He was Plenty Coups, an aged, dignified war chief among the Crow Indians of Montana (see Plate 48). This was one hundred years to the very month after the young Pawnee hero Petalesharro first appeared in the nation's capital wearing a picturesque flowing feather bonnet. During the intervening century the war-bonneted Plains Indian emerged as the widely recognized symbol of the North American Indian.

BIBLIOGRAPHY

Unpublished Materials

American Fur Company Papers, 1828–42. The New-York Historical Society, New York City.

Bradley, James H. "The Bradley Manuscript" in the Montana Historical Society Library, Helena, Montana (published in part in the Montana Historical Society *Contributions*, II, III, VIII, IX).

Ewers, John C. Assiniboin, Blood, Flathead, Piegan, and Teton Dakota (Sioux) Field Notes, 1941–43, 1947, 1951, 1953.

Lewis, H. P. "Bison Kills of Montana" (typescript copy in Missouri River Basin Archaeological Survey Offices, Lincoln, Nebraska.)

Published Materials

Annual Report of the Commissioner of Indian Affairs, 1854–58.

Annual Report of Department of Indian Affairs, Canada, 1892.

American Turf Register and Sporting Magazine (Baltimore), Vol. I, No. 2 (1829).

Arnheim, Rudolf. *Art as Perception*. Berkeley, Calif., 1954.

Audubon, Maria R. (ed.). *Audubon and His Journals*. 2 vols. New York, 1897.

Barrett, S. A. "Collecting Among the Blackfeet Indians," *Year Book*, Public Museum of the City of Milwaukee, for 1921. Milwaukee, 1922.

Blair, Emma Helen (ed.). *The Indian Tribes of the Upper Mississippi Valley and Region of the Great Lakes*. 2 vols. Cleveland, 1912.

204

Bowers, Alfred W. *Mandan Social and Ceremonial Organization.* Chicago, 1950.

Brackenridge, Henry M. *Journal of a Voyage up the Missouri River Performed in Eighteen Hundred and Eleven.* Vol. VI of Thwaites' *Early Western Travels, q.v.*

Bradbury, John. *Travels in the Interior of America, 1809–11.* Vol. V of Thwaites' *Early Western Travels, q.v.*

Bradley, James H. "Characteristics, Habits, and Customs of the Blackfoot Indians," Montana Historical Society *Contributions,* IX (1923).

Brown, Barnum. "The Buffalo Drive," *Natural History,* Vol. XXXII, No. 1 (1932).

Bushnell, David I., Jr. *Villages of the Algonquian, Siouan, and Caddoan Tribes West of the Mississippi,* Bureau of American Ethnology *Bulletin 77.* Washington, 1922.

Cabinet of Natural History and American Rural Sports. Vol. II. Philadelphia, 1832.

Catlin, George. *Letters and Notes on the Manners, Customs, and Condition of the North American Indians.* 2 vols. London, 1841.

———. *O-kee-pa, a Religious Ceremony and Other Customs of the Mandans* (Centennial Edition). Ed. by John C. Ewers. New Haven, 1967.

———. *A Descriptive Catalogue of Catlin's North American Indian Collection.* London, 1848.

Chardon, François A. *Chardon's Journal of Fort Clark, 1834–39.* Ed. by Annie Heloise Abel. Pierre, S.D., 1932.

Clark, William. *The Field Notes of Captain William Clark, 1803–1805.* Ed. by Ernest S. Osgood. New Haven, 1964.

Cocking, Mathew. *An Adventurer from Hudson Bay: Journal of Mathew Cocking from York Factory to the Blackfeet Country, 1772–1773.* Ed. by L. J. Burpee. *Transactions* of the Royal Society of Canada, Ser. 3, Vol. II (1908).

Cooper, James Fenimore. *Notions of the Americans; Picked Up by a Traveling Bachelor.* 2 vols. Philadelphia, 1828.

Curtis, Edward S. *The North American Indian.* 20 vols. Norwood, Mass., 1907–30.

Custer, George Armstrong. *My Life on the Plains, The Galaxy* (magazine), Vols. XIII–XV (1872–73).

Darley, Felix O. C. *Scenes in Indian Life: A Series of Original Designs Portraying Events in the Life of an Indian Chief*. Philadelphia, 1843.

Denig, Edwin T. "Indian Tribes of the Upper Missouri," ed. by J. N. B. Hewitt, Bureau of American Ethnology *46th Annual Report* (1928–29). Washington, 1930.

———. *Five Indian Tribes of the Upper Missouri*. Ed. by John C. Ewers. Norman, 1961.

Denny, Sir Cecil. *The Law Marches West*. Toronto, 1939.

Densmore, Frances. *Teton Sioux Music*, Bureau of American Ethnology *Bulletin 61*. Washington, 1918.

De Smet, Pierre Jean. *Life, Letters, and Travels of Father Pierre Jean De Smet*. Ed. by H. M. Chittenden and A. T. Richardson. 4 vols. New York, 1905.

Ewers, John C. *Artists of the Old West*. Garden City, N.Y., 1965.

———. "The Bear Cult Among the Assiniboin and Their Neighbors of the Northern Plains," *Southwestern Journal of Anthropology*, Vol. XI, No. 1 (1955).

———. *The Blackfeet: Raiders on the Northwestern Plains*. Norman, 1958.

———. "The Blackfoot War Lodge: Its Construction and Use," *American Anthropologist*, Vol. XLVI, No. 2 (1944).

———. "A Blood Indian's Conception of Tribal Life in Dog Days," *The Blue Jay*. Vol. XVIII. No. 1, (1960). (Saskatchewan Natural History Society, Regina, Saskatchewan.)

———. "Charles Bird King, Painter of Indian Visitors to the Nation's Capitol," Smithsonian Institution *Annual Report for 1953*. Washington, 1954.

———. " 'Chiefs from the Missouri and Mississippi' and Peale's Silhouettes of 1806," *The Smithsonian Journal of History*, Vol. I, No. 1 (1966).

———. "Early White Influence upon Plains Indian Painting: George Catlin and Carl Bodmer Among the Mandan, 1832–34,"

Smithsonian Miscellaneous Collections, Vol. CXXXIV, No. 7 (1957).

————. "The Emergence of the Plains Indian as the Symbol of the North American Indian." Smithsonian Institution *Annual Report for 1964*. Washington, 1965.

————. "Fact and Fiction in the Documentary Art of the American West," in *The Frontier Re-examined*, ed. by John Francis McDermott. Urbana, Ill., 1967.

————. "Food Rationing Is Nothing New to the Blackfoot," *The Masterkey* (Southwest Museum), Vol. XVIII, No. 3 (1944).

————. "The Gun of Sitting Bull," *The Beaver* (Outfit 287), Winter, 1956.

————. "Hair Pipes in Plains Indian Adornment: A Study in Indian and White Ingenuity," Bureau of American Ethnology *Bulletin 164 (Anthropological Paper No. 50)*. Washington, 1957.

————. *The Horse in Blackfoot Indian Culture, with Comparative Material from Other Western Tribes*, Bureau of American Ethnology *Bulletin 159*. Washington, 1955.

————. "The Indian Trade of the Upper Missouri before Lewis and Clark: An Interpretation," Missouri Historical Society *Bulletin*, Vol. X, No. 4 (1954).

————. "The Last Bison Drives of the Blackfoot Indians," *Journal of the Washington Academy of Sciences*, Vol. XXXIX, No. 11 (1949).

————. "Mothers of the Mixed-Bloods: The Marginal Woman in the History of the Upper Missouri," in *Probing the American West: Papers from the Santa Fe Conference*. Santa Fe, Museum of New Mexico Press, 1962.

————. "The North West Trade Gun," *Alberta Historical Review*, Vol. IV. No. 2 (1956).

————. *Plains Indian Painting*. Palo Alto, Calif., 1939.

————. "Plains Indian Reactions to the Lewis and Clark Expedition," *Montana, the Magazine of Western History*, Vol. XVI, No. 1 (1966).

————. "Self-torture in the Blood Indian Sun Dance," *Journal of the Washington Academy of Sciences*, Vol. XXXXVIII, No. 5 (1948).

———. "Three Ornaments Worn by Upper Missouri Indians a Century and a Quarter Ago," The New-York Historical Society *Quarterly*, Vol. XLI, No. 1 (1957).

———. "When the Light Shone in Washington," *Montana, the Magazine of Western History*, Vol. VI, No. 4 (1956).

Fletcher, Alice C., "The Elk Mystery or Festival, Ogallala Sioux," Peabody Museum of American Archaeology and Ethnology, *16th and 17th Annual Reports*. Cambridge, Mass., 1884.

Fletcher, Alice C., and Francis La Flesche. *The Omaha Tribe*, Bureau of American Ethnology *27th Annual Report*. Washington, 1911.

Frost, John. *The Book of the Indians of North America, Illustrating Their Manners, Customs, and Present State*. Hartford, Conn., 1852.

———. *Indian Wars of the United States from the Earliest Period to the Present Time*. New York, 1856.

Goodrich, Rev. Charles Augustus. *History of the United States*. Hartford, Conn., 1823.

Goodrich, Samuel Griswold. *The American Child's Pictorial History of the United States*. Philadelphia, 1860.

———. *History of the Indians of North and South America*. Philadelphia, 1844.

———. *The Manners, Customs, and Antiquities of the Indians of North and South America*. Philadelphia, 1846.

———. *Parley's Primary Histories. North America: or the United States and the Adjacent Countries*. Louisville, Ky., 1847.

Grinnell, George Bird. *Blackfoot Lodge Tales*. New York, 1892.

———. *The Cheyenne Indians: Their History and Ways of Life*. 2 vols. New Haven, 1923.

Hafen, Anne W. "Baptiste Charbonneau, Son of Bird Woman," Denver *Westerners Brand Book*. Denver, 1950.

Hamilton, William T. "The Council at Fort Benton," *Forest and Stream*, Vol. LXVIII, No. 17 (April 13, 1907).

Hammond, G. P., and Agapito Rey (eds.). "The Gallegos Relation of the Rodríguez Expedition to New Mexico," Historical Society of New Mexico *Publications in History*, Vol. IV (1927).

Hendry, Anthony. *York Factory to the Blackfeet Country: The Journal of Anthony Hendry, 1754–55*. Ed. by L. J. Burpee. *Transactions* of the Royal Society of Canada, Ser. 3, Vol. I (1907).

Henry, Alexander, and David Thompson. *New Light on the Early History of the Greater Northwest*. Ed. by Elliott Coues. 2 vols. New York, 1897.

Hilger, Sister M. Inez. *Arapaho Child Life and Its Cultural Background*, Bureau of American Ethnology *Bulletin 148*. Washington, 1952.

Hyde, George E. *Red Cloud's Folk: A History of the Oglala Sioux Indians*. Norman, 1937.

Jackson, Donald, ed. *Letters of the Lewis and Clark Expedition and Related Documents, 1783–1854*. Urbana, Ill., 1962.

Jenness, Diamond. "The Sarcee Indians of Alberta," *Bulletin 90, Anthropological Series No. 23*, National Museum of Canada. Ottawa, 1938.

James, Edwin. *Account of an Expedition from Pittsburgh to the Rocky Mountains Performed in the Years 1819 and 1820*. 2 vols. Philadelphia and London, 1823.

Johannsen, Albert. *The House of Beadle and Adams and Its Dime and Nickel Novels*. 2 vols. Norman, 1950.

Kane, Paul. *Wanderings of an Artist Among the Indians of North America*. Toronto, 1925.

Keiser, Albert. *The Indian in American Literature*. New York, 1933.

Kelsey, Henry. *The Kelsey Papers*. Ed. by A. G. Doughty and Chester Martin. Ottawa, 1929.

Kinietz, W. Vernon. "The Indians of the Western Great Lakes, 1615–1760," *Occasional Contributions*, Museum of Anthropology, University of Michigan, No. 10. Ann Arbor, 1940.

Kipp, James. "On the Accuracy of Catlin's Account of the Mandan

209

Ceremonies," Smithsonian Institution *Annual Report for 1872.* Washington, 1873.

Krickeberg, Walter. *Altere Ethnographica aus Nordamerika im Berliner Museum für Volkerkunde.* Bassler-Archive *Beitrage zur Volkerkunde.* Neue Folge Band II. Berlin, 1954.

Kurz, Rudolph Friederich. *Journal of Rudolph Friederich Kurz: An Account of His Experiences Among Fur Traders and American Indians on the Mississippi and Missouri Rivers During the Years 1846 to 1852.* Ed. by J. N. B. Hewitt. Bureau of American Ethnology *Bulletin 115.* Washington, 1937.

Larocque, François. *Journal of Larocque from the Assiniboine to the Yellowstone, 1805,* Canadian Archives *Publication No. 3.* Ottawa, 1910.

Larpenteur, Charles. *Forty Years a Fur Trader on the Upper Missouri: The Personal Narrative of Charles Larpenteur.* Ed. by Elliott Coues. 2 vols. New York, 1898.

La Vérendrye, Pierre G. V. *Journals and Letters of Pierre Gaultier de Varennes de la Vérendrye and His Sons.* Ed. by L. J. Burpee. Toronto, 1927.

Le Sueur, Jacques. *Le Sueur's Voyage up the Mississippi, Wisconson Historical Society Collections,* XVI (1902).

Lewis, Meriwether, and William Clark. *Original Journals of the Lewis and Clark Expedition, 1804–1806.* Ed. by Reuben Gold Thwaites. 8 vols. New York, 1904–1905.

Long, Stephen H. "Voyage in a Six-oared Skiff to the Falls of Saint Anthony in 1817," *Minnesota Historical Society Collections,* II (1889).

Longfellow, Henry Wadsworth. *Song of Hiawatha.* London, 1856.

Lowie, Robert H. "Dance Associations of the Eastern Dakota," American Museum of Natural History *Anthropological Papers,* Vol. XI, Part 2 (1913).

———. "Societies of the Crow, Hidatsa, and Mandan Indians," American Museum of Natural History *Anthropological Papers,* Vol. XI, Part 3 (1913).

———. "The Northern Shoshoni," American Museum of Natural History *Anthropological Papers,* Vol. II, Part 2 (1908).

McClintock, Walter. *The Old North Trail*. London, 1910.

McDonnell, Anne. "Biographical Sketch of Mrs. Alexander Culbertson (Medicine-Snake-Woman), *Contributions to the Historical Society of Montana*, X (1940).

M'Gillivray, Duncan. *The Journal of Duncan M'Gillivray of the Northwest Company at Fort George on the Saskatchewan, 1794–1795*. Ed. by Arthur S. Morton. Toronto, 1929.

McKenney, Thomas L., and James Hall. *History of the Indian Tribes of North America*. 2 vols. Philadelphia, 1836–44.

Mackenzie, Charles. "The Missouri Indians, 1804–1805," in Vol. I of Louis R. Masson's *Les bourgeois de la Compagnie du Nord-Ouest*.

McLean, John. "The Blackfoot Sun Dance," *Proceedings* of the Canadian Institute, Ser. 3, Vol. VI. Toronto, 1888.

Mandelbaum, David G. "The Plains Cree," American Museum of Natural History *Anthropological Papers*, Vol. XXXVII, Part 2 (1940).

Masson, Louis R. *Les bourgeois de la Compagnie du Nord-Ouest*. 2 vols. Quebec, impr. générale A. Conté et cie., 1889–90.

Maximilian, Alexander Phillip (Prince of Wied-Neuwied). *Travels in the Interior of North America*. Vols. XXII–XIV in Thwaites' *Early Western Travels, q.v.*

Morgan, Lewis Henry. *Lewis Henry Morgan: The Indian Journals, 1859–62*. Ed. by Leslie A. White. Ann Arbor, 1959.

Morse, Jedidiah. *A Report to the Secretary of War of the United States, on Indian Affairs, Comprising a Narrative of a Tour Performed in the Summer of 1820*. New Haven, 1822.

Moore, William V. *Indian Wars of the United States from the Discovery to the Present Time*. Philadelphia, 1856.

Morton, Samuel George. *Crania Americana; or a Comparative View of the Skulls of the Various Aboriginal Nations of North and South America*. Philadelphia, 1839.

Nasatir, Abraham P. *Before Lewis and Clark: Documents Illustrating the History of the Missouri, 1784–1804*. 2 vols. St. Louis, 1952.

Ordway, John. "Sergeant Ordway's Journal," ed. by Milo Quaife, Wisconsin Historical Society *Collections*, XXII (1916).

Parkman, Francis. *The California and Oregon Trail*. Boston, 1849.

Parsons, John E. "Gunmakers for the American Fur Company," The New-York Historical Society *Quarterly*, Vol. XXXVI, No. 2 (1952).

Parsons, John E., and John S. Dumont. *Firearms in the Custer Battle*. Harrisburg, Pa., 1953.

Peters, Harry T. *America on Stone*. Garden City, New York, 1931.

Pike, Zebulon M. *An Account of Expeditions to the Sources of the Mississippi and Through the Western Parts of Louisiana*. Philadelphia, 1810.

Point, Nicholas. "A Journey on a Barge on the Missouri River from the Fort of the Blackfeet [Lewis] to that of the Assiniboine [Union], 1847," *Mid-America*, Vol. XIII (1931).

Pond, Samuel William. The Dakotas or Sioux in Minnesota as they were in 1834," Minnesota Historical Society *Collections*, XII (1908).

Radin, Paul. "The Winnebago Tribe," Bureau of American Ethnology *37th Annual Report*. Washington, 1923.

Rhees, John E. "The Shoshoni Contribution to Lewis and Clark," *Idaho Yesterdays*, Vol. II, No. 2 (1958).

Russell, Don. *The Lives and Legends of Buffalo Bill*. Norman, 1960.

Schoolcraft, Henry Rowe. *Historical and Statistical Information Respecting the History, Condition, and Prospects of the Indian Tribes of the United States*. 6 vols. Philadelphia, 1851–57.

Schultz, James Willard. *My Life as an Indian*. Boston, 1907.

———. *Running Eagle, the Warrior Girl*. Boston, 1919.

Shaw, Avery. *A Micmac Glengarry*. New Brunswick Museum. St. John, N.B., 1945.

Skinner, Alanson. "Notes on the Eastern Cree and Northern Saulteaux," American Museum of Natural History *Anthropological Papers*, Vol. XI, Part 1 (1914).

———. "Ethnology of the Iowa Indians," Public Museum, City of Milwaukee, *Bulletin*, Vol. V, No. 4 (1926).

————. "Societies of the Iowa, Kansa, and Ponca Indians," American Museum of Natural History *Anthropological Papers*, Vol. XI, Part 9 (1915).

Smith, De Cost. "Jean François Millet's Drawings of American Indians," *The Century Illustrated Monthly Magazine*, Vol. LXXX, No. 1 (1910).

Spier, Leslie. "The Sun Dance of the Plains Indian," American Museum of Natural History *Anthropological Papers*, Vol. XVI (1921).

Stansbury, Howard. *Exploration and Survey of the Valley of the Great Salt Lake of Utah, Including a Reconnaissance of a New Route Through the Rocky Mountains*. Philadelphia, 1852.

Steele, S. B. *Forty Years in Canada*. London, 1915.

Stirling, Matthew W. "Arikara Glassworking," *Journal of the Washington Academy of Sciences*, Vol. XXXVII, No. 8 (1947).

Stonequist, Everett V. *The Marginal Man: A Study in Personality and Culture Conflict*. New York, 1937.

Tabeau, Pierre-Antoine. *Tabeau's Narrative of Loisel's Expedition to the Upper Missouri*. Ed. by Annie Heloise Abel. Norman, 1939.

Taft, Lorado. *The History of American Sculpture*. New York, 1925.

Taft, Robert. *Artists and Illustrators of the Old West, 1850–1900*. New York, 1953.

Teit, James A. *The Salishan Tribes of the Western Plateaus*, ed. by Franz Boas, Bureau of American Ethnology *45th Annual Report*. Washington, 1930.

Thompson, David. *David Thompson's Narrative of his Explorations in Western America, 1784–1812*. Ed. by J. B. Tyrrell. Toronto, 1916.

Thwaites, Reuben Gold (ed.). *Early Western Travels, 1784–1897*. 32 vols. Cleveland, 1904–1907.

————. *The Jesuit Relations and Allied Documents: Travels and Explorations of the Jesuit Missionaries in New France, 1610–1791*. 73 vols. Cleveland, 1896–1901.

Trobriand, Philippe Regis de. *Military Life in Dakota*. Ed. by Lucile M. Kane. St. Paul, 1951.

Turney-High, Harry H. "The Flathead Indians of Montana," American Anthropological Association *Memoir 48.* Menasha, Wis., 1937.

Vickers, Chris. "Denig of Fort Union," *North Dakota History.* Vol. XV, No. 2 (1948).

Wallis, Wilson D. "The Canadian Dakota," American Museum of Natural History *Anthropological Papers*, Vol. XLI, Part 1 (1947).

Webster, Noah. *History of the United States.* New Haven, 1832.

West, Helen B. *Meriwether Lewis in Blackfoot Country.* Browning, Mont., Museum of the Plains Indian, 1965.

Wheeler, Olin D. *The Trail of Lewis and Clark.* 2 vols. New York, 1904.

Whistler, James A. McNeill. *"Ten O'Clock": A Lecture by James A. McNeill Whistler.* Portland, Maine, 1916.

Winship, George Parker, ed. *The Coronado Expedition, 1540–1842*, Bureau of American Ethnology *14th Annual Report.* Washington, 1896.

Wissler, Clark. "Ceremonial Bundles of the Blackfoot Indians," American Museum of Natural History *Anthropological Papers*, Vol. VII, Part 2 (1912).

———. "The Material Culture of the Blackfoot Indians," American Museum of Natural History *Anthropological Papers*, Vol. V, Part 1 (1920).

———. "Societies and Dance Associations of the Blackfoot Indians," American Museum of Natural History *Anthropological Papers*, Vol. XI, Part 4 (1913).

———. "Societies and Ceremonial Associations in the Oglala Division of the Teton Dakota," American Museum of Natural History *Anthropological Papers*, Vol. XI, Part 1 (1912).

———. "The Sun Dance of the Blackfoot Indians," American Museum of Natural History *Anthropological Papers*, Vol. XVI, Part 3 (1918).

———, and C. D. Duvall. "Mythology of the Blackfoot Indians," American Museum of Natural History *Anthropological Papers*, Vol. II, Part 1 (1908).

INDEX

DATE DUE

NOV 1 1992			
			PRINTED IN U.S.A.